The Fundamentals of
Supply Chain Management

Print ISBN: 978-1-934920-39-8

For permission to use material from this text or for general questions about permissions, submit a request on line to http://www.wordsofwisdombooks.com/contact.asp

Publisher: Words of Wisdom, LLC — Schaumburg, IL
Book Title: The Fundamentals of Supply Chain Management
Author: Editorial Board
Rights: Words of Wisdom, LLC
Publication Date: 2015
Edition: 1

QD 11

ACKNOWLEDGMENTS

We would like to thank the Editorial Board for their time and
dedication to the creation of this book.

Johnny E. Maddox, Ph.D.

Johnny E. Maddox, Ph.D. is an Assistant Professor of Business at Liberty University, Adjunct Professor at Colorado Technical University, Adjunct Professor at North Greenville University, Adjunct Professor at Strayer University, and Adjunct Professor at Southern Wesleyan University. He teaches graduate courses at these Universities in their respective business programs. He has developed courses in Organizational Structure and Design, Supply Chain Management, Operation Management, and the Fundamentals of Executive Management. He earned a bachelor's degree in Manufacturing Engineering from Western Carolina University. He earned a MBA from Southern Wesleyan University, and he earned his Ph.D. from Capella University in Organization and Management. His practical experience began as a Manufacturing Engineer and it has progressed through the various areas in manufacturing.

Dr. Maddox has worked in the manufacturing sector for the last 29 years in which he has held positions in engineering, operations, and quality. He has experience in engineering, engineering management, operations management, supply chain management, operations strategy and planning, quality management, process analysis, inventory management, lean manufacturing, and product design. He is currently the Operations Manager for a major Bearing manufacturer. Dr. Maddox's mission is to help make our world a better place for future generations through learning and collaborating with others in our society.

Jan Palmen

Jan Palmen is a lifetime Certified Purchasing Manager (C.P.M.) member of the Institute of Supply Management (ISM). Due to the dynamic forces that govern global supply chain practices, he has vigorously promoted advanced supply chain training as the founder of Supply Chain Management Training Institute (SCMTI-USA), Access International LLC, and Rocky Peak Training Institute LLC. With more than 20 years of operational, tactical, and strategic sourcing experience, Jan developed proven methods to manage major sourcing projects; train personnel; and assure supplier quality; aimed at improving supply chain efficiencies. He has authored a number of operations and supply chain management training manuals covering a wide spectrum of disciplines including Operations Strategy; Global Logistic Strategies; Product Capacity Planning; Manufacturing and Service Processes; Procurement Maturity Capability Model; and Supply/Demand Planning and Control.

He has led international sourcing teams in bench-marking efforts and developed global sourcing strategies that ensured continuous supply and timely procurement of goods and services. Jan's many years of operational experience enabled him to design and deliver training programs on the development of international sourcing strategies and supply chain management relationships. He has held leadership positions in global commodity and supply chain management with Ingersoll Rand, Woodward Governor Company, and Ampex Corporation. He is a certified Lean Six Sigma Green Belt.

Jan holds a MBA degrees in International Business and Operations Management from Regis University, School of Professional Studies, and a bachelor's degree in U.S., Russian, and Chinese history from San Jose State University.

TABLE OF CONTENTS

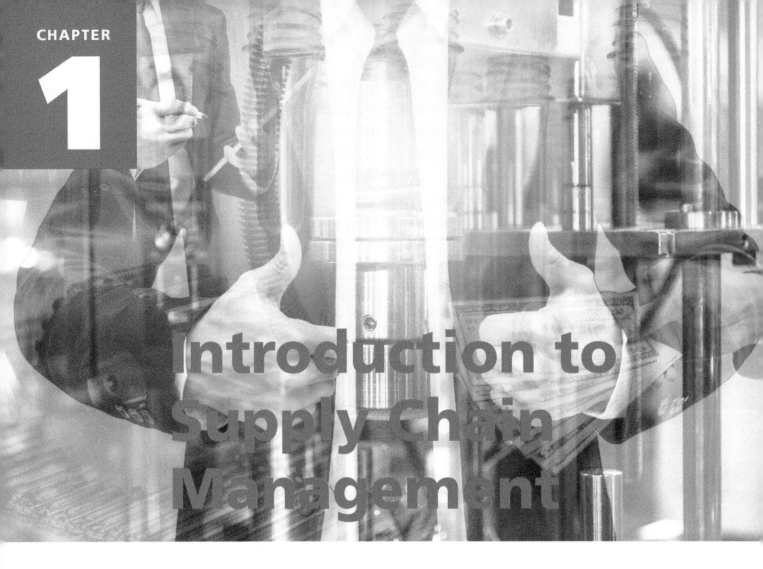

Introduction to Supply Chain Management

Beau goes on a shopping trip to the local food market. She heads back to the milk section to pick up a gallon of milk because it is on sale. On the way, she swings by the produce area and finds no baby carrots. What she does not know is that a heavy blizzard prevented the truck from delivering the carrots. She decides to go with celery sticks this time. Then she looks over the bananas and wonders why they are so expensive. Prices keep going up. Noticing the juices, she ponders, "How do they manage so many varieties of juices?" There are so many choices, and she looks at the shelves for a while before picking up some cranberry juice. Wandering by the cereal aisle, she notices a new type of oatmeal and decides to put it in her cart. She recalls that the doctor told her she needed to bring her cholesterol down. Finally, she heads over to the bakery for her favorite bread. The shelf is empty, so she asks one of the bakers if they have any. The employee responds that they made the normal amount, but the item already sold out. They will have some more later on. Beau figures she will do without and get some next time. She heads to the check out. A typical food store has many challenges to supply all the products it carries. The food chain is a complex system to manage.

WHAT IS SUPPLY CHAIN MANAGEMENT?

Did you ever wonder how a product was made from beginning to end? When you go to a store, you can find hundreds or even tens of thousands of products on the shelves. Each product has its process for production, moving, and handling to get to the customer's hands. Something as simple as a steel frying pan has a series of events that must happen before it reaches its final destination. The product starts from natural resources such as iron ore, coal, and limestone. These components typically need to be transported by rail or ship for further processing. The coal is made into "coke," a type of charcoal and then mixed with iron and limestone. The raw materials are transformed into steel. When the steel is cooled, it can be cut into the pan and handle. Once the two parts are attached, they can be packed for shipment. The frying pan can be transported by rail, truck, ship, and even aircraft. This movement can be direct to the customer, but it usually goes through a series of distribution points and storage. The conventional path would route the frying pan to a retail store where the customer can touch and feel the product before buying it. Finally, the frying pan can end up as scrap to be reused, donated through a second-hand outlet to be recycled, or even end up in a landfill. The lifecycle of a product can go through many stages.

QUESTIONS TO CONSIDER

Consider the following questions as you discuss this scenario:

1. How does a consumer select products?

2. What does the retail store have to consider to keep products on the shelves?

KEY TERMS

➤ e-commerce (p. 7)

➤ greenwashing (p. 19)

➤ links (p. 8)

➤ logistics (p. 8)

➤ mission statement (p. 15)

➤ nodes (p. 8)

➤ quality assurance (p. 11)

➤ quality control (p. 11)

➤ reverse logistics (p. 4)

➤ strategy (p. 15)

➤ supply chain (p. 4)

➤ supply chain management (p. 8)

➤ sustainability (p. 18)

➤ trade agreements (p. 13)

➤ transportation (p. 5)

These stages make up the **supply chain** that involves the processes from natural resources to the final disposition of products. The products or their components need to be managed as they move along the supply chain until they reach the intended customer. These resources are taken out of the ground and transformed into products. Materials need to be transported along the way. Raw materials, components, and final products have to be stored while waiting for further processing. The inventory has to be managed, so the organization knows what quantities and where these items are in the flow. Products require packaging and handling. The distribution of the product from production to the consumer has a path that includes transportation and storage. Finally, the product is disposed of. Disposal can involve many aspects such as recycling, refurbishing, remanufacturing, salvage, or even putting the product into a land fill.

The supply chain attempts to move in one direction, but exceptions happen. **Reverse logistics** is a process that moves products in the opposite flow of the intended supply chain direction that goes from natural resources to the final customer. Products can be damaged and have to flow back up the supply chain until they can be sent back down the supply chain or disposed of. Online purchases such as clothing are frequently returned. Customers expect to return damaged goods. Some companies have an open policy where they will take back any product after the sale. Additional costs to the supply chain for reverse logistics can include customer service, shipping the return, and handling and restocking the product.

SUPPLY CHAIN The processes for producing and supporting a product from natural resources to its final disposition.

REVERSE LOGISTICS Moving products in the opposite flow of the intended supply chain direction that goes from natural resources to the final customer.

Natural Resources

Natural resources are gathered, dug up, or mined. Wood can be gathered for a log cabin. The ground is blasted, and then iron ore is dug up. Coal can be mined. Once the raw materials are collected, they may be immediately moved or temporarily stored and then transported for the next step of the process.

Obtaining raw materials can become a business and even a national priority. Platinum was first discovered by the Spanish during silver and gold mining operations. Initially a nuisance, the use of platinum became important. Currently, the automotive industry uses platinum for vehicle parts. The metal is used to help catalytic converters lower pollution emissions. As a rare metal, sourcing is limited. South Africa produces three fourths of the world's platinum. Other sources come from Russia, Canada, and the United States. Certain raw materials are rare and have limited quantities.

As the world has shifted to being over 50% urban, obtaining food sources creates a demand for a supply chain from the agricultural areas to the city. In a typical large grocery store, food can be found from all over the world. Some stores are marketing more locally grown products in an attempt to connect the customer with local farmers, supporting jobs in the local area. Should the earth warm significantly, futurists predict that farming will be pushed in the Northern hemisphere to Canada, Scandinavia, and Russia and in the Southern hemisphere to Argentina. As the world's population grows, obtaining food can become a national priority. Changes in demographics can create more demand for certain products.

Water is used for human consumption and also for commercial use. Manufacturing can use large quantities of water. Water can be used for cooling heat-producing machinery and cleaning components or products. As the population increases and more manufacturing facilities are built, many predict water will become a scarce resource in the near future. Businesses have to consider the availability of water when constructing new plants. Water is a resource with many uses.

Storage

As natural resources are waiting to be moved or arrive at a production facility, they may need to be stored. Some raw materials can be warehoused right next to the manufacturing facility. Water can be collected from a spring and used for bottled water or in a brewery. Dr. Pepper built its initial facility around a well. The water could be brought up and stored near the bottle filling equipment. Setting up production facilities near natural resources saves on moving costs. Storage can be a large yard in an open space, a building, or some type of container. Iron ore and coal are kept outside until needed. Buildings, typically referred to as warehouses, protect materials from damage and help keep them safe from theft. Spring water is put in a tank until ready for insertion into a consumer bottle or can. Partially processed goods can be stored as they wait for movement to the next step in the supply chain. Finished products may have to be stored until they are transported along the supply chain to their final destinations. Storing materials and goods is a major function of the supply chain.

Along with storing, **inventory management** seeks to have the right quantity on hand at the right place. Supply chain management attempts to balance the demand of inventory with the supply available. Having the data is not a problem in the world of computers and databases. Having the right information in the right format is what managers need. In trying to predict the market, managers often try to store stock for possible customer demand. Because the supply chain is complex and difficult to predict, excess inventory can end up on longer periods of storage than planned. This surplus stockpiling of products that cannot be sold results in the **bullwhip effect**. Inventory management is constantly concerned with the high and lows of stocking products.

INVENTORY MANAGEMENT Seeks to have the right quantity on hand at the right place.

BULLWHIP EFFECT Surplus stockpiling of products that cannot be sold.

Transportation

Most natural resources must be moved to the next stage of the transformation process. From the production facility, the components or products are distributed to the customer. Six basic modes of **transportation** make up the supply chain: water, rail, truck, air, pipeline, and digital. These capabilities form a transportation network to carry goods from one stage of the supply chain to another. Transportation is typically the most expensive cost of the supply chain.

TRANSPORTATION Moving materials and products through one or more of the following methods: water, rail, truck, air, pipeline, and digital.

Water

Historically, water has been the primary means of moving goods over long distances. Rivers and oceans served as the means to move goods across the globe. The Europeans craved silk and spices. These items had to be transported from India and other countries from the East, and the easiest way to do this was transporting the goods over water. Water is still a key means of transporting goods around the earth. Barges are still used to move materials up and down rivers. Container ships carry large loads of cargo across the ocean. New Orleans is typically known for Mardi Gras, the Superdome, and Cajun food; however, the city serves as a major port for the United States. 31 states touch the Mississippi River, and barges can be seen traveling along the river. Water is still a major mode of transportation.

Rail

Rail became a new means of transportation in the late 1800s. Goods and people could be transported faster and more directly. Trains can still move large amounts of bulk raw materials such as coal and grain. They also move containers from port to the destination or to another port for further shipment across the ocean. A container can arrive from Asia in the port of Long Beach, California and moved to New York City by train and be loaded on a ship for Europe. The United States has the most mileage for rail lines, followed by Russia, China, India, Canada, and Germany. Trains still provide a viable means for moving certain goods.

Trucks

Trucks entered the scene as a major means of transport in the 1950s. Trucks started to transport goods earlier, but the advent of the interstate road system transformed the trucking industry. Trucks could travel where trains could not go. They provided a flexibility for transporting cargo faster and could carry smaller loads.

Pipelines

Pipelines move many bulk items such as petroleum and gas. Pipelines actually move large volumes but at a slower rate than other means. The public is generally not aware of how extensive the pipeline system is. According to *The World Factbook* (2013), the United States has natural gas pipelines running for 1,984,321 kilometers (1,232,999 miles) and petroleum products for 240,711 kilometers (149,570 miles) for a total of 2,225,032 kilometers (1,382,571 miles). Russia ranks second with 259,913 (149,570 miles), followed by Canada with 100,000 kilometers (62,137 miles), China with 86,921 kilometers (54,010 miles), and the Ukraine

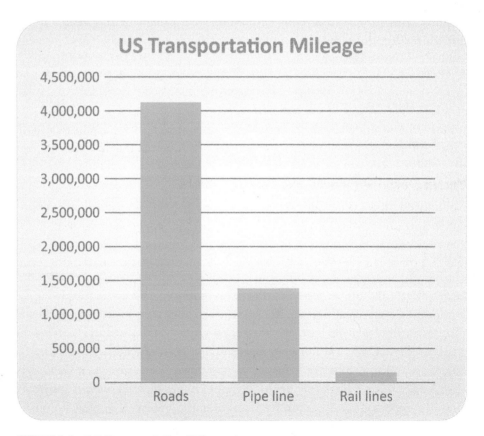

FIGURE 1.1 U.S. Transportation Mileage

with 42,052 kilometers (26,130 miles). Pipelines contribute much to the transportation of materials.

Digital

Finally, digital is a newer form of transport. Many products are delivered through electronic means, such as films, video games, and software programs. Finances are transferred through digital means. Services are provided through technology to support the supply chain. Digital transportation offers a type of transportation throughout the supply chain.

Services Support the Supply Chain

In addition to transportation, services support the supply chain. Organizations are known for their core competencies. Core competencies are the essential functions that the business must do to distinguish itself from other businesses. Walmart is famous for low cost products and an efficient and cost effective supply chain. Users enjoy the ease of use and innovation of Apple products. Colorado Technical University has a core competency for education and students learning at their own pace through Intellipath. Companies find other service organizations to support what is not their primary business strength.

Many companies provide services to supplement the lack of expertise that is not the core competency of an organization. UPS is known for delivering packages. The company also provides managing services to businesses for their transportation needs. They have a business unit that supports other organizations within their supply chain. Their global transportation network can help a company expand into new locations and find ways to save costs for shipping goods. They also offer contracting, custom brokerage, and consulting services. Excel helps companies with supply chain analysis and design; they also support efforts such as warehousing, transportation management, and reverse logistics. Ariba can provide **e-commerce** and payment management solutions. E-commerce uses technology to conduct commercial transactions for customers and merchants and also for merchants with other merchants. Alibaba offers a buyer interface for companies to purchase goods in large volumes. Companies have other firms to turn to who can better support their businesses so that their management and staff can focus on what they are good at.

Technology Supports the Supply Chain

Not only do products flow up and down the supply chain, but technology supports the flow of information. An important aspect of the supply chain is tracking the flow of goods through the system. Computers and handheld devices, such as scanners and smart phones, help to locate shipments, and software tracks the movement of products. Bar code or radio-frequency identification (RFID) scanners can keep track of inventory. Global positioning system (GPS) devices can monitor the location of transportation vehicles and containers. Even drones can be used to move around a warehouse to count inventory. Drones can deliver small packages around a large facility. Inventory is kept in databases that can alert a manager to low quantities or even automatically reorder a product. Knowing where shipments are located in the supply chain helps planning for demand. The quantity of inventory on hand and in transit is also significant for an efficient supply chain. Technology enables a more economical flow of goods along the supply chain.

CHALLENGE

What combinations of the six modes of transportation can you think of for moving products? Water, train, and truck are common. What example covers pipeline and truck? What situation would combine air with another mode of transportation?

E-COMMERCE Uses technology to conduct commercial transactions for customers and merchants and also for merchants with other merchants.

Finances Support the Supply Chain

Finances are passed from one node to another back and forth throughout the supply chain. Most of the finances flow from natural resources to the customer, but in some cases returned or damaged goods may result in money transfer as part of reverse logistics. Organizations are providing goods and services and need to be paid to continue functioning. Managing the payment cycle can keep a business financially healthy and competitive. Cash flow is always a concern for any business. Most small businesses go bankrupt because they are not paid; they are normally capable of doing the work, but they don't have the money. Having working capital enables a company to cover the expenses it occurs and invest more into the business. A successful supply chain has an effective and efficient financial flow.

Supply Chain Management

Supply chain management involves the organization and control of the supply chain. Managing the flow of goods and services is an art and a science. The art involves managing relationships in the supply chain so that they benefit the organization. Although scientific methods are used for planning and executing the flow of goods and services, collaboration is an art for managing organization resources. For example, the market demand and what inventory is required can be estimated. Many organizations have to rely on this estimation to predict the future. Many different types of tools and techniques are used to quantify demand and inventory, yet managers have to make decisions to forecast what the consumers will want.

Supply chain managers have many questions to consider in organizing and controlling the supply chain, and they are as follows:
- How much should be produced?
- Where should the natural resources be taken from?
- How much inventory should be carried?
- How will the products be distributed to the customers?
- How will payment work?
- Are there legal, environmental, or security concerns?
- What is the transportation network?
- Is the technology enabling a more effective and efficient company?

To organize the supply chain, the organization must develop a supply chain network. The network is made up of nodes and links. **Nodes** are locations where supply chain processes happen. Examples are places where natural resources are extracted, production facilities, and distribution warehouses. **Links** are the ways products are moved by the means of the transportation system. Services help keep the network process moving. The nodes and linkages must effectively and efficiently manage the supply chain from beginning to end. Supply chain management tracks and controls these processes of goods and services. The management of the supply chain keeps the products, information, and finances flowing.

Logistics Supports the Supply Chain

Logistics is an essential and major part of supply chain management. Logistics was developed from the military, and the commercial aspect concerns itself primarily with the movement and storage of goods. Logistics looks at the supply chain network to find ways to transport products in an efficient and cost effective way. While waiting for transport or upon delivery, the placement of goods for further processing or delivery to the customer must be considered. Materials handling is also important to protect goods from damage and theft. The equipment used for handling can be found all along the supply chain. Packaging considerations allow products to flow safely. The transportation and storage of goods needs to be considered with the risks of pilferage. Logistics is a significant part of supply chain management.

The Relationship of Operations and Supply Chain Management

An organization has many functional parts. Marketing finds ways to connect with the customer and determine which products the customers want. Sales attempts to sell products. Accounting keeps track of finances. Financing looks at the earnings and expenditures. Technology supports the electronic devices and network of the organization and its Internet presence. Procurement handles sourcing of resources and contracts. **Operations** or operations management focuses on the transformation process for products and the services needed to support these goods. A dairy plant takes cream from cows and materials for the container and transforms both into milk that is convenient to transport and store for consumers. A beverage plant takes water and other ingredients and makes a drink. An automobile repair shop takes a broken car as an input and transforms it, hopefully, into a functional car. Operations has a vital purpose in an organization and usually requires the majority of resources and finances of a business.

Supply chain management works with operations management in many ways. The primary role for supporting operations encompasses logistics. Operations can produce a certain volume of products. Does the transportation network have the capacity to move the products in a timely manner? Where will inventory be stored until it is time to move it to market? Consider a new film or book that will go out to a wide audience around the country and, perhaps, the world. Much coordination has to happen to synchronize the delivery of the product at the right time with the right quantity at the right place. Imagine that a new film or book has a predetermined release date. Depending on the anticipated market popularity, the volume of items could be tens of thousands or even hundreds of thousands of copies that need to be transported to thousands of locations. The transportation network has to run both effectively to make the delivery date and efficiently to have the right quantities at the right place. Operations management and supply chain management have to work together for continued success.

OPERATIONS Focuses on the transformation process for products and the services needed to support these goods.

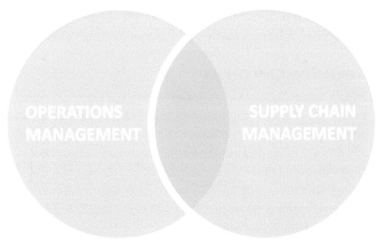

FIGURE 1.2 The Relationship of Operations and Supply Chain Management

This continued coordination has to function both efficiently and cost effectively to maintain the business. Many factors can influence the supply chain. The transportation network can face ambiguous situations. Inclement weather can disrupt deliveries. Strikes can cripple a segment of the supply chain. The supply chain has many threat risks and unknown events that can impact the flow of goods and services. If tsunamis destroy infrastructure so that suppliers could not transport components and products, this affects the supply chain. In some areas, production would have to stop until facilities could be repaired or rebuilt. Several causes can create havoc for the work flow for operations and the supply chain.

Each organizational function has a different responsibility for a product. Marketing looks at packaging the product differently than operations. The "look and feel" of the packaging is important to attract the customer when on display. Something as simple as laundry detergent can have several features to draw in a prospective buyer. What size will the container be? What will be the shape of the container? What kind of handle will it have? How will the spout pour out the liquid? What kind of cap should close and secure the liquid? Operations, though, has a different perspective for the product's design. What materials are need to construct the container? What are the environmental concerns for disposal? Can the manufacturing line be tooled to make this design? Supply chain management views the products in a different way than marketing and operations. Although operations initially packages the product to protect it from damage, there are other factors to consider such as how many can be put in a box and what should be the strength of the box. The supply chain role primarily falls into the logistics role for storing and transporting the product. How many boxes could be stacked in a warehouse without damaging some of the containers? Can the boxes be put into a truck or container to maximize space? As previously mentioned, transportation is one the highest costs of the supply chain. Does the product have sensitively to temperatures? Each function of marketing, operations, and supply chain management has a piece of the overall whole for package design.

Legal Concerns for the Supply Chain

In the interest of public safety, governments pass laws and write regulations affecting supply chain management. For example, truck drivers transporting goods on public roads have rules for how many hours they can drive and how much they need to allocate for rest. Hazardous materials have many rules for proper handling and storage. Vehicles have to meet emissions standards. Supply chain managers must adhere to government requirements.

Security Concerns

Supply chain managers have to look after the safety of their inventory. Employees collaborate in mines to steal minerals such as gold and silver. They know the processes and know how to get around the security system and accountability processes by having more than one person involved; this allows them to bypass the organizational checks and auditing. Customer facing businesses, such as retail stores, deal with customers and internal employees stealing. These problems add to the cost of goods and the competitiveness of the company.

Another concern for the supply chain is counterfeit goods. Fake components can be found in military weapon systems. Electrical products

CHALLENGE

Certain food products require climate controlled environments for shipment and storage. What would be an example of a non-food product that would need temperature control?

can catch on fire because inferior materials were used. Other ingredients can be placed in healthcare products that can actually harm people. Counterfeit products are introduced into the supply chain, some posing as Nike shoes or Gucci bags. The challenge for the current law enforcement system is that even if counterfeiters are caught, they can pay several million dollars and spend only a few months in prison. Many accept the risk and make an underground business quite lucrative. Law enforcement officials struggle to keep up with the volume of goods coming into the country and overseeing those domestically made in the underground system. Customs have to consider the balance of timely movement of goods with inspections to hinder counterfeit flows into the country. Counterfeit components can disrupt the supply chain and threaten an organization's reputation.

To mitigate the risk of counterfeit goods, companies must have good quality assurance processes. **Quality assurance** attempts to create confidence in the processes so that the product meets specifications and customer expectations. Most people typically do not complete a full inspection of their personal vehicles before driving. People have the quality assurance that when they start the vehicle, it will run. Most also have confidence in the food industry. Otherwise, people would grow all their own food or test it out on someone else first before eating. In the growing urban living environment, most people do not have the opportunity to grow all their own food. **Quality control** examines the level of quality for creating and sustaining the products. Quality control has a two-sided function. One aspect checks that the components or product meet the requirements to deliver to the customer. The other side observes substandard performance and possible ways to correct it. Quality control can be expensive, but technology can assist with this work. In the previous example, some may spot check their vehicles by inspecting the tires before driving. Checking the tires is a quality control task. What was once done by humans can be accomplished with the help of technology. Sensors can check beverage lines for foreign materials in the bottles. Infrared sensors can monitor train tracks for weak metals so that they can be repaired. Sound sensors can hear brakes that could be going out. Custom agents use scanners to see into trucks and containers. These capabilities can increase the ability to find contraband or counterfeit goods. Quality control examines the expected requirements and offers ways to improve a product.

Some view quality management as a burden. The extra cost for a robust quality program is not worth the investment. Others advocate that quality is free because defects can cost more than the cost of quality and damage the reputation of the company. Many car manufacturers and producers of other products have spent large sums of money for recalls. In some cases, government prosecution has cost companies significant amounts that impacted their cash flow. Quality is a decision that managers must consider in the supply chain.

THE GLOBALIZATION OF THE SUPPLY CHAIN

The supply chain is very global in nature. As mentioned earlier in the chapter, the European demand for silk and spices led to efforts to find new trade routes. First, they found a way around

QUALITY ASSURANCE
Attempts to create confidence in the processes so that the product meets specifications and customer expectations.

QUALITY CONTROL
Checks the level of quality for creating and sustaining the products.

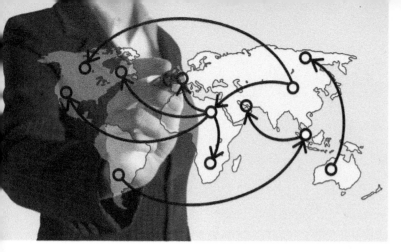

Africa to minimize the expensive network of traders. Then the explorers found new land that opened up new trade routes. Eventually, the supply chain networks became quite complicated and extensive. A global supply chain forms a network that stretches across many nations as different suppliers send raw materials to a manufacturing facilities in the same or different country. Then the product can be distributed anywhere in the world. A product can be produced in South Korea, transported by container on a ship to the port of Vancouver, Canada, loaded on a train to the Port of Montreal on the East Coast, loaded on a ship to Europe, unloaded to a truck, and finally transported to the final destination. The case is clear that an effective and efficient supply chain is important to keep goods moving from the beginning to the end.

Even finding raw materials continues to be a global effort. China buys copper from Chile. India purchases diamonds and gold from the United States. The United States receives oil from Kazakhstan, a former member of the Soviet Union. Obtaining natural resources remains a national and business need for the world. Those requirements influence political and financial decisions between countries. Organizations are trying to acquire raw materials, putting the holder of the goods in a good position to negotiate. Getting resources is often a global operation for the supply chain.

Many factors influence a global supply chain. Consumers have more power with online capabilities. Consumers can compare prices, and some Web sites offer a comparison of multiple vendors. They can choose between actual physical

AN ENGLISH TEACHER CREATED THE LARGEST E-COMMERCE WEB SITE!

Jack Ma was teaching English in 1995. Traveling to Seattle with a trade delegation as an interpreter in 1995, he had an idea that China could make use of the Internet. From his apartment, he created an online directory of Chinese businesses. Then his group of 18 created online buying services called Alibaba; the company grew quite fast. Jack Ma is the wealthiest individual in China. Alibaba is now larger than Amazon and EBay combined. Alibaba.com provides wholesale connections between suppliers and business buyers. As a promoter for small businesses, Jack Ma also formed Taobao.com to meet the needs of Chinese consumers and later created Tmall.com for high end products. AliExpress.com was launched in 2010 to cater to foreign consumers, having most purchasers from the United States, Russia, and Brazil. Alibaba also uses AliPay, similar to PayPal for paying the suppliers. The Alibaba Group opened its shares on the New York Stock exchange in September of 2014 and became the highest entry in history at $25 billion. The Alibaba Group has become quite successful as an e-commerce provider. Goods and finances flow through the supply chain with the support of technology. One of the challenges for e-commerce sites is delivering authentic goods. Many suppliers are using the system to sell fake goods. With so many vendors and transactions online, how does an e-commerce site protect itself and its customers from counterfeit goods?

locations or online shopping. Even though many predicted in the 1990s that the physical store would go away, companies are still expanding physical locations to sell goods. Many people still want to actually see and perhaps touch and feel a product before buying. For online or retail stores, buyers can look at reviews to see if a product is worth purchasing or check which products are highly recommended. They can drill down into details for perspectives from fellow buyers. Consumers also have a platform for issues and complaints. The seller can have a Web site, e-mail, or phone number for feedback. People are empowered with many Web tools to make their plights known. Suppliers have to be more sensitive to the possible damage to their reputation if they do not heed the power of social media.

The supply chain can be impacted by international trade. **Trade agreements** offer advantages to the countries within the arrangements made by the respective governments. The World Trade Organization (WTO) sets the rules for trade among its 161 members. The decisions are made by governments, but the intent is to provide fair trade for businesses and individuals. Conflicts are handled by a negotiation process to solve any disputes. Another well-known trade agreement is the North American Free Trade Agreement (NAFTA). Although the term "Free" is used, these trade agreements have many stipulations. However, businesses can use the trade agreement for a competitive advantage. For example, the Mexican maquiladora is a manufacturing area that allows for duty and tax free incentives along the U.S. borders. Supply chain managers can save on duties and taxes by locating factories to the maquiladora. They can also save on transportation costs due to the proximity of Mexico to the United States. Trade agreements can offer businesses a competitive advantage in the supply chain.

Technology enhances the globalization of the supply chain. Not only is the Web used for selling and buying products, technology has other uses. Communication systems enhance the capabilities of supply chain management. Smart phones can scan, track, and report different statistics. Collaboration Web sites and e-mail allow for a round the clock capability for offering and exchanging information. Supply

TRADE AGREEMENTS
Arrangements made by governments that give duty- and tax-free incentives to promote fair trade.

A SUPPLY CHAIN COLLABORATION WEB SITE

Ariba.com is a collaboration Web site the gives supply chain managers a global network to tap into. SAP, software, used by many companies, acquired Ariba. Ariba provides buyer and supplier management. The network helps supply chain managers navigate around disruptions in the supply chain. Interruptions can be caused by force majeure (acts of nature, strikes, political upheaval, or other reasons). The Ariba network gives users the tools to communicate in real time and to manage their supply chain. The company offers a contract management capability to cut down on processing time. A business intelligence module helps users analyze spending to lower costs. An automated workflow allows sellers and buyers to receive computer or smart phone notifications of order confirmation, shipping, and payment. The software also makes compliance with regulatory requirements more streamlined. Ariba is one technology solution that organizations can use to manage their supply chain.

What kind of disruptions can impact the supply chain? How can companies plan for these interruptions?

chain management depends of the flow of information. Software can transfer funds to minimize the time and cost of paper methods. The technology systems help small businesses survive and thrive. Most small businesses are able to perform the goods and services they offer because of technology. The major cause of bankruptcy is failure to get paid. Web systems allow for immediate payment and minimize the cash flow problems that small businesses deal with. Technology is a major part of the global supply chain.

WHY IS SUPPLY CHAIN MANAGEMENT IMPORTANT FOR BUSINESSES?

The backbone of many businesses consists of the supply chain. In the past, many organizations focused on marketing the product, selling the product, and producing the product to meet demand. However, other aspects of the supply chain were left to the supply chain managers. Companies are more aware of how transportation, inventory management, packaging, materials handling, supply chain security, and other parts of the supply chain can impact a business. A large sum of money is invested in the supply chain. Most of these finances for supply chain management are in manufacturing, transportation, and inventory management. Production requires these expenditures to be equipment and materials, human resources, and raw materials. Research shows that most companies face a supply chain crisis every 4 to 5 years. These threats can come from a variety of directions, such as price competition, natural disasters, government regulation, or poor quality products. Most suffer severe implications for years after the crisis. Nearly half do not recover from a major supply chain crisis. The business must recognize the value that supply chain management brings to the organization.

Financial flow can be critical for some businesses. Timely payment for goods and services in the supply chain can influence the profits or even the functioning of an organization. The amount of financial reserves an organization has must cover supply chain disruptions. Transportation breakdowns can inhibit the flow of goods as can inclement weather. Delays in the delivery of products can impact sales. Workarounds to mitigate transportation issues adds costs.

Technology helps to streamline the supply chain. More processes can be observed for progress updates and completion. Technology helps with the integration of the various business functions. Marketing might have a great idea for a new product, but can operations produce it? Would it be cost effective to do so? Operations may be able to produce a product much cheaper, but will it meet customer requirements? Sourcing of raw materials may be able to find resources much cheaper, but will the quality meet product standards? The ability to use collaboration communication tools helps the company support the supply chain. Information about what demand is anticipated, when the products need to be on location, and what quantity of a product is on hand or where it is in the system are vital to know. The supply chain needs to be connected to the other aspects of the business for an integrated approach to meet the business objectives.

A well-working supply chain maintains the reputation of an organization. When the supply chain becomes ineffective, the image of the company could be impacted.

If expected t-shirts are not delivered on time for an event, the business can suffer embarrassment and possibly lose customers. Poor quality materials and finished products could be delivered in good condition and on time, but customer complaints could wreck the company's reputation. In the same way, businesses that service the supply chain could face penalties or lose contracts. If the company is known for unreliable service, they may not be able to secure enough business to stay afloat.

Commerce is conducted in the United States under the Uniform Commercial Code (UCC). International business falls under the Convention on the International Sale of Goods (CISG). Both of these rule sets provide a means to conduct sales and other business transactions without much legal hassles. Contracts are made according to the UCC in the United States and with the CISG for international business.

HOW SUPPLY CHAIN MANAGEMENT STRATEGY SUPPORTS BUSINESS STRATEGY

The role of strategy for a business is important. **Strategy** is the plan that guides the business to achieve its goals and mission statement. The **mission statement** is a brief declaration about what the business exists for or what its purpose is. For example, the BMW strategy states, "To be profitable and to enhance long-term value in times of change" (2015). And their mission statement reads, "The BMW Group is the world's leading provider of premium products and premium services for individual mobility" (2015). BMW recognizes the requirement to make money to survive as a for-profit business. They also recognize the necessity for change as new models and customer needs change. The focus for BMW is individual mobility. They leave public transport and industrial machines, such as commercial trucks, out of the scope for their business. From a logistics standpoint, they recognize the value of logistics. One of their logistics strategies adapts to customer changes after the order is placed. BMW has a program called customer-oriented sales and production process (COSP); it allows customers to make changes to their orders shortly before the car goes into production. This means the logistics system has to adjust time lines to deliver on the promised date. This change may seem simple, but imagine the impact of many customers making changes at the last possible minute. Manufacturing facilities are set up for efficiency and lower costs.

BMW also has a supply chain strategy to improve its transportation logistics to lower its environmental impact. The two departments, logistics planning and transportation logistics, plan for the movement of vehicles, parts, and materials, a number amounting to 13.7 billion ton-kilometers per year. The raw materials must arrive at the right place, have the right quantity, and come at the right time to make the parts and components of a BMW. The parts are manufactured in different locations and must be transported to the next step of the supply chain. The challenge for this strategy is lowering fossil fuel emissions by coordinating transportation. Using more capacity of the truck, rail, and shipping modes means fuller vehicles, cars, and containers and less empty runs. BMW's supply chain supports the business strategy by improving its logistics functions.

Every organization has certain core competencies. These are important functions of the company that match the strategy and mission statement. A consumer would expect Coca-Cola to be better at the beverage industry than Home Depot, whose core competency is home improvement and building supplies. Even though Walmart has the Sam's brand, and Target has Market Pantry for beverages, they both depend on the beverage industry to provide those products. They are an organizational customer for the drink commerce. Walmart and Target could provide home improvement and building supply products, but they could not offer the magnitude of products and services that Home Depot does. Home Depot's core competencies would be the volume of products to lower costs, the ability to offer larger and cheaper quantities to commercial vendors, and equipment and tool rental. Walmart's core competencies include volume sales of products with acceptable quality, supply change management, and lower operational costs. Customers are comfortable with the level of quality for the price in the United States. However, Walmart failed in Germany because the American strategy of cheap goods did not match German expectations. Germans typically view cheap goods as low quality and will pay more for perceived higher quality.

Coca-Cola has quite a successful history of market share and offering products that consumers like. The company changed its strategy one time and developed a product called *New Coke*. With a new formula, the supply chain had to adapt to produce the new product. The bottling lines had to be modified to produce New Coke. The design of cans and bottles had to be changed as well. Unfortunately, the outrage from the public was so huge that Coca-Cola went back to the original formula. The company had to absorb the cost of retooling the supply chain back to the previous process.

Note how IKEA works supply chain management into their strategy, as seen in the following statement:

> The IKEA Concept starts with the idea of providing a range of home furnishing products that are affordable to the many people, not just the few. It is achieved by combining function, quality, design and value - always with sustainability in mind. The IKEA Concept exists in every part of our company, from design, sourcing, packing and distributing through to our business model. Our aim is to help more people live a better life at home. (IKEA, 2015)

The design of products attempts to balance customer wants with the cost effective ways to produce the products. Sourcing is a supply chain function for obtaining raw materials for producing the products. Packing involves how the products are presented to the customer, and logistics functions are used for the way products are protected from damage during shipment. Finally, distributing considers the logistics of transportation, storage, and inventory management.

Companies also have to be aware of cultural issues when developing a global strategy. Home Depot went into China and flopped, whereas IKEA is doing quite well. Home Depot strategists thought the rapid change of Chinese owning their own homes would be a target of opportunity. In the United States, people often go to Home Depot to solve a problem or upgrade their homes. In China, most of the population lives in apartments or condos. They do not have much room for tools and the do-it-yourself products. However, culturally, no one expected Chinese to be do-it-yourself customers. IKEA saves customers money with an assemble yourself model. The Chinese needed examples for how to decorate their living spaces. IKEA's use of showrooms captured the Chinese need for different ways to decorate. From a supply chain management perspective, IKEA can save logistic costs. Many products are produced in China, and IKEA can turn around and offer products to an emerging market closer to the manufacturing facilities.

SPOTLIGHT ON A LOGISTIC'S COMPANY STRATEGY, MISSION, AND PROMISE

Fred Smith wrote a paper in 1965 about the need for a fast delivery system. He envisioned a network that would move medicine, computer parts, and electronics quickly. He earned an average grade on his work. He took the concept and developed FedEx into a global logistics company. The following details different aspects of FedEx and its mission (2015):

Corporate Strategy

The unique FedEx operating strategy works seamlessly and simultaneously on three levels.

Operate independently by focusing on our independent networks to meet distinct customer needs.

Compete collectively by standing as one brand worldwide and speaking with one voice.

Manage collaboratively by working together to sustain loyal relationships with our workforce, customers and investors.

Mission Statement

FedEx Corporation will produce superior financial returns for its shareowners by providing high value-added logistics, transportation and related information services through focused operating companies. Customer requirements will be met in the highest quality manner appropriate to each market segment served. FedEx Corporation will strive to develop mutually rewarding relationships with its employees, partners and suppliers. Safety will be the first consideration in all operations. Corporate activities will be conducted to the highest ethical and professional standards.

In order to fulfill its strategy and mission, FedEx has made the Purple Promise.
"I will make every FedEx experience outstanding."
To keep The Purple Promise, we must:
Do whatever it takes to satisfy our customers.
Always treat customers in a professional, competent, polite and caring manner.
Handle every customer transaction with the precision required to achieve the highest quality service.
Process all customer information with 100 percent accuracy

What aspects of FedEx's strategy and mission statement are directing related to supply chain management? Do you think the Purple Promise is realistic? Why or why not?

Because digital products require a digital transportation network, the logistics function requires servers in the form of memory and storage capacity, electronic network connections, and cyber security.

THE ROLE OF CORPORATE RESPONSIBILITY AND THE SUPPLY CHAIN

SUPPLY CHAIN SUSTAINABILITY The actions an organization takes to minimize damaging the environment by mitigating threat risks and eliminating waste in the supply chain.

The customers want their products and expect the producer to minimize the impact on the environment. **Supply chain sustainability** comprises the actions an organization takes to minimize damaging the environment by mitigating threat risks and eliminating waste in the supply chain. Due to public scrutiny and social media, organizations must be sensitive to the carbon emissions and pollution they produce. Placing trash into landfills is a cost issue for corporations, but the perceived efforts for going green must be balanced when assessing the company's reputation. No organization wants to be accused of contributing to destroying the planet. Yet consumers drive what products the company can produce. Manufacturing can produce what the customers want, but will the buyers consider the extra costs for making environmental friendly products?

The pressure from customers and environmental activist groups pushes organizations to greener standards. Organizations have to develop a strategy for sustainability. The supply chain consumes many resources; therefore, leaders look for ways to lower pollution. The supply chain carbon footprint is the amount of carbon dioxide and other carbon by-products released into the air. Chemicals poured into water and stripped forests and vegetation are other types of contamination. Industrial waste are materials left over after the transformation process. Industrial operations can produce residual contaminants in solid, semi-solid, liquid, or gas forms. The primary contributors to pollution are manufacturing and logistics. Manufacturers have wastewater from cleaning or degreasing metals. The coke process later used in iron production creates ammonia lime sludge. Some by products are classified as hazardous materials, such as pesticides and nuclear waste. Industrial waste can include biodegradable waste such as food processing, animal slaughterhouses, and textile manufacturing. Although people typically think of biodegradable material decomposing in a matter of weeks or months, the U. S. government defines the process as less than one year. Over one year would be considered composting. Under this definition, banana peels are considered compost material. The supply chain creates pollution, and organizational leaders must consider sustainability as part of their business strategy.

Logistics carries a large carbon footprint. The heavy use of diesel trucks and trains adds greatly to carbon emissions. Truck manufacturers are looking for ways to improve on engines to lower the amount of pollutants created. Innovative policies can help with mitigating pollution. UPS implemented a system of delivery in which the trucks avoid left turns and make as many right turns as possible. This simple procedure saved time and gas for the trucks. Companies are using software to analyze transportation routes and vehicle capacity. One of the challenges for logistics is empty loads. Transportation systems have more empty loads than one would think. Trucks often travel empty to pick up another load. Companies resist sharing transportation resources because of the lack of control. Disruptions to the supply chain can hurt a business. Trains carry coal across the United States and return empty to pick up another load. Cleaning scores of railroad cars is more expensive and adds other environmental hazards to the process. For every four containers that reach the

United States from Asia, three return empty. The challenge for the United States is how to lesson that ratio. Logistics can add a lot of contamination to the environment.

Although alternative energy sources are available, the cost of creating and implementing them is often too high. For example, one U. S. city has a fire in its coal burning facility that produces electricity. The leaders had the opportunity to create new forms of energy to lower the carbon footprint. The existing logistics support structure was in place, and many were making good money from its operation. Rather than invest in a new generation of technology, financial gain from the current infrastructure and lack of innovation led the city to rebuild the plant. Alternative energy projects continue, but make up a small percent of the energy created.

Some companies try to innovate new technologies to form a viable business. Tesla manufactures an electric Roadster. To lower costs to attract customers and streamline the logistics system, they offered cars direct from the factory. Some states have or are in the process of passing legislation to force the company to establish dealerships. The car dealership has a strong lobby and can influence officials to counter this type of logistical structure.

Futurists see a network of electric stations set up in the fashion of gas stations. Customers can hook up their electric cars for a fee or perhaps a monthly rental cost. Delivering electricity is a supply chain with several challenges. The first is the initial set up cost to establish the logistics network. Does the supply of electricity come from the local power grid, or can the company create an alternative power source? Where do they place the electrical connections, so the car owners can easily access them? Is there financial support to invest in the business? How low will the payback period be? A **payback period** is the time the initial investment for the project is recouped. How does the new method survive the threat of competition from the traditional auto industry? Any strategy has to consider the consumer perception for cheaper and convenient modes of individual mobility. Creating a sustainable logistics system that can create, store, and move electricity is very costly for the time it might take to get a return on the investment.

PAYBACK PERIOD The time the initial investment for the project is recouped.

Almost every medium to large company has a corporate responsibility section on their Web site. The company can present their sustainability for energy use in manufacturing and logistics. Deforestation concerns have brought in a heavily regulated environment for procuring wood. Countries have various environmental laws. Those with lower standards can draw manufacturers in to build factories. This opportunity provides jobs and capital for these countries. Activists claim that the foreign companies are exploiting the people and should do more to raise living standards. The conditions are not considered acceptable to standards in other nations. The corporations respond with the rationale that they can influence the manufacturing but cannot control it. Each country is sovereign and can make their own laws and rules. Many companies also counter that the workers earn an average or above average income in that country.

One of the keys for sustainability is accountability. A company can make many claims, but are they actually doing what they claim to do? Many operations are using independent auditors to verify their green actions. This practice raises the bar for integrity because a third party group is checking the sustainability record of the company.

The popularity of consumer desires for sustainable products can have drawbacks for businesses. In an effort to promote their image, some companies have been accused of greenwashing. **Greenwashing** is marketing green friendly products and deceiving the consumers of green practices. Many organizations have been brought to accountability through various activist groups. The list not only includes for-profit businesses, but also government, political leaders, and non-profit groups. Source

GREENWASHING Marketing green friendly products and deceiving the consumers of green practices.

Watch, Greenwashing Index, and Greenpeace Greenwashing educate the public and post information about actual or perceived violators. The Asian Pacific Environmental Network attempts to address issues related to the Asian Pacific regions and the United States. For the United States, the Federal Trade Commission (FTC) works to inform the public on consumer issues. The Web site offers a guide to businesses about green marketing and practices. Although the FTC has many cases, the number of greenwashing are few and far between. Those campaigning against greenwashing have focused more on social media and organizing demonstrations.

Corporations spend money to counter green regulations. Business leaders claim to advocate going green while covertly trying to lobby the government to mitigate future initiatives and even remove or restrict current environmental laws and regulations. These leaders are attempting to protect their wealth and may also justify the business' need to lower standards.

Sustainability has many approaches but the following model of four ways for a sustainment strategy is a good one to look at. Recycling is the most known. Remanufacturing encompasses remaking a product. Refurbishing would consist of making old products useable. Salvage is a way to reuse scrap or take apart products and using them for other purposes.

Recycling is famous and becoming worldwide. Germans recycle glass and subdivide the containers into the various colors of white, brown, and green. However, most European waste ends up in China. The pressure to raise the cost of landfills caused the Europeans to export more waste. China processes about 70% of global waste. The Chinese recently passed legislation called the "Green Fence." Because about a quarter of waste is contaminated by food and mixed products, the Chinese are enforcing higher standards of waste. The added cost for storage while waiting for inspection and rejection rates causes countries to relook at internal means of disposal. Recycling can be a profitable business. Many states have deposits on bottles. One of the main collectors of bottles are homeless people. New technologies can create opportunities to recycle bottles for manufacturing.

Remanufacturing is a common process for taking used products and putting them back in the market as new products. Automobile parts distributers charge for certain used parts. These components are sent back to the manufacturer and returned to the market in a new condition. Printer manufacturers include pre-paid mailers with print drums. Users can simply mail the old cartridge back to the source. The resources to make a new cartridge is much higher than the reused process.

Refurbishing takes used products and renovates them to a satisfactory state for resale. Damaged computers that are returned by customers or damaged in transit or storage can be repaired. If a laptop was scratched and the screen cracked, a refurbish facility could replace the screen and offer the product at a discounted price. Many consumers could overlook a scratched case.

Salvage takes on many forms. Scrap steel is remanufactured into steel that can be used for other products. Containers are sent to West Africa with network cables and other electronic parts. Many teenagers needing work burn the cables in open air to extract the copper. They sell the day's work for about $1 to $2. Developed countries are sending waste to developing nations, and this can result in health hazards for those who try to find a way to support themselves and their families. Old vehicles can be sent to a lot, and the parts are sold. Salvage can involve the breaking of old ships or train locomotives to be distributed for other uses. Scrap can be viewed differently from waste because scrap can always be used for another purpose. Salvage is taking consumed products and finding ways to reuse them.

DISCUSSION QUESTIONS

Consider the following questions as you review this chapter:

1. What is a supply chain? Describe the basic supply chain for a product that you are familiar with.

2. What are the implications for businesses operating in a global supply chain?

3. How does the supply chain support a business?

4. Why is sustainability important for supply chain management? What is greenwashing and how can consumers be sure organizations are truly green?

REFERENCES

Alibaba. (2015). *Products*. Retrieved from http://www.alibaba.com

Alibaba Group. (2015). *About us*. Retrieved from http://www.alibabagroup.com/en/about/businesses

Ariba, Inc. (2015). *Solutions*. Retrieved from http://www.ariba.com

BMW Group. (2015). *Company portrait. Strategy*. Retrieved from http://www.bmwgroup.com

Central Intelligence Agency. (2013). *The world factbook: Pipelines*. Retrieved from
    https://www.cia.gov/library/publications/the-world-factbook/index.html

Container Research Institute. (2015). Retrieved from
    http://www.container-recycling.org/index.php/publications

EnviroMedia social marketing. (2015). Retrieved from
    http://www.greenwashingindex.com/about-greenwashing/

Excel. (2015). *What we do*. Retrieved from http://www.exel.com

Federal Trade Commission. (2015). *Going green*. Retrieved from
    http://www.consumer.ftc.gov/features/feature-0013-going-green

FedEx. (2015). *About FedEx*. Retrieved from http://about.van.fedex.com

Greenpeace. (2015). *Greenwashing*. Retrieved from http://www.stopgreenwash.org/

Home Depot. (2015). *Investor FAQ, What is Home Depot's mission statement?* Retrieved from
    http://ir.homedepot.com/phoenix.zhtml?c=63646&p=irol-faq#37549

Huff, B. (2014). *How to optimize supply chain operations for strong cash flow*. Retrieved from
    http://www.industryweek.com/cash-is-king

IKEA. (2015). *This is IKEA*. Retrieved from http://www.ikea.com/cn/en/

Lajoie, M., & Shearman, N. (2014). *What is Alibaba?* Retrieved from
    http://projects.wsj.com/alibaba/

NAFTA. (2012). *North American Free Trade Agreement*. Retrieved from
    http://www.naftanow.org/default_en.asp

Office of the United States Trade Representative. (2015). *Countries and regions*. Retrieved from
    https://ustr.gov

Sherman, E. (2013). *Resilient supply chain management: Turn disaster response into a competitive
    strength*. Retrieved from http://www.middlemarketcenter.org/expert-perspectives/
    resilient-supply-chain-management-turn-disaster-response-into-a-competitive-strength

SourceWatch. (2015). *Greenwashing*. Retrieved from
    http://www.sourcewatch.org/index.php/Greenwashing

United Parcel Service of America, Inc. (2015). *UPS supply chain solutions*.
    Retrieved from http://www.ups-scs.com/

Introduction to Logistics

Bubba is looking online for a Christmas present for his mother. He is more of a spontaneous person and finally gets around to finding a gift. He thinks that it will be no problem because everything on the Internet is fast. He is in Pennsylvania, and his mother is in Ohio. It is December 23, and he searches for an appropriate gift. There is something he likes, but the business is in Florida and that would be too far away. He finds some nice jewelry from a vendor in Indiana. He thinks to himself that that it will be no problem for an overnight delivery service. The posting offers next day delivery, and it is still morning. So he orders the item and pays for gift-wrapping and next day delivery. When he makes his yearly evening call to his mom on the 24th, there is no present. He follows up on the evening of the 25th and still no gift. Finally, he calls the delivery service when they open on the 26th and waits for a long time to get someone on the line. He finds out the package will be delivered that day. After giving the customer service a piece of his mind, he hangs up angry and frustrated. "Why did they promise next day delivery if they could not keep their word?" he says.

Consider the following questions as you discuss this scenario:

1. How does a consumer select products?

2. What does the retail store have to consider when keeping products on the shelves?

WHAT ARE THE BREADTH AND DEPTH OF LOGISTICS FUNCTIONS?

The Christmas season is a challenge for logistics. The amount of packages sent and received surges to a yearly high, and logistics companies struggle to manage the flood of deliveries. Even though they know it is coming every year, planning for the overwhelming number of freight to move stretches the system beyond its limits. UPS ships 18 million packages a day, and FedEx ships about 9 million. The United States postal system delivers around 512 million letters and packages on a normal day. Even when these organizations plan and execute for the holiday season, their capacity is still less than the demand. When the holiday comes, this increase in movement goes beyond their capabilities. How does the industry capitalize on a peak season? And how do consumers prepare? E-commerce sites are learning the perils of offering next day delivery on the 23rd of December. Logistics takes on a very wide role in the business world.

LOGISTICS The movement and storage of products along the supply chain.

Logistics is the movement and storage of products along the supply chain. Fundamentally, logistics comes in three types. Business logistics encompasses the movement of products from the raw materials to the formation of the product to the customer and finally its disposal. Companies producing electronic products focus on developing new technology and supporting current products, meaning that they outsource logistics functions to other companies. Some organizations maintain logistics, such as Walmart. The Walmart trucking fleet and distribution

KEY TERMS

- ➤ big data (p. 33)
- ➤ electronic data interchange (EDI) (p. 36)
- ➤ enterprise resource planning (ERP) (p. 32)
- ➤ internet of things (IoT) (p. 34)
- ➤ inventory management (p. 25)
- ➤ just-in-time (JIT) (p. 25)
- ➤ logistics (p. 23)
- ➤ materials handling (p. 25)
- ➤ radio frequency identification (RFID) (p. 31)
- ➤ sourcing (p. 24)
- ➤ transportation (p. 24)
- ➤ vendor-managed inventory (VMI) (p. 32)

centers sustain the supply chain; although, they add outsourced companies to supplement the demand. Military logistics involves the movement of personnel, equipment, and supplies to support military operations. Event logistics looks at a large gathering, such as a concert or sports venue. Another example could be a disaster relief effort anywhere in the world. When Nepal was hit by a devastating earthquake, their main shipping hub, the airport, was damaged. Relief agencies had to find other ways to send supplies through the mountainous terrain to help those in need. When Hurricane Katrina hit New Orleans, the U.S. government found out that it could not respond as well as the military and other large commercial businesses such as Walmart and Home Depot. The military and certain companies are used to the logistics required to move people and materials to respond to a large event.

Sourcing

Sourcing is the organizational function that finds and coordinates the raw materials, materials, and support that is required for products moving along the supply chain. Logistics supports sourcing by moving what sourcing has acquired. Sourcing has to consider the costs for the logistics system. When a company is looking for natural resources, the market can be the entire world. China brings in copper from Chile. Companies are negotiating oil from many sources, such as the Middle East, Russia, and Venezuela. China and Indonesia have large supplies of tin. But when large deposits of tin were found in Mongolia, the tin market adjusted to a new supplier. Sourcing serves the supply chain by finding out what the organization needs.

Sourcing manages the contracting for other aspects of the supply chain. When the logistics system needs new equipment, sourcing gathers the requirements and looks for suitable sellers. A warehouse may need a new forklift. Administration may need new office supplies. The organization may outsource parts of the logistics system, and contracting manages them. Sourcing sustains the supply chain with acquisition and contract management.

Production

The production of a product falls under operations management. Operations can transform raw materials into products. Often, this process can involve multiple stages to produce one product. A typical car can have 700 to 900 parts that, in turn, require movement and storage. Logistics moves these components from one facility to another. The suppliers also have to manage the flow of parts and store enough inventory to keep the production line moving. There is a tier structure that supports the original equipment manufacturer (OEM). For example, the radiator and cap have five tiers in the supply chain. The radiator comes from a facility in Tennessee, and this will be a tier one supplier. The cap would be a second tier that comes from India. The rubber and steel frame could come from two different companies in England to form the third and fourth tier, and the fifth tier is the delivery of the actual steel from Germany. This long supply chain requires coordination and collaboration among the various suppliers so that the parts can arrive at the vehicle manufacturing facility.

Movement of Goods

Moving materials and products through one or more of the following methods: water, rail, truck, air, pipeline, and digital is known as **transportation**. Usually,

transportation is the highest cost for logistics. Raw materials need to be transported to production facilities. Components of a final product may need to be moved. Usually, the final product must be delivered to the customer. In special cases, a person may special order a BMW and travel to pick up the vehicle in Munich, Germany. Parents may travel to a foreign country to pick up an adopted child. In a twist of the definition of a product, some companies move people as is the case with public transport and the military. Consider the supply chain for an airline company such as Delta or TransAero. The aircraft requires maintenance and consumables such as food, beverages, pillows, blankets, headphones, and other items. Even transportation has its own supply chain management.

Storage

Often, raw materials, parts, and products must be stored while waiting for their next move along the supply chain. Storage can be generally divided into open spaces, buildings, or tanks. Iron ore and coal can be placed in large yards until needed. Buildings often referred to as warehouses are safe places that contain items. Tanks can store liquid or gas products. Storage is frequently the second highest cost in logistics. The cost per square foot or square meter must be factored into the overall cost of a product. Maximizing the capacity of storage is an important element for logistics.

Inventory Management

Closely related to storage is **inventory management;** this is where a supply chain or company seeks to have the right quantity on hand at the right place. As a logistics function, timely movement of items is critical to the success of the supply chain. Managing inventory can be a time consuming effort, even for a small business. Westone is a small manufacturer of custom earplugs and earpieces. Their customers range from people who are hearing impaired and need earpieces, manufacturing earplugs, military pilot earplugs, to wireless earpieces for bands. With a parts inventory of over 125,000 items, keeping track of the required inventory is important for the business. Inventory management strives to balance the organizational needs with the flow along the supply chain.

Just-in-time (JIT) manufacturing is trying to minimize inventory to save on costs and deliver what is needed to the next stage in the supply chain. The amount of safety stock is a constant challenge, so keeping the inventory down saves money, but the supplier does not want to cut it too close. JIT requires more planning and coordination among the members of the supply chain. The level of quality must be extremely high because defects can negatively impact the process. Just-in-time manages inventory levels to maximize efficiency for the organization.

Materials Handling

The stock must be handled as it is moved from place to place within a facility. The volume of stock moving through the system makes the efficiency of movement beneficial to the operation. **Materials handling** involves the processes and equipment needed to move, store, protect, and control inventory. In high labor rate countries, handling the stock during production is not cost effective. Equipment facilitates

INVENTORY MANAGEMENT Seeks to have the right quantity on hand at the right place.

JUST-IN-TIME Minimizing inventory to save on costs and deliver what is needed to the next stage in the supply chain.

MATERIALS HANDLING The processes and equipment needed to move, store, protect, and control inventory.

that are faster, safer, and store larger quantities of materials are desired. Celestial Seasons produces about 8 million tea bags a day in its Boulder, Colorado facility. The company imports large volumes of tea from multiple countries around the world. The tea is stored until its production schedule calls for that type of tea. Some tea is aromatic, such as peppermint, and to avoid contamination with other teas, it has to be stored in a separate, cooler storeroom. The tea is moved by forklift to a giant hopper to feed the production line. The individual bags are filled and sealed along a conveyer belt and put into the boxes. The construction of the boxes is too thin for automated packing, so human labor packs the tea boxes into larger boxes for shipping. The smaller boxes are run down a conveyer belt to a robotic arm that loads pallets for shipping. Materials handling then moves items efficiently within a facility.

Materials handling also involves the transfer of material to a distribution center, transportation terminal, or cross-dock. A distribution center may have to stock up on seasonal items and hold them until the proper time. Equipment such as forklifts, conveyers, and overhead cranes can move items around the facility. Transportation terminals may take in freight and prepare them for another mode of transportation. A container can come into a hub and then be broken down into various sizes so that trucks can carry the products farther. In a cross-dock operation, such as an airfreight carrier, the cargo can be taken off of the plane to a dock and immediately put into a truck for delivery. The logistics system has to determine what equipment and procedures will work best for the situation.

Packaging

The perspectives of marketing, operations, and logistics influence the design of packaging. Marketing intends, for some products, to have an attractive "look and feel" to attract customer. Some products have surrounding material, such as plastic or cardboard, so the displayed item draws attention in the store. A laundry detergent bottle has to take into consideration many marketing decision. What is the shape of the container? How should the handle be designed for customer convenience and look good on the shelf? What should the size of the cap be?

Operations consider the product from the completion of the product to the hand off to logistics. Packaging needs to be just enough to protect the items as they move along the processes until the end of production. Packing the finished products costs labor, and the efficiency of the material handling equipment must be taken into consideration. Operations would prefer larger boxes, and the higher the pallet load, the better.

Logistics is concerned with the potential damage during transit. Heavier loads have a higher negative risk for damage. Products or their parts need a different criteria to protect them from water damage when traveling in containers across the ocean or along inland waterways. Also, maximizing transport space must be planned to minimize shipping empty space.

Finally, packaging needs to meet customer demands for sustainability. Logistics deals more with the final disposal of the packaging material. Up to three quarters of the material can end up in landfills. Companies are under more pressure

LOGISTICS FAILURE: WEBVAN EXPANDED ITS LOGISTICS TOO FAST

The pizza industry was known for fast delivery. It would seem logical that a grocery business could use the same model and provide a service for busy Americans. Louis Borders, who cofounded Borders Bookstore, tried to start an online grocery delivery business. Webvan started in the bubble of the dot.com era in 1996. The business concept involved paying by credit and delivery non-perishable groceries within 30 minutes. The company started off in Silicon Valley, California, and at its first opening in the stock exchange, it had $375 million in assets and the company was worth $1.2 billion. The company expanded to 10 cities and planned for 26 more. What they discovered is that the other cities were slower to come on board. Webvan planned for $1 billion to expand its logistics infrastructure but ended up filing for bankruptcy in 2001. Shares had fallen from around $30 to 6 cents. Webvan is considered one of the biggest dot.com failures in history.

Do you think Borders started Webvan too early, had too aggressive of a business plan for the number of customers, or did not have the logistics infrastructure to support the expansion?

to use environmentally friendly materials and to lower their carbon footprint when moving goods. Marketing managers, operations directors, and logisticians need to collaborate to reduce the amount of pollution as materials, components, and products flow through the supply chain.

BRIEF HISTORY OF ITS GROWING IMPORTANCE
Historical Aspects of Logistics

The concept of logistics has been around for thousands of years. Construction used logistics in the pyramids in Egypt, the great wall of China, and the building of St. Petersburg, Russia. Military operations depended on good logistics systems to sustain victories on the battlefield. Alexander the Great had to strategically consider multiple climates, terrains, and supplies during his many campaigns. The Mongolians developed a strategy of using two horses for its mounted warriors, one for battle and one for carrying supplies. Napoleon, who subdued most of Europe, stated that an army marches on its stomach. The D-Day invasion in 1944 required a significant amount of logistical planning and support to sustain the beachhead in France.

From a commercial perspective, logistics developed from a compartmentalized approach to an integrated system to stay competitive in the global marketplace. The decentralized methods could not measure costs effectively, and much waste resulted from the fragmentation of functions. Sourcing and many of the functions that led into production, such as demand forecasting and production planning, transitioned into inbound logistics by the 1980s. Transportation for distribution, distribution, and others merged into outbound logistics. Manufacturing inventory, inventory management for the finished goods, logistics packaging, material handling, and storage split into the inbound and outbound logistics. That change brought the manufacturing process as the dividing point for logistics managers. Operations management became the integration of the manufacturing processes. By the 21st century, the logistics functions were brought into a system known as supply chain management. Businesses can now look at the total cost of the system. The supply chain developed the model of the value chain so that business intelligence and planning could utilize this model for a competitive advantage. Senior management and investors have quantifiable data to analyze the cost effectiveness and efficiency of the supply chain.

Logistics companies exploit this opportunity to provide a competitive service for other organizations. Some governments control the postal and telephone system. Many are privatizing these operations as Germany did with the Deutsche Post in 1995 and German Telecom in 1996. The commercial aspects of mail and communications means that governments depend on these services for part of their logistics support. The military relies on some commercial ventures to move people and supplies around the world; they put vehicles on commercial trains to transport to a port for overseas deployment. Imagine a local police force with its own tow trucks for illegally parked vehicles.

Enhancing core competencies in logistics allows companies to compete on a global scale. When Fred Smith envisioned a fast delivery system, he initially exploited the concept to form FedEx. Now, FedEx is enhancing its service with the Purple Promise. FedEx is trying to gain market share with excellent customer service and a goal to handle all customer information with 100 percent accuracy. This requires FedEx to have a high quality, trained staff and a reliable technology infrastructure to support these promises.

For the United States, several deregulation policies affected logistics. By the early 1980s, the entire transportation industry was changed to allow companies to set their own rates for freight and expand beyond their allotted areas. This change forced logistics companies to collaborate with other logistics companies to offer better prices and maximize the use of vehicles. Previously, many companies were constrained, goods moved with less than truckload (LTL) capacity, and, often, trucks came back completely empty to return for the next delivery. Logistics companies have an advantage because they can coordinate two-way shipments, whereas businesses, such as Walmart and Safeway with their own trucking fleet, frequently deliver products and return empty.

The financial sector experienced deregulation, offering the opportunity for many financial institutions to expand on services. Cash flow is always a concern for businesses. Many corporations delay payments to invest current capital to make more money for shareholders and to invest into the company for needs such as expanding services and new facilities. For small businesses, offering an online payment system has mitigated the potential for failure from slow or non-payment. Credit cards have dramatically lowered the cost of doing business. Financial institutions can become more competitive and can respond to customer needs both for organizations and individuals. However, the crisis of 2008 with the subsequent bailouts has put more government oversight on financial institutions and businesses. In spite of these setbacks, the financial arena is still beneficial, and businesses can survive and thrive in this arena.

The communications industry drives much of the technology and habits of consumers. When the Supreme Court broke AT&T into several entities, the ability for competition brought communications to a new level. The capabilities for communication have enhanced the use of technology. Costs continue to go down, and automated systems improve customer service. Managers and customers now have a round the clock ability to monitor and control the supply chain. Order status can be checked on demand. Logistics systems scan bar codes and have real time visibility about the location of products and shipments. For example, many consumers want fresh food. With the use of smart phones, a company in Japan has developed an application where a person can order a particular fish from Japanese waters and have it shipped directly to that person's location anywhere in the world. The company has to be quite confident in the logistics system to meet these customer expectations.

The final characteristic of the history of logistics involves the growing infrastructure to support a global market. Super ships increased the number of container capacity. Carrying 2,000 to 3,000 containers has been benchmarked by ships carrying 11,000 containers. The sheer volume has made sending a ship across the ocean cheaper than land transport between two large cities by truck. The United States can handle large volumes of truck transit with the advent of the interstate road system. Originally designed during the Eisenhower administration as a military and then commercial capability, the multiple lane construction of the interstate highways allows trucking companies to operate on a public funded transportation system. Commercial vehicles contribute to the operations but not nearly enough to pay for the construction and maintenance required to expand and upkeep the roads. For some countries such as India, Russia, and in Central and South America, the road infrastructure is inadequate, and much transport still relies on rail. India has the heaviest rail transport system in the world. The country is investing heavily in infrastructure, but it is limited by government bureaucracy and corruption. Commercial airlines can also take advantage of public airports, but they have developed their own air super hubs, such as Louisville, Kentucky for UPS and Memphis, Tennessee for FedEx Railroads. These centers rarely experience inclement weather and are strategically placed to serve most of the population of the United States. Pipelines must build and maintain their own infrastructure. Political interests can often delay or block new ventures for pipelines. Investment in infrastructure is changing the dynamics of logistics.

Questions that Logistics Answers

The value chain provides an organization with the means to determine the total cost of a product. Setting a price for a product has many factors such as the cost of materials, manufacturing, handling, storing, transport, and the potential back order and reverse logistics figures. Because 50 to 90% of organizational costs are in operations and the supply chain, logistics is a significant part for the business. Organizations have to determine what their core competencies are and whether logistics is beneficial to keep in house or outsource. A logistics company can provide the services better, faster, and cheaper, but the organization can lose control of the movement and storage of products.

Logistics considers the following questions:
- How can logistics provide value to a business and save costs?
- Where can waste be eliminated in the logistics system?
- What will the transportation network look like?
- What are the requirements for material handling?
- How much storage capacity is needed?
- Where should logistics facilities be located?
- How will logistics sustain the firm and lower pollution?
- With whom should logistics collaborate to work more efficiently and lower costs?

A TRUCK AND CAR RENTAL COMPANY BECOMES A LOGISTICS PROVIDER

Most people think of Penske as a truck rental company for do-it-yourself moves. However, Penske has expanded to provide logistics solutions to other firms. "Whirlpool Corporation is the world's leading manufacturer and marketer of major home appliances with annual sales over $19 billion and more than 80,000 employees and more than 60 manufacturing and technology research centers globally." With products going to over 170 countries, the market cycle can be very unpredictable. Whirlpool realized that its core competency lies in manufacturing and supporting home appliances. Their business strategy could not focus on logistics, so they learned to hand that task over to a third-party (3PL) provider. As many companies consider the opportunities and threats of managing several logistics providers, Whirlpool decided to contract with a single source as the lead logistics provider (LLP). Hiring the staff to manage such a large supply chain network did not prove feasible, so Whirlpool put the entire responsibility on Penske to replace previous 3PLs. Within four months of the start of managing logistics for Whirlpool, Penske LLP was able to do the following:

- Increase on-time loading by 13 %
- Increase on-time departure by 13 %
- Increase on-time delivery to logistics data centers by 12 %

When Whirlpool decided to acquire Maytag, Penske handled the transition of Maytag's logistics support. Maytag had a decentralized method for handling inbound logistics. Whirlpool had already migrated to a centralized system, so Penske had to work on consolidating storage and distribution of products. The transportation network needed adjustments to take advantage of an economy of scale to move larger volumes of items and lower costs. Penske filled a niche for Whirlpool by focusing on logistics so that Whirlpool could dedicate its efforts on manufacturing and marketing their home appliances.

Impact of Logistics on Industries

Senior management has to include supply chain management into its company's performance. The company must project its total costs to set pricing for products. The strategy and planning must include the capabilities of logistics to support the organization's objectives and goals. Businesses have many options, but can the logistics support these efforts?

Marketing responds to the demands of the customer. Sourcing deals with contracts made with sellers to bring the raw materials and other needs of the organization. Logistics and operations work together to connect marketing with sourcing to form a unified supply chain. Dysfunctional logistics drains precious resources for an organization. Marketing, sourcing, operations, and logistics must collaborate to effectively support the supply chain.

Many company decisions influence the logistics. Most food chains maintain their own trucking fleet to control the flow of goods into their stores. Because grocery stores have weekly specials, they want to have the correct inventory on hand to meet customer expectations when the customers come to pick up the advertised specials. Large food stores carry items in the tens of thousands.

Some organizations have to plan for the release of a new product. Coordinating a new item requires synchronization so that products arrive on the shelves in thousands of locations at the same time. A film may have multiple products to stock when released. Seasonal items have to be produced and stored until the timing is right. Imagine the tulip industry in Holland; tulips have a short life cycle, and millions of fresh tulips need to be distributed around the world. Even donation centers have peaks after "spring cleaning" and the end of the year for those trying to increase tax donations.

Disruptions in the supply chain can impact a company. Human intervention or equipment failures can alter the logistics system. Strikes, such as the train engineer strikes in Germany, can put stress on the logistics system. They can influence movement of goods much like with the 40-hour dock strike in Hong Kong in 2013. The BP platform explosion not only stopped the flow of oil, but the cleanup effort consumed much time and money.

Force majeure events can cause mild to complete disruptions in the supply chain. The tsunami in Japan crippled many electronics and car parts firms. Honda survived because the company developed a system of small businesses to support the flow of products. Massive floods devastated Malaysia and Pakistan. Blizzards in the United States can stop the transportation network for days.

Political events can impact the supply chain. Political decisions, such as the vote for Crimea to join Russia, triggered economic sanctions on Russia. Many European Union nations such as Finland, the Baltic States, Poland, Hungary, and more had to curtail the flow of goods to Russia. This action impacted up to 8% of their exports. These firms had to find other buyers to make up that loss. Armed conflicts can stop the flow of products, and this has happened in Iraq, Israel, Syria, and the eastern Ukraine. Violent conflicts rise up quickly and give businesses little time to react.

The Significance of Technology to Support Logistics

The use of technology is critical to logistics success. Logisticians frequently refer to the visibility up and down the supply chain. Knowing the levels of inventory and its location determines if the supply is keeping up with the demand. Lead times are important to know so the company has knowledge about when to order or reorder products. The time for work in progress in the production facility must be calculated into lead time for distribution. The entire process from the beginning to the customer has much to do with customer expectations.

At a minimum, supply chain staff need to track as much inventory as possible with bar codes and scanners. Accurate numbers are facilitated by automated processes that scan items as they move down the supply chain. **RFID** tags can transmit information to a reader. RFID technology relies on line-of-sight signals and are limited in range. RFID tags can transmit data to a sensor and would not be subject to a fixed scanner. The other challenge for RFID tags is with the item code or stock-keeping unit (SKU) number and a unique identifier being correctly read so that machines do not pick up duplicate numbers of inventory. Logistics operations try to minimize the manual passing of boxes and items. The ideal situation is that a package is loaded into the system and handled automatically around the world until a person has to deliver the product to the customer.

RFID Technology that uses tags that can transmit data to identify and track its movement.

Many organizations are looking to cloud computing, a system where software and information is stored. Logistics managers can access this information in a timely manner. The challenge is not so much the technology to store information, but the ability to retrieve what the logistics mangers' needs at the time.

Enterprise resource planning (ERP) software helps logistics managers see how the supply chain is operating. ERP is basically a software application that helps managers plan and control business functions. They have a holistic view of the structure and processes of the supply chain. Initially, ERP was for manufacturing planning and control but has expanded to other areas of organizations. The business functions of accounting, finances, human resources, sourcing, manufacturing, ordering, and more can use the software to benefit the organization.

ENTERPRISE RESOURCE PLANNING (ERP) A software application that help managers plan and control business functions.

Managing the Logistics System

The logistics managers oversea a complex network to make a supply chain successful. Many independent and dependent variables factor into supply chain management. An independent change in the price of fuel can have a ripple effect up and down the supply chain. A dependent change could be converting metal radiator caps into plastic ones. The spout of the radiator may need to be reengineered to fit a plastic cap. A dependent change could have multiple changes affecting the process. Hybrid vehicles require a number of adaptations to produce.

Bottlenecks occur within the supply chain. One or more nodes or links will be a bottleneck in the system. Goldratt came up with the theory of constraints (TOC) to deal with bottlenecks in a system. The narrow points in the logistics structure can be the layout or use of equipment, the processes people use to accomplish work, or policies written or accepted that inhibit a higher flow of goods. If the goal is clear and there is a way to measure the goal, the following steps help to eliminate the constraint. In the supply chain, the goal is to create and move inventory and eliminate unwanted safety stock. The following are points of the TOC:

- Identify the system's constraint(s).
- Decide how to exploit the system's constraint(s).
- Subordinate everything else to the above decision(s).
- Elevate the system's constraint(s).
- Warning! If in the previous steps a constraint has been broken, go back to step 1, but do not allow inertia to cause a system constraint.

A common methodology for managing inventory is **vendor-managed inventory (VMI)**. VMI is a technique for suppliers to replenish stock for the next stage of the supply chain. Ownership of products remains the same, but the supplier is managing the inventory flow. A typical scenario would be a beverage supplier stocking shelves with its drinks or a cosmetic vendor monitoring and resupplying lipstick for a store. With VMI, the buyer is passing the risk over to the vendor who then has to manage the level of inventory.

VENDOR-MANAGED INVENTORY (VMI) A technique for suppliers to replenish stock for the next stage of the supply chain.

Often, logisticians talk about the flow of information. Actually, managing logistics follows the following method when combining technology with people: data to information to knowledge to knowledge management. Data is the basic numerical representations of numericals or logistics concepts seen in something like truckloads. Information would be represented by 98% filled truckloads. Knowledge examines ways to fill the trucks to 100% capacity. Could trucks be scheduled to pick up other freight rather than traveling back empty? Knowledge management takes the data, information, and knowledge available and combines it with the institutional knowledge of those involved in maximizing trucks. Is the current truck fleet adequate for the organization's needs? Are the trucks constructed to maximum legal size and weight? Can an exception be submitted to increase size and weight constraints? What sustainability issues need to be solved? What other ways could the truck transportation network improve? Knowledge management finds innovative ways to improve logistics.

Current and Future Trends in Logistics

Managing inventory is a constant challenge for the supply chain. As previously explained, just-in-time inventory minimizes excess inventory. The buffers are smaller, requiring better planning and coordination. Vendor-managed inventory improves the logistics system because the supplier is closer to the capabilities of its part of the supply chain than its successor. So to sell product, the seller takes on the risk of satisfying the next link in the supply chain. The theory of constraints is one way to improve the flow of goods. These concepts are being adopted more and more by members of the supply chain.

Sustainability

Sustainability continues to rise to the top of consumer concerns. Customers are expecting companies to be more environmentally responsible. Consumers are savvier with the open information provided on the Internet. Logistics managers have to find ways to lower the consumption of resources and eliminate waste. Going green is touted by everyone these days, but actually following through is a matter of integrity. Many companies are claiming green practices but are ignoring them in real practice. Because much of the pollution comes from logistics, practitioners are trying to find ways to use more environmentally friendly materials for packaging. Rather than put waste in landfills, logistics is working to recycle. Software is used to plan routes and lower the time on the road. Companies will have to be more transparent about their sustainability practices. Due to green washing, reliable third party organizations will need to watch over the company's scorecard. Sustainability will be a trend as the world realizes resources are limited.

Enterprise Applications

As businesses manage the supply chain, enterprise applications offer new ways to track trends in the marketplace. One of the challenges in the current environment is the amount of information available; this is referred to as **big data**. Big data is an extremely huge amount of data tables that analysts examine to find trends in human behavior. Databases are storing so much information that business analysts are overwhelmed with the items and numbers. Finding the anomaly in the market to offer a new product takes patience and the ability to recognize what people will actually purchase. When demand is high, the logistics system needs to respond to the surge of activity. If logistics is tied down with normal operations, companies need the flexibility to expand, even if it is a short duration. Enterprise applications help the companies plan for normal product flow and plan for contingencies. The software can also place triggers to notify logistics managers of capabilities or problems with nodes and links. These applications can be shared with partners and other supply chain relationships to better utilize assets and control inventory. Finances can flow faster through electronic transfer. Although many applications are moving

BIG DATA A huge amount of data tables that analysts examine to find trends in human behavior.

to the cloud, the organization has to have the proper security in place to protect its finances and intellectual capital from theft. Enterprise applications will continue to dominate the business scene for years to come.

Artificial Intelligence

Much of the logistics system is repetitive. Planning follows the same process, and an interactive database can enhance automation of the process. Inventory managers and purchasing agents repeat the same process at least one-third of the time. Much of quality assurance can be built into an algorithm. People would need to control the decisions made. Organizations are so busy managing the day-to-day activities that knowledge management and organizational learning is not captured in the enterprise systems to predict a process for automation. The leaders who can exploit this capability will be ahead of the others.

Service-Oriented Supply Chains Will Surpass Product-Only Ones

Many companies are experiencing the negative impact of providing a product without service support. Even Apple had to apologize for distributing many products without Chinese language support. The companies that do offer support are finding that the next generation of consumers has a lower tolerance for simply products and nothing else. They also have a negative view of support personnel who speak in their own language but have heavy accents that are difficult, at best, to understand. The future winners in the supply chain will invest in the service chain and provide multi-lingual support to their global customers.

Internet of Things

INTERNET OF THINGS (IoT) Connecting devices on humans, animals, and objects to send and receive data.

The **Internet of Things (IoT)** connects devices on humans, animals, and objects to send and receive data, and this idea is growing in significance. The importance for improving supply chain management provides real time data to logistics managers. IoT is predicted to save $1.9 trillion within a decade because of improved connectivity among transportation, materials handling, and storage. Fifteen billion devices are currently linked with an estimated 50 billion more by 2020. More and more vehicles and equipment are tagged to track inventory and movement. In an unusual case, a vendor sent a container of supplies with a military unit to a foreign country. Two years later, the operations officer received a communication that the company had discovered a lost container in the country. The container had a global positioning service device attached to it that no one had noticed. IoT is attracting more organizations to attach communication devices on their inventory and assets.

RFID

Radio frequency identification (RFID) is currently in use in many logistic operations. RFID technology uses tags that can transmit data to identify and track movement. RFID usage continues to increase in double-digit percentages each year. RFID continues to prove useful. One challenge for implementing RFID technology lies in the cost of a tag compared to the cost of the item. As usage spreads, economies of scale has begun to kick in to make it more affordable. The second issue is the range of the wireless transmitter. Logisticians are longing for the day when an entire truck can pass through a sensor without unloading. Grocery stores are looking for the ability to scan a full cart as it passes through the checkout. This capability will increase handling of products and move larger volumes of items. The reliability for RFID on that scale is still lacking. RFID can handle individual and small amounts of items that are in clear range of the sensor, but not anything much larger.

On the commercial side, logistics tends to focus on goods and services. However, many organizations move and track living beings. The future will see more biochips used for such purposes. The ethics of doing this is still under debate. Biochips have an RFID transmitter to communicate with another device. Already, animals have chips for tracking location and monitoring biological functions. Not only would pet owners find this helpful, but zookeepers and park rangers could also keep an eye on animals. Tags are currently used to follow movement, but a biochip could be placed in an animal to check for disease. The military will probably use biochips for monitoring its deployed personnel in violent regions. Healthcare benefits seem promising because a biochip can detect anomalies in the human body. They could monitor the effects of hazardous materials or workers in a dangerous chemical environment. Law enforcement would see value in tracking hardened criminals. Biochips can be used for identification, and no external identification is needed, making it easier for someone with a company badge to enter into secure areas or to make financial transactions. The question will be how far society will go regarding monitoring humans and using technology inside the body that transmits signals.

Drones

Drones initially had a military purpose, but now logistics is seeing uses for unmanned flying vehicles to assist logistics. Experiments are underway to develop a drone to deliver small packages. Each country will need to decide how to regulate the movement of drones. A person could order a product online from a nearby store. A store employee could fill the order and attach the package to the drone. The drone could then drop off the package and return to the store. The carbon footprint for an electrical drone is much less than a person getting into a vehicle, driving to a store for one item, and driving back.

Another use for drones is in the natural gas field. Natural gas pipelines must be monitored for safety. A natural gas leak can be quite dangerous. Much of the work is conducted on the ground or by helicopter. Drones can be fitted with sensors to travel along the pipelines to check for leaks or potential cracks.

EXAMPLES OF APPLICATION
Food Industry

Kroger

Kroger has over 2,600 supermarkets in 34 states and in the District of Columbia. They combine 2,111 pharmacies and 1,330 supermarket fuel centers to add value to their strategy for one-stop shopping. They also claim a customer first strategy. The company also runs 782 convenience stores and 328 jewelry stores. They employ over 400,000 people. Their market share in the states they have a presence in is number one or two in 38 of the 41 major markets. They earned $108.5 billion and have a 7.1% growth rate in fiscal year (FY) 2013. In comparison, Walmart had 5% and Safeway had 1.3%. Kroger continues to grow in a highly competitive market. The food industry typically has profit margins from 1% to 3% so, economies of

scale are an important key to financial success. Kroger is one of the largest food chains in the United States and continues to expand.

The company operates 36 distribution centers. The company operates on a three-tier system in which many products, such as food, are produced within the tier one radius of 200 miles. The second tier expands in about a 350-mile radius to include slower moving items such as pharmaceuticals, health and beauty care items, and dry grocery merchandise. The third tier is made up of products that come from all over the world, such as seasonal, promotional, and other general merchandise products. Kroger operates a complex and dynamic distribution system.

Kroger keeps some of its manufacturing processes in house. To support its private label products, 40% of its products are manufactured at its 37 manufacturing facilities. These plants are broken into 17 dairies, nine bakeries, five general grocery products, two beverage plants, two meat plants, and two cheese plants. For other suppliers, Kroger operates an **electronic data interchange (EDI)** portal to manage vendors. EDI allows the submission of electronic files from one computer to another with standardized formatting to lower the need for human interaction to process documents. The more automated the processes, the more the company can save on repetitive and labor consuming tasks. Kroger combines internal manufacturing for some of its items with sourcing from local, regional, and global vendors.

Regarding the transportation network, the logistics manages 2,770 tractors and 10,500 trailers that coordinate 3,300 daily truckload deliveries. The actual mileage equates to 329 million miles a year. Third party logistics handle 20% of the trailers and 55% of the tractor fleet. Transportation managers use software to plan routes and maximize truck space. Vehicles have on-board computers to monitor their status and improve on-time delivery.

To lower costs and make changes to lessen their impact on the environment, the company states in its sustainability report the following efforts:

- Improving the aerodynamic design of tractors and trailers for better fuel economy
- Utilizing the latest clean engine technology that also improves tractor fuel efficiency
- Installing an automatic tire inflation system
- Expanding the usage of multi-temperature trucks to transport frozen, refrigerated, or dry goods in one truck
- Improving the insulation of its refrigerated trucks
- Standardizing top speeds and idling protocols

Kroger provides a model of a successful food industry system with complex logistics processes and efforts to support its customer first and one-stop shopping strategy.

Whole Foods

The natural and organic food market is representative of Whole Foods Market, Inc. With an overall growth of 24% annually since 1991, Whole Foods is worth around $14 billion. Private label sales increased by 3% in 2014, and the national brands increased by 1%. The company operates in a highly fragmented natural foods environment, and it tries to focus on local and regional sources. One of their major

ELECTRONIC DATA INTERCHANGE (EDI) The submission of electronic files from one computer to another with standardized formatting to lower the need for human interaction to process documents.

weaknesses is the cost of reverse logistics that has been seen in many product recalls in recent years. The increase of consumer demand for organic products and the growing popularity of private brands, such as their 365 label, offers potential for continued growth. The company has stores, and its employees come in at around 87,000.

The organization encourages its buyers to work with local and regional suppliers. The corporation produces an approved vendor list. This kind of authorization means each store can choose which products to buy from the accepted suppliers. Whole Foods uses a decentralized system to manage the purchase of products.

Whole Foods outsources its logistics to United Natural Foods, Incorporated (UNFI). UNFI is an independent distribution network that provides products and logistical support to the natural food industry. Next to Whole Foods, its second largest customer, UNFI provides distribution support of non-proprietary natural, organic, and specialty products for Safeway. UNFI operates 33 distribution centers. Most are on the West Coast and in the Eastern United States with only one distribution center in the Denver and Dallas areas. Although the risk is low, both the areas around these cities can be impacted by inclement weather, such as snow, ice, high winds, or tornadoes.

The transportation management system runs from a carrier and supplier portal. The carrier portal coordinates inbound shipments to its warehouses and distribution centers. The system manages times for pick-up and delivery. They also offer opportunities for new lanes to provide service for its customers. The supplier portal manages the quantities and timelines for shipping products. They also allow vendors to mark purchase orders as ready to ship. The UNFI transportation network coordinates products and movement through two separate portals.

To lower its carbon footprint, UNFI has implemented several initiatives in its logistics practices. Transportation managers use more rail than truck. UNFI implemented EcoPower recycled engine oil in Denver, saving 85% energy in the production of the oil. UNFI built some warehouses and other facilities, achieving LEED (leadership in energy and environmental design) certification. LEED is governed by the U.S. Green Building Council and sets standards for greener design, building, and operation and maintenance costs for buildings. The categories progress from certified, to silver, to gold, and then to platinum standards. LEEDS offers companies an independent auditor for constructing more ecological friendly facilities.

The company's existence is primarily within the United States. Although it has over 95% of its revenue there, it does have a small presence in Canada and the United Kingdom. The company has an opportunity to expand overseas if it can develop a strategy to market and support its brands in other countries.

Retail Goods Industry

Walmart

Walmart combined its retail goods with the food industry. With over 11,000 stores, Walmart is the largest retailer in the world. The company is basically an American business that has an international division. The company has had various successes and failures in other countries. The annual income for the fiscal year of 2015 was $485 billion. The company employs over 2 million people. Its growth rate was consistently positive, but now it is possibly facing the peak of its momentum. The volume of consumers and products provides the company with big data to process. Big data for the retail industry comes in the form of extremely huge amount of data tables that analysts examine to find trends in human shopping behavior. Walmart tries to use this data to predict future customer wants and to estimate sales.

Walmart logistics serves a massive operation. With 158 distribution centers, the transportation fleet is made up of 6,500 tractors, 55,000 trailers, and over 7,000 drivers. Local distribution centers support around 90 to 100 stores, typically within a 200-mile radius. They will have over one million square feet of space and more than five miles of conveyer belts. Regional centers have hundreds of thousands of cases each day that they ship to other centers or stores. Walmart keeps nine distribution centers located around the country to respond to natural disasters.

The transportation system relies on EDI to manage routes, pick-ups, and deliveries. The trucking fleet travels 700 million miles a year, meaning each driver averages 100,000 miles. Walmart set a goal to double its fleet efficiency from 2005 to 2015 and claims to be 84% on target. Walmart states in its transportation strategy the following sustainability objectives:

- Effective driving techniques, such as minimizing idle time and progressive shifting, to ensure optimal performance
- Advanced tractor-trailer technologies, such as electrification, lightweighting, improved aerodynamics, and fuel-efficient tires
- Improved processes and systems to drive efficient loading and routing of merchandise

Walmart has a core competency in supply chain management. Their logistics system is massive, and they could expand more in other countries. The question is more related to how they can adapt to the consumers and logistics systems in other areas around the world.

IKEA

Originating in Sweden, IKEA now spans the globe. The company is truly a global business that seeks to improve home living. With only 315 stores in 27 countries, the company employs 147,000. Its revenue is 29 billion Euros ($32 billion) annually. IKEA has over 12,000 products and is one of the largest wood consumers in the retail industry. The company has a niche for designing furniture that is compact and some requires some assembling for the consumer. This concept is helpful for consumers who have small vehicles and those who depend on public transportation.

The logistics system benefits from the ready-to-assemble model. Many items are reduced in volume to lesson shipping through "air." The stores use a combination of warehousing and retail to lower logistics costs. The company manages 1,074 suppliers and uses a decentralized 3PL approach with 251 transport service providers for distribution to stores. They also contract with 90 global food suppliers. IKEA has established the IWAY code of conduct for suppliers to set standards for work hours, child labor, and safety. IKEA manages this relationship with on-site visits to monitor compliance, but they also do this to collaborate with vendors on improving the supply chain. IKEA also belongs to the Global Social Compliance Programme (GSCP) to contribute to improving working and environmental conditions for the global supply chain. The company uses independent auditors to oversee its sustainability progress.

IKEA operates 32 distribution centers and 11 customer distribution centers. As a global company, they require 28 trading offices in 24 countries to support their movement of goods around the world. Because 50% of the raw materials are sustainable or environmental friendly, the company controls costs with the designs of all products and manufactures as much as possible. The prices continue to drop and volume increases, showing that the business model is successful.

Electronic Industry

Samsung

The company has quite a range of interests, but this section will highlight the electronics business. Overall, Samsung makes $305 billion each year and employs 489,000. Samsung Electronics pulls in $180 billion and has 326,000 employees. Samsung emerged as the number one producer of mobile phones. Samsung provides parts for Apple, and this relationship has created a tense atmosphere between the companies. Samsung uses eight domestic plants to produce its products. The company is a conglomerate of subsidiaries that support the overall business objectives for a high tech company.

Samsung runs much of it operations and logistics through subsidiary companies. The logistics system operates out of Incheon Airport in Korea and then distributes throughout the world. Samsung Electronics, Logitech, and Samsung Digital System (SDS) control a sophisticated logistics and global enterprise research planning (ERP) system. Logitech handles the transportation management system and warehouse management system. They manage 22 distribution centers in South Korea. Logitech supplies 3,200 businesses in the country and has 600 buyers from overseas. The logistics follows two models. One supply chain moves from manufacturing to a logistics center to a store and then to a customer. The second model goes from manufacturing to a logistics center to a customer.

The international buyers handle their own supply chain, but Samsung offers logistics consulting primarily for those businesses using Samsung products and software. Logitech manages Samsung Electronics, Samsung Display, and some affiliates for products bound for the global market. The company runs 77 offices in 30 countries to forward freight and assist with the process of transnational shipments. Samsung Electronics and Logitech supports Samsung with domestic and international logistics.

Samsung Digital Systems offers the consulting area for the technology side of logistics. They offer supply chain design consulting and a logistics software solution known as Cello. Cello helps organizations plan, execute, and analyze their supply chains. SDS also supports the integration of logistics activities and the service supply chain with IT solutions.

Regarding sustainability, the company reports using recycled plastics for refrigerators, washing machines, air conditioners, and vacuum cleaners. Due to its rapid growth, its carbon emissions continue to rise. However, since 2009, the company has invested $6.3 billion in lowering its carbon footprint and has halved its carbon emissions. The company claims to have had an independent agency verify its sustainability report with the Business Institute for Sustainable Development (BISD), led by the Korean Chamber of Commerce and Industry (KCCI). Samsung is making efforts in its manufacturing and logistics system to become more environmental friendly.

Apple

The company is known for its growth in personal computers, software such as iTunes, and electronics such as its iPhone. With $182.795 billion in annual revenue, the company currently is second to Samsung in technology and is the world's third largest producer of cell phones. In 2014, it became the largest publically traded business in the world. Apple has over 400 retail stores in 16 countries and has a workforce of 98,000.

Apple is often referred to as the number one supply chain system in the world. The sourcing of materials and manufacturing of components comes from the United States, China, Europe, and other Asian countries. The final assembly is done in China. The warehousing is primarily in Elk Grove, California, and from there, products are distributed to retail stores, direct sales forces, and other wholesalers, retailers, and network carriers. Intermediate warehouses receive products from China via UPS and FedEx to handle online orders. Oddly enough, the logistics system is quite simple compared to other large corporations.

Apple has kept the design and control of its products internal and has mixed the supply chain. They invest billions of dollars into their operations and logistics to improve the movement and handling of products and the service supply chain. Normally, large corporations have thousands of suppliers, but Apple maintains only 156 key vendors. This puts them at an advantage when developing strategic relationships. Vendor management can then focus on better collaboration.

Due to criticism of activist groups, Apple now runs 100% of its U. S. operations and data centers on renewable energy. Eight-seven percent of its global operations use renewable energy. In its logistics system, it claims no ozone producing substances in its packaging. They have a service to recycle packaging at most retail stores. Apple is proactive in banning hazardous materials and produce brominated flame retardant-free (BFR-free) and polyvinyl chloride-free (PVC-free) products. The company has found a way to invest in sustainability and stay profitable.

DISCUSSION QUESTIONS

Consider the following questions as you review this chapter:

1. What are some logistics functions that support the supply chain?

2. Why should senior management pay attention to logistics?

3. What is an example of a technology that logistics uses? What would be a new technology that could be implemented in the future?

4. What are some sustainability efforts of commercial companies?

REFERENCES

Apple. (2015). *Investors*. Retrieved from http://investor.apple.com

Aronow, S., Hofman, D., Burkett, M., Romano, J., & Nilles, K. (2014). The 2014 supply chain top 25: Leading the decade. *Supply Chain Management Review, 18*(5), 8–17.

British Broadcasting Corporation. (2007). *Addicted to cheap shopping? Why the real cost of goods keeps going down* [Video file]. Retrieved from http://digital.films.com/play/UJZ4L9

CNN Money. (2001, July 9). *Webvan shuts down*. Retrieved from http://money.cnn.com/2001/07/09/technology/webvan/

Commercial Section of the Canadian Embassy in the Republic of Korea. (2012, February). *Global value chain analysis on Samsung Electronics*. Retrieved from http://albertacanada.com/korea/images/GlobalValueChainAnalysisSamsungElectronics.pdf

Coyle, J., Langley, C., Novack, R., & Gibson, B. (2013). *Supply chain management: A logistics perspective* (9th ed.). Mason, OH: South-Western Cengage Learning.

D'Onfro, J. (2014, April 18). The founder of a dot-com disaster is giving his old grocery delivery idea another shot. *Business Insider*. Retrieved from http://www.businessinsider.com/louis-borders-webvan-founder-hds-2014-

FedEx. (2015). *Our story*. Retrieved from http://about.van.fedex.com/our-story/company-structure/corporate-fact-sheet/

Goldratt, E. M. (2004). *The goal: A process of ongoing improvement*. Great Barrington, MA: North River.

Inbound Logistics. (2015). *Articles*. Retrieved from http://www.inboundlogistics.com

IKEA. (2015). *About the IKEA group*. Retrieved from http://www.ikea.com/ms/en_US/this-is-ikea/company-information/index.html

Ikea Group. (2015). *Ikea Group Marketline company profile*, 1–20.

Johnson, J. R. (2015). *Supply chain, RFID 24-7*. Retrieved from http://www.rfid24-7.com/

Kovalenko, V. I., & Yarmolyuk, V. V. (1995). Endogenous rare metal ore formations and rare metal metallogeny of Mongolia, *Economic Geology*, *90*(3).

Kroger Co. (2015). *Kroger Co. MarketLine company profile*, 1–36.

Kroger Company. (2015). *Investor relations*. Retrieved from http://ir.kroger.com/CorporateProfile.aspx?iid=4004136

Leger, D. L., & O'Donnell, J. (2013, December 26). UPS driver: 2013 'worst Christmas ever' for delivery. *USA Today*. Retrieved from http://archive.burlingtonfreepress.com/article/20131226/BUSINESS/312260031/More-delays-as-UPS-staggers-under-holiday-crush

Marketline. (2015, April 28). Whole Foods Market, Inc. SWOT analysis. *Business Source Complete*, 1–8.

Marketline. (2014, November 7). Wal-Mart Stores, Inc. SWOT analysis. *Business Source Complete*, 1–11

Penske. (2015). *Whirlpool Corporation: Evolution of a supply chain*. Retrieved from http://www.penskelogistics.com/casestudies/whirlpool2.html

Samsung. (2014). *Sustainability report*. Retrieved from http://www.samsung.com/us/aboutsamsung/investor_relations/corporate_governance/corporatesocialresponsibility/downloads/2014sustainabilityreport.pdf

Samsung to overhaul logistics operation. (2001). *Frontline Solutions*, *2*(12), 58.

Sanders, N. R. (2012). *Supply chain management: A global perspective*. Hoboken, NJ: John Wiley & Sons.

Sengupta, S. (2013). *10 supply chain trends for the next 10 years, supply chain 24/7*. Retrieved from http://www.supplychain247.com/article/10_supply_chain_trends_for_the_next_10_years

SupplyChainOpz. (2015). *Is Apple supply chain really the no. 1? A case study*. Retrieved from http://www.supplychainopz.com/2013/01/is-apple-supply-chain-really-no-1-case.html

United Natural Foods, Inc. (2014). *Products and services*. Retrieved from https://www.unfi.com

United Natural Foods, Inc. (2014). *Sustainability reports*. Retrieved from https://www.unfi.co

United Parcel Service of America, Inc. (2015). *World wide*. Retrieved from http://www.ups.com/content/us/en/about/facts/worldwide.html

United States Postal Service. (2015). *Just one day in the life of the U.S. Postal Service... by the numbers*. Retrieved from https://about.usps.com/who-we-are/postal-facts/one-day-by-the-numbers.htm

United States Green Building Council. (2015). *Overview*. Retrieved from http://www.usgbc.org/leed#overview

Walmart. (2015). *Walmart logistics*. Retrieved from http://corporate.walmart.com/our-story/our-business/logistics

Webvan.com. (2009). *Webvan, a part of Amazon.com family*. Retrieved from http://www.webvan.com/

Westone (2014). *The in-ear experts*. Retrieved from http://www.westone.com/hhc/index.php/about/about-westone

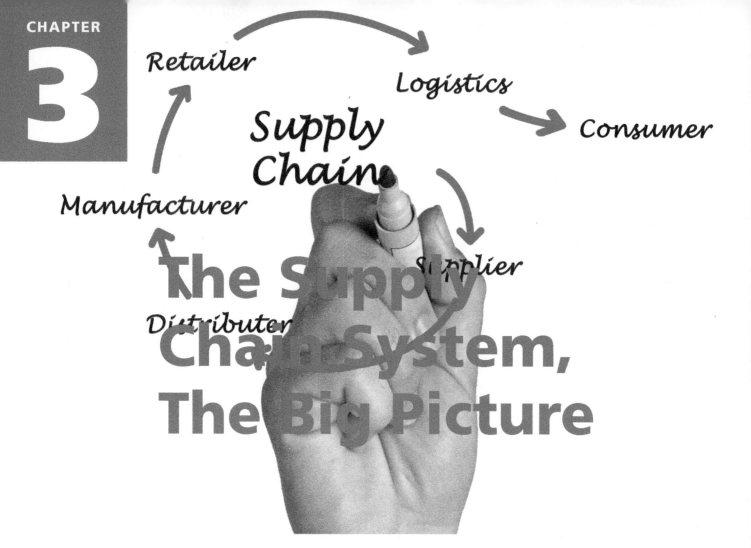

THE BIG PICTURE

Have you ever wondered how that bottle of water got to you? What is a supply chain, how does it work, and how does it directly or indirectly affect customer expectations?

There are a lot of steps required to get any product to the consumer. Products flow all over the globe daily, and there seems to be no method to the madness. But everyone knows expects exemplary customer service and immediate shipment. This product flow has many steps that are coordinated at each level to ensure the following:

- The right product
- At the right time
- In the right condition
- At the right price
- With a profit for the company

In the 1800s, the movement of product could take months or years. Today, customers in many situations expect products within hours or minutes of requisition. What has changed within the supply chain that has made this possible, and how will expectations change in the future?

Technology, in all of its forms through time, has been a vital part of the changes within supply chains.

The mining of ore was a one-man job that could be hazardous to the miners' health and was done with a pick-axe and backpack that required movement from a remote site based on the season. Today, mining operations for the most part are technology driven operations that move tons of ore within minutes.

In the past, a sailing ship moving product across the sea may have taken months. Today, technology and transportation improvements can move tons of products within hours from one point on the globe to another.

1. What is demand, how does it affect supply chain decisions, and who generates demand?

2. What is a supply chain, who are the members of a supply chain, and how do they interact?

3. What are the different strategies within the supply chain, and how are they used to make decisions.

4. What is a strategic fit, and how is it achieved?

5. What is a target segment, and how does the supply chain innovate to meet these needs?

KEY TERMS

- bullwhip effect (p. 55)
- business strategy (p. 54)
- competitive strategy (p. 53)
- constraint (p. 60)
- continuous improvement (p. 57)
- demand uncertainty (p. 44)
- economic risks (p. 57)
- economies of scale (p. 46)
- efficiency (p. 53)
- environmental risks (p. 57)
- geopolitical risks (p. 57)
- information flow (p. 55)
- lead time (p. 52)
- logistics strategy (p. 52)
- operations strategy (p. 52)
- opportunity (p. 56)
- point-of-sale (POS) (p. 44)
- pricing strategy (p. 53)
- product availability (p. 46)
- product flow (p. 54)
- push/pull cycle (p. 46)
- responsiveness (p. 52)
- revenue flow (p. 55)
- reverse flow (p. 46)
- risk (p. 56)
- stakeholders (p. 48)
- strategic fit (p. 53)
- supplier strategy (p. 52)
- supply chain (p. 46)
- supply chain management (SCM) (p. 48)
- supply chain network design (p. 49)
- target market segment (p. 54)
- technological risks (p. 57)

In the past, retailers received scarce products occasionally and could not count on a managed inventory beyond using a pencil and paper. Products may or may not be available or may be seasonal. Over time, the supply chain has reduced **demand uncertainty,** the accuracy that a company has in projecting customer demand for products in the future.

Customers may have had to plan to go into the closest town to order the products they needed and then wait for the products to be delivered to the retailer; when the products arrived, they would plan another trip into town to pick up the product. Today, the customers can order the products they need on the Internet or smartphone and expect delivery to their front door within hours through express delivery.

The supply chain has undergone an exponential change in just the last twenty years, and this has altered customer expectations. Technology has been a big part of this rapid change but so has the way people think about the supply chain and how people measure supply chain performance.

Early supply chains were vertically integrated siloes, and each function was conducted in house. As supply chains evolved over the last couple hundred years, supply chains have taken on external partners that specialize in a function, such as logistics, manufacturing, sales, warehousing, and transportation.

Increasingly, strategic partnerships are formed by customers and suppliers to reduce cost and improve profit margin through operational collaboration. Today's supply chain integration can use any combination of supply alternatives to achieve maximum efficiency and responsiveness.

Today, retailers have **point-of-sale (POS),** technology that uses an automated system to link computers that transmit sales data to an account that can control inventory. This system accounts for product sales to the customer but can send data requesting replenishment across the supply chain and the globe in nanoseconds.

SYSTEMS: THE BIG PICTURE
Customer Demand

A company must define the needs of the customer. Customers have expectations and choose companies that meet their expectations. Customer demand is differentiated and varies with the following attributes:

- Quantity of product by lot
- Responsiveness tolerance by customer
- Variety of product
- Level of service required by customer
- Price of product
- Product desirability of innovation

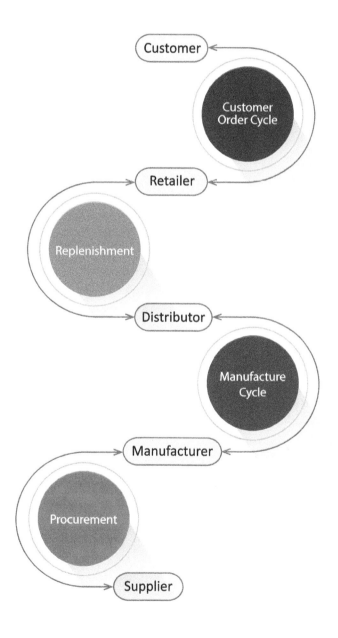

FIGURE 3.1 Cycle View

The parties that directly or indirectly integrate within the supply chain to meet demand are as follows:

- Customer
- Retailer
- Distributor
- Manufacturer
- Supplier

Two views of processes performed in the supply chain are the cycle view and the push and pull view.

The **cycle view** is where the supply chain may have any of the following series of cycles that integrate to meet demand:

- Customer cycle
- Replenishment cycle
- Manufacturing cycle
- Procurement cycle

In the cycle view of the supply chain transaction, the customer requests a product or service, and the retailer converts the customer request into a customer order. The retailer passes the invoice to a distributor within the distribution channel to fill the demand. The distributor interacts with the manufacturer to request a product. The manufacturer interacts with the supplier to replenish stock through production.

Not all transactions within the supply chain require every step and every transaction, but some variation is usually used to meet customer demand.

The push and pull cycle is another process to move product. The push cycle is providing product in anticipation of customer demand, and the pull cycle is providing product upon customer demand. The pull cycle is when the execution of the order is based on the customers' actual requisition.

If you as a customer do not buy your daily cup of coffee from the corner store but decide to buy it at the office store, how have you affected the customer demand at the corner store, at the office store, and within the coffee industry?

A **reverse flow is** when a customer returns products back through the supply chain. An example of reverse flow is when you return a product or turn in a bottle for credit.

Economies of scale occur when the customer attempts to reduce price by purchasing products in a sized lot to reduce cost. An example of this is when you purchase a case of cereal at your bulk store, so you can get a box for half price.

Product availability is how much of a product is available at specific point in time.

The supply chain is all of the organizations that are interlinked upstream and downstream within the supply chain flow of services or products that source customer expectations. Supply chains require efficient collaboration by organizations to perform at optimal levels. Companies no longer have complete control of market success because they must rely on partnerships within their supply chain. Supply chains are as follows:

- Collaborative
- Cooperative
- Constantly changing
- Interdependent

PUSH AND PULL CYCLE The push cycle is providing product in anticipation of customer demand, and the pull cycle is providing product upon customer demand. The pull cycle is when the execution of the order is based on the customers' actual requisition.

REVERSE FLOW When a customer returns products back through the supply chain (such as returning a product or turning in a bottle for credit).

ECONOMIES OF SCALE The customer attempts to reduce price by purchasing products in a sized lot to reduce cost (such as purchasing a case of cereal at your bulk store so you can get a box for half price).

PRODUCT AVAILABILITY How much of a product is available at specific point in time.

THE SUPPLY CHAIN All of the organizations that are interlinked upstream and downstream within the supply chain flow of services or products that source customer expectations.

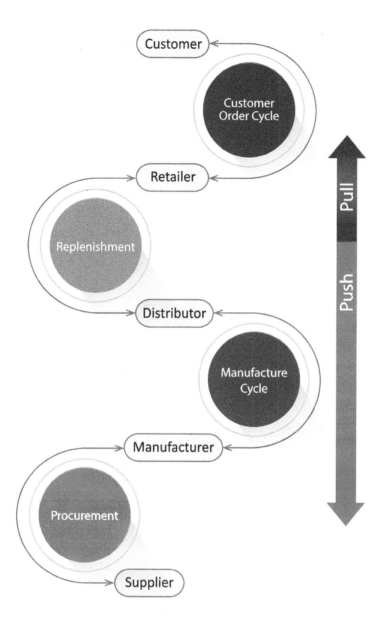

FIGURE 3.2 Push Pull Cycle View

A **collaborative** supply chain is when each member within the supply chain has chosen to work together, and they have an agreement on how and where they will fit into the chain, what their responsibilities will be, and what steps they will take to keep the supply chain members informed of any changes that happen or need to be addressed.

A **cooperative** supply chain is when each member of the supply chain agrees to build trust through cooperation, to work in the best interest of the team, to provide information, and to make decisions that will improve their competitive advantage over external competitors.

A **constantly changing** supply chain is when variability from internal and external mechanisms will cause the supply chain to adapt. As changes are anticipated or occur, the supply chain must have the flexibility to address the changes in a timely manner and effectively make the right decision for successful future operations.

A **interdependent** supply chain is when each member must be cognizant that they are reliant on the other members to openly communicate information that will affect the supply chain and that they will be proactive in meeting change because each member is dependent on the support of the other team members.

Supply chain management (SCM) is a systematic management approach to the flow of goods or services from supplier to the customer and involves all of the stakeholders within the transaction. This includes raw material, inventory, services, or finished products at the point of consumption. It is also the design, planning, execution, control, and monitoring of services and products in the upstream and downstream flow that create value.

Supply management functions are as follows:
- Sourcing
- New product development
- Marketing
- Operations
- Distribution in the forms of order management, shipping management, and delivery management
- Finance
- Customer service

A few of examples of supply chains are as follows:
- When you order a custom built computer online, and you have it delivered to your home address
- When you go to a large store, choose the computer that best fits your needs from a shelf, and take it home with you
- An auto manufacturer builds the car, delvers it to a retailer for sale, and you choose a car from the lot to take home

These supply chains have been designed to meet the specific customers' needs at a specific point in time. The customers' expectations change based on type of product, quality, cost, and many other factors. The supply chain's primary task is to meet the customers' expectations.

So, what are **stakeholders**? Stakeholders are the entities involved in the supply chain transaction from start to finish who promote the movement of services, product, information, or funding to the customer. Some stakeholders may include the following:
- The miners of raw material
- The manufacturers that turn raw material into products
- The transporters that move material
- Administrators that document the supply chain transactions
- Brokers that contract and facilitate the legal movement of product or funds (wholesale and distribution)
- Warehouse workers that receive and ship products
- Retail sites that provide access to products
- The customers that use the products

As you can see, there are a lot of stakeholders, especially if you consider that in some transactions there are multiple, repeated handlers. These multiple handles can include forklift operators at each phase of moving the product from production to transportation, or administrators at each phase documenting the movement of product. When considering all that goes into a product, it is surprising to think of the low price customers expect to pay for the end product.

This is where flow efficiency becomes the key to value added performance and to maximize value. The supply chains profitability is the financial objective. Flexible supply chains change at the least cost or lead in innovation.

SUPPLY CHAIN NETWORK DESIGN
Supply Chain Network Design

It is a wonder how you can order an item, and you can expect the delivery within hours to a week from requisition with a 90% or better accuracy rate. How does this happen, and who are the members of the supply chain team behind the scenes that are so efficiently executing your order?

The **supply chain network design** is the decisions suppliers make to design the configuration of the supply chain and can include information flow, inventory management, operating facilities, and transportation.

The supply chain network design is not just a business processes to be analyzed for performance, but it is also the infrastructure used to move products and services.

Information flow is what information will be kept, how it will be kept, and for what purpose. This information is vital to the supply chain's overall performance. How is this information collected (scanner, database), and where will the results be maintained for forecasting and business capturing?

These questions about information must be synchronized through the members of the supply chain to bring continuity of action. Today, most of the information is passed through the supply chain using information technology (IT).

Inventory management is how much inventory will be kept at the manufacturer, the distribution center, or the retailer. How much inventory is kept by whom is a calculated decision, so the flow of product or service can be anticipated to maintain a level of certainty. There are three types of inventory to be considered, and they are as follows:

- *Cycle inventory.* This is the average amount of inventory over a specific time that will be required to meet customer demand for the same specific time period.
- *Safety inventory.* This is the amount of inventory projected to meet uncertain customer demand because customers are not predictable in the specific time period.
- *Seasonal inventory.* This is the added amount of projected customer demand for a season. An example would be ordering an additional amount of inventory for the winter season.

Some of the questions supply chain managers must analyze are how much safety inventory will be maintained, what is the cycle inventory, and what is the lead time to receiving replenishment or seasonal inventory?

The cost of inventory being in the store and not being sold is what supply chain managers have to contend with because of the cost of space and the revenue tied up in maintaining the product on the shelf.

Operating strategy examines how large the facilities will be and where they will be located. Hub operations are a common occurrence in today's supply chain. But the members of the supply chain must decide how to operate their individual facilities and how their facilities will support the other members of the team. There are three considerations for supply chain managers at facilities, and they are as follows:

SUPPLY CHAIN NETWORK DESIGN The decisions suppliers make to design the configuration of the supply chain.

LARGE RETAIL STORES

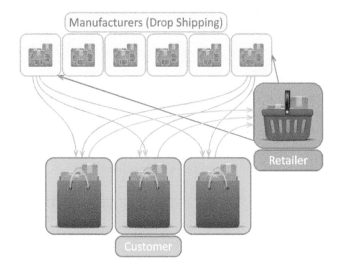

Centralize inventory at manufacturer
Manufacturer aggregates demand
High level of availability
Lower levels of inventory
Retailer no inventory

Retailer Information Flow   ⟶
Customer Information Flow   ⟵
Product Information Flow   ⟶

MANUFACTURER TO TRANSIT CARRIER

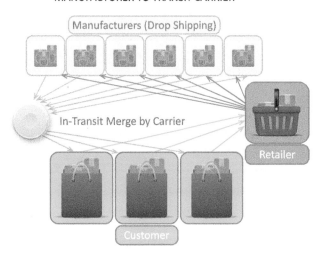

De-centralize inventory at manufacturer
Manufacturer aggregates inventories
High level of availability, little customization
High value items, lower levels of inventory
Inventory at factory, demand difficult to forecast

Retailer Information Flow   ⟶
Customer Information Flow   ⟵
Product Information Flow   ⟶

DISTRIBUTOR

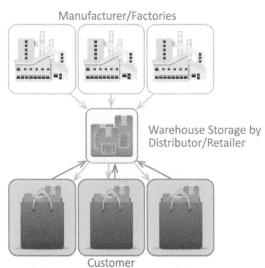

De-centralize inventory at factory
Factory aggregates inventories
High demand, little customization
Transportation costs lower
Facility costs higher, lost aggregation

Retailer Information Flow   ⟶
Customer Information Flow   ⟵
Product Information Flow   ⟶

FIGURE 3.3   Supply Chain Network

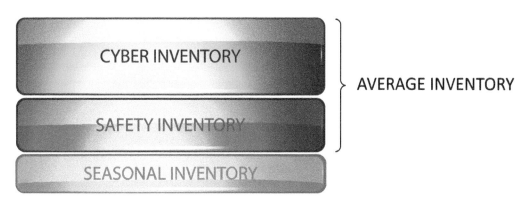

FIGURE 3.4 Inentory Levels

■ *Capacity.* This is large amounts of product that provide ready responsiveness but incur a cost for shelf time. The movement of product, the maintenance of product, and the facility cost in manpower and utilities are a few costs to consider here.

■ *Location.* Companies must decide where to place facilities to maximize distribution at a manageable cost. Some companies locate stores around their distribution centers to service the area and plan distribution centers based on projected customer sales over a long-term supply model.

■ *Role.* Companies within the supply chain must decide what the role of the facility is to the supply chain function and what process will be used to move product. *Flexible.* This type of facility is used for many types of products.

■ *Dedicated.* This type of facility is used to manage a limited amount and type of product. Many soft drink companies use dedicated facilities.

Transportation examines who will provide transportation. Should internal resources be used, or will it be cheaper to outsource? Transportation is a large cost that is affected by external pressures. Fuel prices can be volatile, and the cost of fuel can have a large impact on the cost to deliver products and services. Companies must be able to forecast cost but, more importantly, must be able to reduce cost within the supply chain.

These questions are the beginning of a long process of deciding how to best meet customer needs while remaining profitable. The members of the supply chain team must be complementary to their partners and support the teams' strategic goals.

There are three components to the transportation decision, and they are as follows:

■ *Transportation network design.* This includes all the modes of transportation, locations, and routes by which products travel.

■ *Transportation mode.* This is the manner by which products are moved within the supply chain. Some of the choices are air, ground, or sea.

■ *Transportation metrics.* Transportation expenses drive profitability within the supply chain. Supply chain members must decide through metrics if the network is efficient and if the mode is applicable to the optimization of supply chain resources.

Supply chain network designs are strategic decisions about the structure of the supply chain, who the members are, if the companies use their own resources or outsource to perform optimized supply chain functions. How do the members of the supply chain increase profitability while meeting customer expectations?

Supply Chain Strategy

What differentiates company supply chain strategies is the company's desire to meet customer expectations. For a trucking company within a supply chain, how should it configure its operations to fit into a supply chain, and what innovations would it need to remain in the supply chain?

Long-range supply chain decisions are driven by the **supply chain strategy.**

When you order a product or service online and receive an immediate response, a digital download or a transportation tracking code was used. If you go to your local convenience store to purchase you favorite soft drink, you have become part of that company's supply chain strategy.

Supply chain strategy includes the following:

- Logistics strategy
- Operations strategy
- Supplier strategy

LOGISTICS STRATEGY Each member of the supply chain creates one or more logistics strategies that define the service levels that the organization finds most cost-effective.

Logistics strategy is where each member of the supply chain creates one or more logistics strategies that define the service levels that the organization finds most cost effective. Sometimes because of product or service diversity, the organization must make multiple strategies to match each product's or service's specific need to the customer.

Components to consider in a logistics strategy are as follows:

- Competitors
- Information
- Logistics systems
- Outsourcing
- Strategy review
- Transportation

OPERATIONS STRATEGY The decisions made that cause cohesion of the team's actions, policies, programs, and systems in response to other competitors.

SUPPLIER STRATEGY Members of the supply chain working to improve performance by communicating effectively and integrating processes.

Operations strategy is the decisions that are made that cause cohesion of the team's actions, policies, programs, and systems in response to other competitors. Operations strategy is a long-term use of resources. Integration throughout the chain can be both internal to the company and externally with the team members of the supply chain, and integration is paramount to a supply chain's success at the operational level.

Supplier strategy is when the members of the supply chain work to improve performance by communicating effectively and integrating processes. The team must be cognizant of the entire chain's cost and value upstream and downstream for the effective use of resources and cost control. This will require sharing vital information about the supply chain amongst all team members and the routine management of contingencies to meet future expectations.

There are two strategies to consider in the supply chain strategy: responsiveness and efficiency.

RESPONSIVENESS (Sometimes known as *agility*) the speed at which a supplier reacts to a customer's request.

LEAD TIME The wait time between the placement of an order and the delivery of the item to the customer.

Responsiveness (sometimes known as *agility*) is the speed at which a supplier reacts to a customer's request. Company responsiveness is the ability to recognize and respond to demand fluctuations, maintain short lead times, support diversity of products, and retain the edge on supply chain innovation while producing highly innovative products and maintaining a high level of service to the customer.

Lead time is the wait time between the placement of an order and the delivery of the item to the customer.

An example of a very responsive system is when a customer orders a product over the Internet, and it is delivered the next day. The response is indicative of a computer technological supply system integrated with flight, cross docking, and trucking to provide a seamless logistics system. The cost to the supplier is higher because the responsiveness is more immediate.

Improving responsiveness shortens lead times. In a typical transaction for responsiveness, the customer may incur a higher price to receive the product faster.

Efficiency is the cost of delivering and producing products for the customers.

Supplier cost is reduced when the supplier chooses more efficient supply chain options. When a customer orders a product and requests delivery on a longer timeframe, a week or more, the price of transportation can be greatly reduced for the supplier and customer, but this means reduced responsiveness.

EFFICIENCY The cost of delivering and producing products for the customers.

Competitive Strategy

What differentiates each company from its competitors within the supply chain? How will companies compete within the supply chain but also retain their position in this supply chain from other competitors or be able to remove competitors from their supply chain by offering a better value?

Competitive strategy is the plan that clearly defines a company's strategy to satisfy its customers' needs for products and services. Competitive strategies differ from company to company, and consumers experience it because some companies the offer the lowest prices with adequate quality, and some offer exceptional quality no matter the cost. The company's competitive strategy should align with the supply chain strategy, otherwise known as strategic fit.

COMPETITIVE STRATEGY The plan that clearly defines a company's strategy to satisfy its customers' needs for products and services.

There are three types of competitive strategies, and they are as follows:
- Cost leadership
- Differentiation
- Pricing strategy

Cost leadership allows a company to manage costs and hopefully become the lowest priced competitor. Increasing sales and reducing costs assists in the supply chain's profitability, providing the team with a competitive advantage over competitors.

Differentiation is the marketing and supplying of products or services within the supply chain that provide a competitive advantage within the marketplace. How does a company's difference make it a better choice than other competitors?

Pricing strategy is the pricing of products or services by the members within the supply chain that provides a competitive advantage. One of the strategies to control pricing is to provide bundling or bulk pricing to reduce cost.

PRICING STRATEGY Pricing of products or services by the members within the supply chain that provides a competitive advantage.

STRATEGIC FIT The continuity between competitive strategy and customer supply chain strategies.

Achieving Strategic Fit

Strategic fit refers to the continuity between competitive strategy and customer supply chain strategies. To achieve a successful strategic fit, a company's supply chain strategy and competitive strategy goals must be as follows:
- Facilitate supply chain decisions that best meet the target segment customers' priorities and reduce uncertainty
- Align customer needs by products or services
- Synchronize supply chain functions and capabilities within supply chain constraints

Companies typically fail when they cannot align strategic fit, processes, and capabilities to support strategic goals. Conflict typically arises from management's inability to provide the supportive environment, initiate alignment, and sustain and correct for variation when the strategy matures.

Consider if a company boasts consistently low prices and ready supply on hand what their strategic fit (supply chain strategy and competitive strategy) would need to look like. How about high quality and customized products? What would that strategic fit look like?

Business Strategy

How does each company decide how to conduct its business? What process can the company use to make it unique but, competitive? What processes are being used by competitors within the industry?

Business strategy is the plan that companies use to establish business goals and objectives; this plan can include product design, process management, and collaborative business initiatives. Strategies differ from company to company, and this is seen when consumers experience customer expectations. When you visit a food restaurant, your expectations drive your choice.

When you choose a meal in less than a few minutes through the drive-up window, you have chosen a business strategy. If you choose a food restaurant that is sit down for the family in a nice atmosphere, you have chosen a business strategy.

The restaurant has developed a business strategy to capture the customers' expectations of a target market segment of the population. Companies that compete at the top of their game establish, sustain, and improve their business strategy to meet changing customer expectations.

Target market segment is a plan by a company to specifically choose a segment of an appropriate customer market. A company's decision on a strategy that can meet customer expectations is important. There are four steps to establishing the target market segment, and they are as follows:

- Define the target market
- Conduct customer demand analysis
- Analyze sub-targets
- Identify a segment

Businesses must decide how they will interact with their customers. Business strategies are the core of a company's competencies and strengths and how they apply a competitive advantage over their competition.

Who is a company's customer? No, it is not just people. Customers have demographic tendencies. As a provider of products or services, companies need to know specifically who the customer is, what their specific expectations are, how customer will change, and how to provide a supply chain that can evolve to meet those needs in the future and retain the customers.

Supply Chain Flow

What are the flows within a supply chain that need to be considered, how does a company use those flows, and how does the company improve the flows to maintain a competitive advantage?

There are three types of flows in a supply chain, and they are as follows:

- Product flow
- Information flow
- Revenue flow

Product flow is the movement of material from raw to the end product (downstream) or this process in reverse (upstream). An example of upstream would be to recycle or return a product to the manufacturer. Product flow has improved measurably. As discussed earlier, looking back through history, product flow was uncertain at best and sometimes nonexistent. The flow of services and products is much more reliable, and to compete a company must a flow be at optimal levels of performance. With the advent of enterprise resource planning (ERP) supply chains are more manageable, reliable, and predictable.

Information flow is the shared information in all its forms that is used by all stakeholders in the supply chain to manage resources. Information flow is critical to the efficiency of supply chains. Technology such as ERP now allows for the movement from POS throughout the chain with pinpoint accuracy. The manufacturer can forecast production requirements, inventory managers can usually predict consumer requirements over a specific time period, and all entities can account for revenue.

Revenue flow is the movement of funds through the supply chain to all stakeholders; this can be upstream and downstream. The bottom-line is who is spending what where and how much profit is generated from the supply chain for all the entities in collaboration.

The success of a supply chain is about managing the change from individual functions to highly integrated activities in a trusting, collaborative environment. One negative factor within supply chain flow is the bullwhip effect.

The **bullwhip effect** is defined as how demand uncertainty and lead times can cause order sizes to rise and fall quickly within the supply chain, and it is based on the excess product on hand or shortages of product that also affect costs and profit margin.

Resource Planning

What resources will be needed to maintain customers? How should a company improve its processes and innovate for future changes? What is the cost to maintain the supply chains competitive advantage?

Resource planning is how supply chain managers analyze and prepare for the future. What could happen? And how does a company prepare potential contingencies?

You do this when you prepare for your day. It is somewhat unconscious for some tasks, but others require articulate planning. It looks like it could rain, and the forecast says there is a 90% chance, so you choose to close the windows in your home in case it does rain. Supply chain managers must also anticipate transportation breakdowns, potential natural disasters, and sometimes political disturbance.

Supply managers may have to plan to shift operations to another location to compensate for production loss. A prime example would be supply managers preparing for a holiday surge. The complete supply chain must forecast possible scenarios and enact contingency plans to meet increased customer demand.

Supportability analysis is a process to integrate various analytical techniques to solve a variety of potential problems with the objective of designing, developing, and implementing an effective and efficient supply plan that will be consistent with established requirements.

First, the supply chain managers must identify the potential problems, define the analysis goals, set the rules for implementation, and understand the constraints of the situation. Fortunately, there are software tools that can provide a solid basis for designing, implementing, and monitoring supportability analysis plans.

INFORMATION FLOW The shared information in all its forms used by all stakeholders in the supply chain to manage resources; critical to the efficiency of supply chains.

REVENUE FLOW The movement of funds through the supply chain to all stakeholders; can be upstream and downstream; includes bottom-line, who is spending what where to what expectation, and how much profit is generated from the supply chain for all of the entities in collaboration.

BULLWHIP EFFECT How demand uncertainty and lead times can cause order sizes to rise and fall quickly within the supply chain based on excess on hand or shortages of product, which also affects costs and profit margin.

PROCESS MANAGEMENT WITHIN THE SUPPLY CHAIN

Members of the supply chain must manage their processes with the intent of improving the performance of the entire supply chain, not just their own organization. The supply chain is a collection of processes, and each process integrates to provide a seamless flow of information, product, or service along with revenue.

Processes may be analyzed from a quantitative point of view known as the analytics or metrics or from qualitative point of view, and this is the organizational integration of processes by each supply chain member.

Some quantitative supply chain performance measures are the following:

- *Demand rate.* This is the amount of product required to meet customer expectation within a specific time period.
- *Economic order quantity (EOQ).* This is the amount of product ordered to minimize total cost of inventory held.
- *Inventory stock levels.* This is synchronizing inventory by efficient forecasting of minimum stock quantity and minimum reorder quantity.
- *Inventory turnover rate.* This is a measure of the amount of times inventory will be sold in a specific period of time.
- *Product availability.* This is the amount of product that is available to be purchased at a specific point in time. It is a key to customer loyalty.

Some qualitative supply chain process analyses are the following:

- Transportation integration
- Production integration
- Sales integration
- Customer integration
- Service integration
- Administrative integration

Opportunity and Risk Management

What opportunities or risks are within the supply chain, how will they affect the supply chain, how should these opportunities or risks be resourced, what innovations will come from the opportunities or risks, and how should the bad risk be mitigated?

Opportunity is identified as a shortcoming in system or process that may allow a chance to provide or improve a product or service with a competitive advantage. Supply chain relationships rely on each partner improving the supply chain by identifying opportunities, improving processes, and providing the chain with cost saving while adding value. Some opportunities may be improved.

Communication is frequent, articulate communication; it is a key indicator of supply chain performance. Companies that communicate at high levels of efficiency are always passing information to improve the supply chain performance. The companies that used communication are usually the innovators within their industries.

Risk is any issue that impacts the supply chain's performance; there are good risks and bad risks. Risk can be divided into the following two categories:

- *Demand risk.* This is the potential that a supply forecast will not match actual demand, and this will incur a cost because of surplus or lost sales.
- *Operational risk.* This is the potential that loss will occur due to the failure of the supply chain members' internal organizational shortcomings.

OPPORTUNITY
A shortcoming in a system or process that may allow a chance to provide or improve a product or service, gaining competitive advantage.

RISK Any issue that impacts the supply chain's performance; there are good risks and bad risks.

Some risk factors to be considered by supply chain teams are the following:

- Environmental
- Geopolitical
- Economic
- Technological

Environmental risks are natural disasters, extreme weather, and disease. Supply chain members have little ability to control these risks and can only plan to mitigate the risk through planning and insurance.

Geopolitical risks are political instability, trade restrictions, terrorism, theft, and piracy. These risks can be influenced but require a mitigation plan; they can be controlled. The supply chain can be impacted by global situations. This has been seen repeatedly when a situation occurs in a country that causes supply disruption that affects prices and demand.

Economic risks are demand shock, price volatility, currency fluctuations, and energy. These risks can be controlled or influenced with planning and management by supply chain members. Fuel has had a high impact on supply chains because the cost of fuel and the supply of fuel are volatile.

Technological risks are IT disruptions and infrastructure risks. These are controllable and can be influenced by the supply chain members with planning and management.

Opportunities and risk must be continuously reviewed to allow the supply chain members to forecast future operations. Changes within the supply chain provide opportunity and risk that can be mitigated or exploited to improve the profit margin.

SUPPLY CHAIN PERFORMANCE MANAGEMENT

Members of the supply chain are under pressure to meet market requirements. Companies large and small must foster relationships that are cost effective, efficient, and responsive to meet customer expectations. Smaller companies may need to segment or differentiate themselves from competitors to compete in established supply chain relationships. This differentiation may require finding value added services, high delivery performance, or any improvement opportunity a large company may not be able to exploit.

Supplier Performance Management

Who in the supply chain is meeting their contractual obligations? Why are they not meeting contractual obligations? Are all the team members performing efficiently and contributing the value and revenues of the supply chain? What metrics will the supply chain use to manage performance, and how will that information be evaluated to mitigate risk and exploit opportunities within the supply chain?

Each member of the supply chain is important. Members' performance directly or indirectly impacts supply chain performance. Supplier performance management is used to measure, analyze, and manage the supply chain, to cut cost, reduce risk, and seek continuous improvement within the supply chain.

- **Continuous improvement** is monitoring the performance and processes of the supply chains, and it is paramount to getting and retaining leadership within the industry. Companies that continuously analyze current performance and processes

ENVIRONMENTAL RISKS Natural disasters, extreme weather, and disease; supply chain members have little ability to control these risks and can only plan to mitigate the risk through planning and insurance.

GEOPOLITICAL RISKS Political instability, trade restrictions, terrorism, theft, and piracy; these risks can be influenced but require a mitigation plan and can be controlled; the supply chain can be impacted by global situations.

ECONOMIC RISKS Demand shock, price volatility, currency fluctuations, and energy; these risks can be controlled or influenced with planning and management by supply chain members (for instance, fuel has had a high impact on supply chains because the cost of fuel and the supply of fuel is volatile).

TECHNOLOGICAL RISKS IT disruptions and infrastructure risks; controllable and can be influenced by the supply chain members with planning and management.

CONTINUOUS IMPROVEMENT Monitoring performance and processes is paramount to getting and retaining leadership within the industry; companies that continuously analyze current performance and processes for opportunities remain innovative and are prepared for changes.

for opportunities remain innovative and are prepared for changes. The following are just a few of the improvement systems within supply chain that are used:

– Lean
– Performance-based logistics
– Six Sigma
– Total quality management (TQM)

▪ **Delivery performance** is when customers seek 100% on-time delivery with zero defects. This is extremely hard to attain and maintain without constant vigilance on the variables of performance within the supply chain.

▪ **Process accuracy** is when the customer expects zero defects. The reality is there will always be discrepancies. Manual processes allow for more variation within processes while automated ones should be perfect, but human error is still a factor. Supply chain software products assist supply chain teams with improving supply chain accuracy.

When companies measure supply chain performance, they return to the design of the chain. The following are some of the metrics used to measure a supply chain's performance:

▪ **Facilities**

– *Average flow and cycle times.* These are used for setting the due to customer date, and measures the average of the actual time it takes to process a product in a specific time period.

– *Capacity.* This is used in design or construction of facilities and measures how much product the facility can process in a specific time period.

– *Flow-time efficiency.* This is used to measure product flow efficiency and how much actual time versus an established standard it takes to move product in a specific period of time.

– *Product variety.* This is used to increase product flow and measures the variety of product moving through the facility in a specific period of time.

– *Utilization.* This is used to understand how well the facility is being used for what it was designed to do.

▪ **Inventory**

– *Average inventory.* This is used to understand how much inventory is being maintained and measures the average amount of inventory in a specific period of time.

– *Average safety inventory.* This is used to understand how much safety inventory is being maintained and measures the average amount of safety inventory in a specific period of time.

– *Fill rate.* This is used to understand how quickly orders are being processed in a specific period of time.

– *Inventory turnover.* This is used to understand how quickly inventory by type is being processed in a specific period of time.

▪ **Transportation**

– *Average inbound transportation cost.* This is used to understand the cost of a type of product within cost of goods sold and how much the supplier is charging the company for the product.

– *Average outbound transportation cost.* This is used to understand the cost of a type of product within sales and how much the customer is costing the company for the product?

– *Average outbound shipment size.* This is used to understand the size and amount of product leaving the facility.

■ **Information**

- *Forecast horizon.* this is the specific time a forecast is designed before the actual event.
- *Forecast error.* This is used to understand the difference between the actual demand and forecasted demand.
- *Variance from plan.* This is used to understand the difference between what was forecasted and the actual event.

■ **Source**

- *Average purchase price.* This is used to understand the average price of a product or service for a specific period of time.
- *Average purchase quantity.* This is used to understand the average quantity of a product moved in a specific period of time.
- *Supplier lead time.* This is used to understand the average time it takes a product to be ordered and delivered in specific period of time.

■ **Pricing**

- *Average sales price.* This is used to understand the average price of a product or service for a specific period of time.
- *Average order size.* This is used to understand the average order size or amount of product for a specific period of time.
- *Profit margin.* This is used to understand the amount of net revenue generated from sales within a specific period of time.

These are just a few measures of performance per category. There are many more that provide a more in depth look at the supply chain's performance. All of the metrics used are combined to identify opportunities or risks within the supply chain.

Supply chain managers must not only be constantly vigilant of how activities internally and externally are currently affecting the supply chain, but they must also be aware of how the activities in the future will impact the company and what changes or innovations will need to take place to meet customer expectations.

Supply Chain Software

What technology is being used within the supply chain or industry? Is the company being as efficient as the competition? How is software optimizing the supply chain?

Supply chain software is a tool that is applied to manage supplier relationships and control business processes, providing a competitive advantage. Supply chain software assists team members in the forecast, supply disparity, and demand management within the supply chain. Some of the benefits of supply chain software are the following:

■ Lower costs
■ Improved collaboration
■ Cycle times
■ Response to conflict

There have been many software products that have been used to analyze customer information within the supply chain. Management must decide how to incorporate these products into the project and forecast customer trends. Management can use the following to project and forecast:

■ *Electronic data interchange (EDI).* This early version has been used since the 1970s and has sped up the transmission of supply chain information from the previous non-automated system of supply tracking.

■ *Enterprise resource planning (ERP).* This real-time system (scanners) tracks supply chain information using computer-based technologies and has global connectivity due to the Internet.

■ *Supply chain management (SCM).* This provides analytical support to the ERP system. This assists the supply chain members in decision making.

■ *Radio frequency identification (RFID).* This system uses radio frequency tags to track supply movement. RFID has greatly improved the accuracy of producing, tracking, and reducing theft of product within the supply chain.

SYSTEM CONSTRAINTS

What are constraints and how do they affect the functions of the supply chain? How do organizations manage the constraints so as to improve profit and maintain supply chain flexibility? What is the value of performing outside established system constraints within a specific time period for the supply chain?

CONSTRAINT Restricts a system from being able to achieve its goal; the term most often used is *bottleneck*.

A **constraint** is something that restricts a system from being able to achieve its goal. The term most often used is a "bottleneck." The supply chain has constraints at various times and places, and these constraints can cause production slowing, incurred costs, and limit resources.

Some of the constraints that the supply chain must contend with are the following:

■ Capacity constraints
■ Inventory balance constraints
■ Overtime limit constraints
■ Workforce constraints

Capacity constraint is the amount of product that can be produced, delivered, or retained in inventory for a specific period of time.

Inventory balance constraints are the amount of value the inventory is worth as an asset and includes finished goods, raw materials, stock, or works in progress.

Overtime limit constraints are the time in excess of regular established work hours within a specific time period.

Workforce constraints are the accumulated time of full time employees (FTE) and the cost of hiring and termination of employees during a specific time period.

CRITERIA FOR DECISION MAKING ON OPTIMUM SUPPLY CHAIN DESIGN

How do organizations make supply chain decisions? What mechanisms are in place to assist supply chain members in meeting customer demand upstream and downstream to manage profits and risk?

Consumers do not often think about all of the decision making that is accomplished to get a product or service into the marketplace. There are a myriad situations and issues that must be addressed to get the right item to the right place at the right time in the manner the customer desires.

Some of the supply chain decisions include the following:

■ *Optimizing inventory.* This is determining the amount of customer demand for a specific period of time and being able to match that quantity without expending more funds than necessary to meet demand.

■ *Optimizing of supply chain flexibility.* This is the measure of how responsive and efficient a supply chain reacts to fluctuations in demand or strategic change when a situation arises within a specific period of time.

■ For example, imagine if a shipment is not sent or received in the specified time. How quickly can the supply chain respond to this problem to meet the demand and retain customer loyalty while keeping cost to a minimum?

These are directly related to the following supply chain capabilities:

■ *Optimizing consumer response.* This is the supply chain's customer service performance strategy provides a customer experience that retains loyalty. Service excellence, listening to the voice of the customer, and innovating to meet transcendental customer demand.

■ *Optimizing cycle time.* This is efficiently maximizing value added activities while minimizing non-value added activities by reducing cost, increasing quality, and increasing responsiveness within the supply chain.

■ *Reduce supply chain costs.* Costs for supply chains are increasing due to global dispersion. Supply chain managers must constantly monitor costs from taxes, new product development, inventory, transportation, and infrastructure.

There is a plethora of information for managing a supply chain. It seems amazing that customers get their products and services in a timely manner. Supply chains are complex systems that require intricate coordination and exemplary management to meet customer expectations.

So the next time you get your bottle of water, think about all of the negotiations, coordination, and management needed to get that product to you, where you want it, when you want it, how you want it, and, most importantly, for the price you want it at.

There are a lot of parties involved in a supply chain, and much like an orchestra, they must all play their part when they are supposed to, how they are supposed to, and make it all seem so easy.

DISCUSSION QUESTIONS

1. Have you ever wondered how that bottle of water got to you? What is a supply chain, how does it work, and how does it directly or indirectly affect customer expectations?

2. It is a wonder how you can order an item, and you can expect the delivery within hours to a week from requisition with a 90% or better accuracy rate. How does this happen, and who are the members of the supply chain team behind the scenes that are so efficiently executing your order?

3. What opportunities or risks are within the supply chain, how will they affect the supply chain, how do companies resource these opportunities or risks, what innovations will come from the opportunities or risks, and how do companies mitigate bad risk?

4. Who in the supply chain is meeting their contractual obligations, and why are they not meeting contractual obligations? Are all the team members performing efficiently and contributing to the value and revenues of the supply chain? What metrics will the supply chain use to manage performance, and how will that information be evaluated to mitigate risk and exploit opportunities within the supply chain?

5. What technology is being used within the supply chain or industry? Is the company as efficient as the competition? How is software optimizing the supply chain?

6. How do organizations make supply chain decisions? What mechanisms are in place to assist supply chain members in meeting customer demand upstream and downstream to manage profits and risk?

SUCCESS

Metrics to Assess Success

A young, inspiring person has been promoted to chief executive officer (CEO) of a Fortune 500 company. This organization has sales of $10 billion dollars annually. The organization has a very complicated business that requires an extremely complicated supply chain. The organization is beginning to lose customers due to poor delivery times. The new CEO was put in place to correct this major issue. The new CEO has been given a short time frame to correct the poor performance of the organization. The CEO has many options to work with, but the priority is to work on the supply chain. In an effort to get the right focus on the supply chain, the CEO hired a supply chain manager to work through the complicated supply chain and correct the issues that the organization is currently facing. This new manager started out with a basic level of knowledge of how the supply chain and leadership process works. How will the performance be assessed?

INTRODUCTION

Supply chains are critical to the success of an organization because they are responsible for staying current with supply and demand so that products or services are delivered to customers. To be successful, the performance of the supply chain must be measured and monitored. There needs to be a focus on the customer and internal performance levels. These performance levels should be measured through metrics. Metrics that measure the performance throughout the supply chain must be created. Leadership creates these metrics, and leadership uses planning, organizing, leading, and controlling functions to effectively manage the supply chain. These metrics must be able to give the management team immediate feedback on how the supply chain is operating.

The supply chain is time-sensitive, and the metrics should be heavily focused on time. The customer wants a product or service at a certain time, and it is the supply chain that must meet this requirement. Managers have three key responsibility areas: legal, economic, and ethics. Legally, managers should understand the laws and regulations and abide by all them throughout the supply chain. Economically, managers should work to produce and supply products and or services as efficiently and effectively as possible. Managers must perform business activities by the moral standards of society. This means that work safety, quality, financial measures, community, employees, environment, and all other aspects of the business must be conducted according to the moral standard.

The critical items that a manager must understand extremely well in any business are supply and demand. These are the fundamentals for understanding the market that the organization is competing within and must be utilized to build a robust supply chain. In a market where supply is greater than demand, waste is being created. If demand is greater than supply, then the organization is losing out on opportunities, and the customer will be dissatisfied. The ideal state is when supply equals demand. Variations in supply and demand are something managers should work to understand.

A supply chain has four sources of variation: the variety of product and services that are being offered; structural variations in demand; random variation; and assignable variation. An organization that offers a large variety of products or services will experience much variation in their production and service requirements. Structural variations that are in demand are planned and predictable. Random variation is the natural variation that all

KEY TERMS

processes experience. Assignable variation is variation that can be assigned to a cause that management can correct and eliminate.

A **supply chain** consists of the suppliers all the way to the customers and everything that is in between; this includes all functions and operations. In essence, the supply chain is the sequence of organizations and their facilities, functions, and activities that are used to create a product or service. The supply chain starts with the basic raw materials and suppliers, and it includes warehouses, factories, processing centers, distribution centers, and offices all the way to the customer. The activities and functions found throughout the supply chain includes the following items:

- Forecasting
- Purchasing
- Inventory management
- Information management
- Quality assurance
- Scheduling
- Production and delivery
- Customer service

This activity requires management to coordinate, organize, and integrate supply and demand for the complete supply chain. It requires strong management to develop and lead the supply chain so that the organization can obtain a competitive advantage. A manager must be able to perform four major functions and must have authority for those operations. Those functions are planning, organizing, leading, and controlling. It is necessary to create plans to achieve a supply chain that gives an organization a competitive advantage.

Planning

To be successful, there must be a sound foundation in place. This foundation is the plan that will be used to achieve the goals. Managers must define the activities, tasks, resources, time, and responsible person to carry out a systematic approach to leading an organization on a journey. The plan must utilize the current situation that the organization is facing and compare it to the future situation that the organization wants to achieve. The plan will define how the gap between the current situation and future situation will be closed so that the organization can reach its destination. The manager must have a very strong understanding of the supply chain so that the appropriate approach is being used to achieve the plan. This means that the manager decides what type of activities the company will engage in throughout the supply chain so that complex plans can be completed successfully.

Organizing

Managers must coordinate and assemble information, people, financial resources, equipment, and many other resources to meet the required goals. It is necessary to define job responsibilities, staffing needs, and operation layouts for the supply chain so that the wants and needs of the customer can be met. Information is critical to the success of the supply chain. Information will flow through every stage of the supply chain, and it affects quality, cost, and customer service. People are the number one aspect of any business. It is people that will define the organization and use the information to build and deliver products and services. People should be treated with the highest level of respect because they are the heart of every business and will determine the level of success that will be achieved.

Teams of people can help make improvements in all areas of the supply chain, and this will help lead the organization to new heights. It is highly recommended to have team activities in place for the people so that they can collaborate to make improvements. To execute the necessary plans and to operate on a daily basis requires financial resources. Financial resources are required in any organization and will allow an organization to make the pertinent investments and maintain their equipment. The operations of an organization require equipment to be effective and efficient, so the organization must purchase the appropriate equipment that is needed. This equipment needs to have preventative maintenance (PM) schedules that will allow the equipment to be effectively utilized for long periods of time. The organization should have metrics that measure the preventative maintenance schedules. The number of PM schedules completed is an ideal metric. Other metrics in this category are percent of downtime, percent of unplanned downtime, and number of breakdowns.

A leader is a manager with influence, and the leader must understand the fundamentals of leadership to build a robust supply chain for the organization. Leadership is critical when attempting to align the people in the organization so that the complete organization is working toward the same goals. An effective leader builds a supply chain that keeps people and groups at the center to drive the organization toward success. The key elements that a leader must possess to build a successful supply chain are the ability to influence, understand organizational objectives, able to be a change agent, able to follow, and understand others.

A leader has to be able to influence the complete supply chain. The leader communicates the plans and ideas throughout the supply chain and must gain agreement between different the nodes and people. For the leader to be successful, it is necessary to motivate the appropriate employees to accept and implement the plans that have been defined. These plans may require changes to be implemented, ones that could cause disruptions in the organization if they are not properly supported. It is necessary to gain commitment and enthusiasm from everyone in the supply chain. The manager can gain this commitment by creating clear organizational objectives.

Managers must understand the organizational objectives throughout the supply chain. It is necessary to set objectives that are specific, measurable, attainable, realistic, and time bound (SMART). These objectives should be challenging but clear. The objectives shall also be measurable. A manager should only set objectives that are attainable and realistic. All objectives need a date associated with when they will start and when they will finish. Objectives that are challenging typically require an organization to be willing to change.

Change needs to be a common event in organizations for them to be competitive in the global economy. It is imperative that organizations use change to drive continuous improvements. This cycle is never-ending, and it should be on going when an organization is being highly competitive. An organization can always improve from their current position. Managers must lead this change and build a culture that accepts change. Managers should explain to their employees why change is required to gain acceptance for the change, and this conversation should take place prior to implementing the change. Managers must also be open to ideas and suggestions from the people throughout the supply chain and must be able to follow instead of lead. A formal change process is necessary for an organization to effectively manage change. A basic fundamental of a change management system is to have a defined group that must approve the changes.

Being a follower is critical when leading an organization to being competitive. It is necessary to understand when to lead and when to follow. Managers need to build relationships with people and enjoy collaborating with people to achieve the goals that have been defined. While building these relationships, it will be necessary for the manager to follow others who may have better expertise in certain areas. It is also important to allow others to lead so that the manager can gain their respect and trust. The trust factor is critical when building a team that collaborates and achieves the stated objectives. In all aspects of being a manager and a leader, people are required to be included.

People are the most important part of any organization, and managers must build a deep appreciation of the people who work in the supply chain. It is necessary to encourage people and motivate them to perform at the highest possible levels. People that perform at high levels lead to high performing organizations. High performing organizations throughout the supply chain build a high performing supply chain.

Controlling

To maintain high performance, an organization needs to have controls in place to maintain this level of performance. There needs to be individual controls, department level controls, product line level controls, plant level controls, divisional level control, corporate level controls, and company level controls so that the complete supply chain is being controlled. This leads to metrics that can be used to assess the supply chain. The performance will be monitored, and the needed changes must be implemented to successfully control the organization.

Managers do not necessarily use the four functions of management over a course of a 4-hour period. It is important to understand all four functions so that the manager can be effective in the role. A critical role that most organizations employ today is the supply chain manager position. The supply chain manager determines the appropriate level of outsourcing, manages suppliers, manages customer relations, manages procurement, manages risk, and solves problems.

METRICS

METRIC The measurement that is used to gauge a component of a company's performance.

A **metric** is used to measure the performance level of an individual or organization. This measurement system must be taken across the complete supply chain to assess its success. Organizations in today's environment must build better quality products at the lowest possible cost, and these expectations are expected to improve every day for the organization to remain competitive. Competitiveness is how well an organization meets the wants and needs of its customers relative to its competitors that offer similar products and services. The complete supply chain must address the internal and external customers' wants and needs to achieve a competitive advantage. Internal customers are those customers internal to the organization. The customer may be the next operation step in the process. This would be considered an internal customer. External customers are individuals or organizations that a product or service to help is delivered to so as to meet their wants and needs. To be competitive in the supply chain, it is crucial to understand how businesses compete.

Businesses compete by using many methods to create a competitive advantage. Items such as cost, location, product design, service design, location, and supply chain management are examples of what is used by businesses to compete. The supply chain can use all the items listed plus many others to develop a competitive advantage. Fundamentally, the supply chain must have a mission, goals, strategy, and tactics to achieve objectives. A mission is the reason why an organization exists, and it defines the purpose of the organization. The goals define the scope of how the organization will achieve the mission. The strategy is the roadmap used for achieving the goals that have been defined. Tactics are the actions and methods that will be taken to achieve the strategy. Metrics are used to determine how an organization is performing. These metrics are critical for a manger to understand so that the manager can gauge the level of performance of the supply chain.

CREATING METRICS

Many years of working in a manufacturing environment has yielded a process of creating metrics for a service or manufacturing environment. The foundational piece for creating metrics is being able to understand the complete supply chain from start to finish. Once the supply chain is understood, metrics should be created utilizing the following approach:

- A cross-functional team should select metrics that impact and measures the pulse of the supply chain.
- The metrics must be SMART.
- Metrics should be available for viewing by all team members.
- Updating the metrics must be very easy to do.
- A system to address metrics that are not at target or trending the wrong direction must be in place.

A cross functional team must select the metrics to ensure that many perspectives are included to assess the supply chain. While assessing the supply chain, the suppliers and customers should be included so that the complete supply chain is being measured. The team should use metrics that are composed of suppliers, warehouses, manufacturing, service organizations, functional areas, and customers. This approach will help secure a robust systematic view of how the supply chain is measuring up against its domain. This team approach to setting metrics will help drive the ability of the supply chain to reach it maximum potential.

SMART metrics make it clear to all parties in the supply chain what is important for the supply chain to build or deliver that meets the customers' wants and needs. A metric that is specific eliminates all ambiguity and allows a measurable item to be developed. If it is not clear how to measure performance, then it is difficult to determine if improvements have been made. In the environment that organizations operate in today, it is required to continuously improve to remain competitive. Continuous improvement has become part of the culture of successful organizations, and this success must be visible throughout the organization.

The manner in which most companies make improvement visible is through displaying this information in front of all the employees throughout the supply chain. All departments and functions are encouraged to have an area to place the metrics in so that it is very obvious whether the supply chain is meeting or not meeting the targets. It is necessary to keep these metrics up to date at all times so that employees have a current view on how the supply chain is performing. The metrics should be taken down to the smallest possible levels. This means measuring individual's quality levels, outputs, and other measures by the second. This will not be possible at first, and it will require an organization to develop this culture by starting at a higher level of measurement.

To maintain this metrics system, it is required for the data to be retrieved very easily. It is also required that the actual charts that are being displayed can be updated with very little effort. If metrics are tough to update, then they will not be updated as needed because people will work on other areas that are easier to maintain. Metrics are critical to the success of an organization, and must be treated that way by all employees. The power of metrics is centered in the heart of the supply chain and will drive the supply chain to produce an effective an efficient product or service.

Metrics that are not on target or trending in the wrong direction must be dealt with so that the supply chain can improve. If a target is not being met, then a manager must identify this gap and work with the team to define an action plan that will eliminate this gap. This same approach must be used when the metric is trending in an unfavorable direction. If the metric is trending in a favorable direction, then the manager should also recognize this situation by defining why the metric is on an upward trend. This will help organizations become better and improve the supply chain.

Areas to Avoid When Creating Metrics

It is critical to understand what to avoid when creating metrics. When developing metrics, the approach should be to keep it simple and to not create complicated metrics. Metrics that are complicated will not be understood by all employees in the supply chain. Understanding is needed by all employees in the supply chain because it will be the people of the supply chain who will be developing improvement ideas, and these people must understand how the metrics are measuring items throughout the supply chain. Avoid ambiguity as to why these metrics are being measured. Not sharing why there are metrics is the reason many good ideas fail in the business environment. When people are told why the metrics are important and being measured, the people are more willing to accept the metrics and will work to make improvements. Managers must avoid losing the trust of their employees. Employees that trust their managers and supervisors are engaged with the business and are willing to give an all-out effort to help build the best supply chain for the organization. Managers must avoid utilizing charts that are too complicated. The charts must be clear and concise so that they will be maintained. An organization creates a strong environment when it develops internal and external metrics.

Internal Metrics

Internal metrics are those metrics used internally. This includes metrics at corporate, divisional, plant, product line, and department levels. A department should have metrics that are internal for the department. These metrics could be as simple as employee's attendance rates, employee's turnover rates, or safety levels. The metrics could be as complicated as productivity, orders completed on time, or scrap rates. These metrics are used to determine the internal level of success for the department. The department can measure their level of performance from these metrics. The metrics that are selected should match-up with the strategy for the department. The metrics allow the department to control and monitor the performance so that the mission can be achieved. Productivity is a metric that most organizations use to help drive toward a competitive edge. It is a measure of how well the resources are being used, and it is output divided by input. Higher productivity is an indicator of an organization that is effective and efficient, and it helps protect an organization from foreign competition. If an organization has an output of $200, and the labor, material, and overhead costs are $10, then the productivity rate is figured as follows:

Output = $200

Input = $10

Productivity = Output / Input

Productivity = $200 / $10 = 20

The factors that affect productivity are labor, quality, management, technology, methods, and capital. Productivity improvements are necessary for an organization to continue toward becoming a successful supply chain. The first step to improving productivity is defining which areas will be measured. The next step is to determine where the bottleneck areas are in the process. By focusing on bottlenecks, an organization can improve the output. Next, the organization should develop tactics to improve productivity. Reasonable goals are needed so that it is clear as to where the organization must head. It must be clearly shown that top management supports productivity improvements. A productivity metric must be tracked, and it should be publicized.

Customer-Focused Metrics

External- or customer-focused metrics are used to assess the performance level of the supply chain from the perspective of the customer. Managers monitor and control these metrics so that its operations are controlled throughout the supply chain. The goal in the supply chain is to be effective and efficient. This means that responsiveness is required in the supply chain, and it must be conducted with safety, quality, and cost in mind. From a customer's perspective, the supply chain must have the ability to meet their expectations. Customer service expectations are the primary drivers for measuring the supply chain's performance. The customer is looking for the right quantity of the right product at the right time that is at the right quality level. In essence, the customer is measuring the following items:

- Delivery
- Quality
- Cost

Delivery has many components that will need to be identified and measured to control this aspect of the supply chain. The quality of the product must meet or exceed the customer's expectations. Quality measures show the level of quality that is being delivered. Cost is a measure of how effective the supply chain is at producing the output with the correct level of resources, and this drives profitability for the end customer. A supply chain is in place to service a market so that customers can compete and be successful.

Lagging Indicators

A supply chain must understand that the external metrics are lagging indicators. Lagging indicators are those indicators that are used to measure when the product was delivered, what the product cost at the end of the supply chain, and how many customer complaints were experienced. **Lagging indicators** are indicators that follow an event. It is too late to change the product once it has occurred. Once an organization gets a delivery rating, it is too late to change this rate. Once a company finds out the number of customer complaints that they have, it is too late to change that metric. A successful supply chain places focus on leading indicators. Another good example of a lagging indicator is weight loss. If a person wants to lose weight

LAGGING INDICATOR
Indicator that follows an event.

and then steps on the scale, the actual reading is a lagging indicator. Lagging indicators are typically easier to measure but extremely hard to change.

Leading Indicators

A **leading indicator** is a signal of an event that will happen later. If used correctly, it will help control a lagging indicator. Managers must understand the metrics that control quality, delivery time, and cost. Once an organization defines the metrics that control these lagging indicators, then improvements can be implemented throughout the supply chain in these focused areas. Although this is a very simple approach, many companies do not focus on the leading indicators. Focusing on the leading indicators drives performance in a controlled approach. Using the weight example, if a person is trying to lose weight, then the number of days the person worked out for 30 minutes or more is considered to be a leading indicator. If the answer is zero, then the weight loss will more than likely not be at the expected lower target. Leading indicators are hard to measure but easy to change in the supply chain. It is important to understand the difference between lagging and leading indicators. Figure 4.1 gives examples of lagging and leading indicators.

LAGGING	LEADING
Weight of a person	Amount of exercise each day
On-time delivery	On-time completions
Customer complaints	Internal audit findings
Inventory value	Inventory turns
Number of sales	Advertisement budget

FIGURE 4.1 Examples of Lagging versus Leading Metrics

METRICS DEALING WITH TIME

Meeting customer service requirements is extremely critical for the supply chain. The supply chain in today's environment needs to be agile and flexible due to the changes that occur in supply and demand for the products and services that are being delivered. Managers want to achieve outstanding performance throughout the supply chain. This outstanding performance can be achieved by controlling and monitoring the performance for the supply chain. This requires a specific set of metrics that will need to be controlled and monitored. These metrics should fall in three key categories. They are as follows:

- Customer service
- Effectiveness and efficiency
- Flexibility

Customer service includes many key areas that must be controlled. The supply chain requires metrics that define effectiveness and efficiency to be used and met. Flexibility allows the supply change to adapt to changes in supply and demand that is present in the current marketplace. An agile supply chain emphasizes a flexible approach for the supply chain that drives and adapts to changes, and this will allow the supply chain to thrive in a dynamic environment. In each of these categories, a common theme is present. They all include a time based component that must be measured. Holistically, these categories can drive the time based strategy for the supply chain. A time based strategy drives reductions in time for tasks throughout the supply chain. Reduction in time leads to lower costs, better quality, lower inventory, improved customer service, and higher employee morale throughout the supply chain. The following items have been identified as some key time based metrics for the supply chain:

- Planning time
- Product and service design time
- Processing time
- Changeover time
- Delivery time
- Response time for complaints
- Product development

Each of these categories help lead an organization to improved customer service levels, better effectiveness and efficiency, and improved flexibility.

Planning Time

Planning time refers to capacity planning. Capacity is the maximum amount that can be produced from the operations in a specified time period. Areas in the supply chain that can give a good measure for capacity are equipment, space, and employee skills. Metrics for these areas are needed in the supply chain to help monitor and control the time a product or service can be delivered; this is based off of the capacity level of the supply chain. It is recommended for the supply chain to implement a strategic capacity plan with the goal being to match the long-term supply capabilities of the organization and supply chain with the long-term demand requirements. This will prevent an organization from over committing delivery promises to its customers. A supply chain needs to understand if it is over or under capacity because these items also drive the cost side of the supply chain. Over capacity leads to high costs, and under capacity leads to a loss of customers because the organizations are not able to deliver on promises. In an effort to understand the capacity levels, there are some key questions that an organization must be able to answer. Those key questions are as follow:

- What type of capacity is needed in the supply chain?
- What type of capacity is needed to match demand for the supply chain?
- When is the capacity needed in the supply chain?
- Where is the capacity needed in the supply chain?

The following metrics can help an organization understand the level of capacity, and the measurement of these items can help a supply chain meet the delivery needs of its customers. These metrics are design capacity, effective capacity, and actual output. Design capacity is the maximum output rate or service requirements that the supply chain, organization, facility, operation, or process has been designed to handle. Effective capacity refers to the design capacity minus downtime that is caused by maintenance, changeover, or quality issues. Actual output is the rate of output that was actually produced. Actual output will not exceed effective output. Other items to measure are efficiency and utilization. Efficiency equals actual output and effective capacity, and utilization equals actual output and design capacity. These measures are shown as percentages, so they must be multiplied by 100%.

Efficiency = Actual Output and Effective Output × 100%

Utilization = Actual Output and Design Capacity × 100%

Examples of Efficiency and Utilization

If the design capacity is 100 computers per day, and the effective capacity is 90 computers per day with an actual output of 80 computers per day, then compute the efficiency and utilization.

Design capacity = 100 computers per day

Effective capacity = 90 computers per day

Actual output = 80 computers per day

Efficiency = 80 computers per day / 90 computers per day $\times$ 100% = 88.9%

Utilization = 80 computers per day / 100 computers per day $\times$ 100% = 80%

Understanding capacity needs are extremely critical to the success of the supply chain. A forward view of the supply chain's capacity needs is required so that capacity adjustments can be made in advance of the needs that the supply chain may require. Tracking capacity needs and performance allows the supply chain to be proactive in meeting customer demand. Many organizations build a capacity cushion into the system when demand uncertainty is present. The capacity cushion normally is 100% minus the utilization. This cushion will help protect the customer from demand uncertainty. Looking at the previous example, the utilization was 80%, so it would be necessary to put a capacity cushion in place if the demand was uncertain.

Capacity Cushion Example

Utilization = 80%

Capacity cushion = 100% − Utilization

Capacity cushion = 100% − 80% = 20%

The steps in determining a capacity plan are as follows:

1. Define future capacity requirements.
2. Evaluate existing capacity and facilities, and identify gaps.
3. Select alternatives for meeting requirements.
4. Review financials.
5. Evaluate key qualitative issues.
6. Determine the best alternative for the long-term.
7. Implement alternative chosen measure.
8. Monitor results.

The capacity process is ongoing because capacity needs are understood and being modified to meet the customer requirements for the supply chain. The first step in defining capacity is very fundamental. Future capacity requirements must be identified from the aggregate plan and MRP. Once this information is clear and concise, the organization is ready to evaluate the future capacity against the current capacity and establish the gap. Any gaps that are identified in this planning process should be closed through action items that are defined to eliminate the conditions that are affecting the supply chain's capacity. A key step that is sometimes missed is a review of the financials. This is necessary to understand the impact on the profitability of the organization. Issues that must be reviewed are not all quantitative. Qualitative issues such as policies, procedures, political, and or economic policies may need to be evaluated. The best approach to meet the capacity requirement must be defined at this stage, and then the approach must be implemented to achieve the requirements. The monitoring of the results is the next step, and it is critical so that management controls the direction the organization must head in.

Product and Service Design

It is necessary to first understand why organizations design or redesign products and services. It is done because market opportunities or threats caused by economic, social, and demographic, political, legal, competition, cost, or technological changes are the driving forces for the need to design or redesign products or services. The key questions that the supply chain has to answer are as follows:

- What is the market size and demand profile for this product or service?
- Can the supply chain manufacture and service this product?
- What are the customer's expectations for the quality level?
- What are the economic implications to the supply?

To achieve a successful supply chain, it is necessary to measure the product life cycle for products and services that are new and redesigned. The product life cycle goes through four phases: introduction, growth, maturity, and decline. This will help a supply chain monitor and control when the product must be replaced.

Processing Time

Processing time is the time it takes to complete one complete unit of a product. In an effort to place this time in customer terms, it is referred to as Takt time. **Takt time** is defined as the cycle time needed to match customer demand to the final product. This is also called the heartbeat of the system, and it is normally shown by work shifts. The first step is to determine the net time available for a work shift. If there are multiple shifts available for this process or operation, then the net available time is multiplied by the number of available shifts. The next step is to figure the Takt time, and then divide the net available time by demand. To understand this Takt time in the changing environment, it should be measured, at least, on an hourly basis. This metric should be used to drive improved cycle time through the complete supply chain.

TAKT TIME The cycle time needed to match customer demand to the final product.

Example of Takt Time

The available time in a process is 21 hours per day with a customer demand of 300 pieces per day. Define the Takt time for this process.

Available time = 21 hours / day (3 shifts at 7 hours or $3 \times 7 = 21$)

Customer demand = 300 pieces per day

Takt time = Available Time / Customer Demand $\times$ 60 minutes / hour = 21 hours / 300 pieces per day $\times$ 60 minutes per day = 4.2 minutes per part

Changeover Time

Changeover time is the time it takes to switch from one part to another part on a line, product, facility, or organization. An organization should work aggressively to reduce changeover time. In a lean process, the ultimate lot size is one piece. To achieve this small lot size, changeover reduction has to be a strategic goal for the organization. The benefits of small lot sizes can help drive quality, delivery, and cost improvements for a supply chain. It has been proven that inspection, scrap, and rework costs are lower with small lot sizes. Inventory levels are also reduced, and this leads to lower carrying costs and less required storage space. The lower inventory causes problems to become more visible, and they must be solved at a very fast pace to prevent the supply chain from being disrupted. A process called single-minute exchange of dies (SMED) has been used by many organizations to reduce changeover times. This process is based on understanding the external and internal parts of a changeover. The external portions of the changeover are items that can be completed while the process is operating. The internal portions of the changeover are items that cannot be completed while the process is operating. The key to this process is to first move as much of the changeover as possible to be external. The next step is to reduce the time to complete the internal and external items.

Delivery Time

Customers expect to receive products from suppliers on time. The customers monitor the on time shipments by measuring how effective the suppliers are achieving this metric. Suppliers should also measure on time shipments. On time shipment is a lagging indicator, and the supply chain must focus on the leading indicators that drive on time shipments. Areas that are important for the supply chain to focus on to achieve an acceptable on time shipment rating are as follows:

- Aggregate planning
- Sales and operations planning
- Master scheduling
- Material requirement planning
- Inventory management
- Types of inventory
- Economic order quantity
- Purchasing
- Bullwhip effect
- Order fulfillment
- Logistics
- Scheduling

Aggregate Planning and Sales and Operation Planning

Aggregate planning is essentially intermediate capacity planning that covers a time horizon of 2 to 18 months, and it is used to create a production plan to match the supply chain resources with demand. In today's economy, many organizations experience demand variations. Aggregate planning works well in these types of environments. Sales and operations planning is considered the same as aggregate planning, and this term is used by many organizations to match the resources with demand. This term states that sales, finance, and operations are included in this planning process. This data is used in most organizations to make sure that supply and demand match resources in the supply chain. The business plan that defines the capacity and operations strategies feeds into the aggregate planning process. It is necessary to measure and monitor this plan at least once per month so that capacity and resources match, or so adjustments can be made with demand and or resources. The aggregate plan synchronizes the flow throughout the supply chain, and this helps drive customer service, resources (equipment and employees), and cost. The inputs for the aggregate plan are work force, production rates, facilities, equipment, policies, demand forecast, and inventory.

Master Scheduling

Master scheduling determines the amount of product or services that are needed to meet demand. This function is responsible for utilizing all sources to meet the objective that are set in the business and aggregate plan. The sources worked with are marketing, operations, capacity planning, and production planning. The master scheduler must provide delivery dates for orders. It is necessary to measure capacity, inventory, forecast accuracy, completed orders by the due date, and resource availability. These metrics will allow an organization to measure the performance level of the organization's delivery function.

Material Requirement Planning (MRP)

Organizations have complex raw materials, components, and subassemblies that make up a final item. It is necessary to have a system in place that can handle this complexity for a product structure. Material requirement planning (MRP) is a system that can be used to transform the master schedule requirements of an end item into raw material, components, subassemblies, and assembly requirements. The key metrics for MRP are expected demand, scheduled receipts, inventory on hand, planned order receipt, planned order releases, and net requirements.

INVENTORY MANAGEMENT

Inventory is an amount of a product or service that is in storage or on hand. It is necessary to manage this inventory for two primary reasons. The first reason is to maintain a certain level of customer service. The second is to understand the cost of ordering and or carrying cost for inventory. Inventory management's main objective is to protect customer service while balancing carrying cost. Managers utilize the measure of inventory turns, asset utilization, inventory investment, backorder quantity, and customer complaints; they take these measures and use them as metrics to monitor and control the performance levels. Management needs to establish a system for tracking inventory and make decisions as to when to order and how much to order. Inventory turns tracks the speed of how fast inventory is sold. An organization wants to achieve a turn rate that is high for the most part. The only time a higher turn rate is not desirable is when demand flexibility is required to meet customer service. Inventory value is a metric that should be measured at specific times but should also be measured over an average time. Inventory is checked through the complete supply chain and will typically carry a very high value. This is an area every organization should target for reductions. Excess inventory is not desirable for the supply chain.

Inventory turns = Annual Cost of Sales / Annual Average Inventory Value

Types of Inventory

Understanding inventory allows organizations to improve their level of customer service. Inventory is broken into six major categories: raw material, work in process, tools and supplies, finished goods, maintenance and repairs, and goods in transit. Each of these categories should be measured so that control of the inventory can be realized. Inventory control is important because inventory is cash that has been converted into the categories mentioned above. A system should be in place to evaluate the amount of inventory that is in place in each of the categories. Physical inventory is required to occur in an organization, and it must be controlled. A physical inventory is an actual count of the inventory that is in place. In most organizations, this physical count of inventory should occur at least annually. It is also a very good practice to have a classification system for the inventory. There is a system called

A-B-C that is used very frequently where the inventory is classified by importance. The A items are considered the most important items and make up approximately 20% of the number items and 70% of the annual dollar value of the inventory. The B items are moderately important, and they make up approximately 10% of the number items and 20% of the annual dollar value. The C items are the least important and they make up approximately 70% of the number items and 10% of the annual dollar value.

Economic Order Quantity

Inventory costs are very important to understand. The costs for inventory are purchase cost, holding or carrying cost, ordering cost, setup costs, and shortage costs. The purchasing cost is simply the amount required for buying the inventory. The holding or carrying cost is the amount it costs to carry inventory for a specific amount of time. The ordering cost is the cost to make the order and receive the order. The setup cost is the amount it costs to change machines or equipment to create the order. The shortage cost is the cost that impacts an organization when it runs out of an item. It is necessary to order the optimal quantity of a product by minimizing the costs that vary with order size and frequency. This is known as the economic order quantity (EOQ).

Purchasing

Purchasing evaluates potential suppliers and supports the needs of operations on purchased goods and services. The purchasing department plays a critical role in making sure that customer service is being met. This department is responsible for obtaining the materials, parts, and supplies and services that are required by the supply chain to produce a product or provide a service. The purchasing group should have a list of approved suppliers for the products or services that are required. The group should also put in place contingency plans in case the primary supplier is not able to supply the product or service. The metrics for this group should be centered on delivery time. Metrics should be in place to define the amount of time it takes to place an order, time to receive an order, amount of defects, supplier certification rating, and service time.

Bullwhip Effect

The **bullwhip effect** is the variation in demand and how it ripples back through the supply chain and causes control situations for suppliers. This variation can be caused by many different items. The main causes are reactions to shortages, forecast inaccuracies, and periodic ordering. It is important to minimize these causes. Metrics should be in place to measure shortages, forecast inaccuracies, and periodic ordering. The bullwhip effect results in higher costs and poor customer satisfaction.

Order Fulfillment

It is necessary to fulfill orders that have been accepted by the organization to ship to the customer. This is known as order fulfillment. There are many approaches organizations use to fulfill these orders. The common approaches are as follows:
- Engineer-to-order (ETO)
- Make-to-order (MTO)
- Assemble-to-order (ATO)
- Make-to-stock (MTS)

An organization should understand which category their products are being produced within and track the number of orders that are produced per week in that particular category. In an engineer-to-order (ETO), the customer orders a specific type of product that requires engineering work. Next, a make-to-order (MTO) is a special product that a customer may order. A good example of this type order is a new automobile because the customer can customize it. An excellent metric that could be used to monitor this type order is on-time completion rate. Assemble-to-order (ATO), utilizes components and subassemblies, and these items are assembled once the customer places an order. This could be a special piece of manufacturing equipment for the operations for one facility in the supply chain. A make-to-stock (MTS) is normally a commodity type product that is supplied to a large market. Examples of this type product are typically the normal products that the organization builds on a regular basis. Order fill rate is an excellent metric for this type of order.

Logistics

Logistics refers to the movement of materials, components, services, money, and information through a supply chain. The movement of these items in a facility should be defined on a diagram so that it is clear and well-defined. The team should review and work to improve this flow on a monthly basis. It is also critical to understand the movement of products and services in and out of the facilities of the supply chain. A metric that can help control and monitor the movement of the product and services is transportation cost.

LOGISTICS Refers to the movement of materials, components, services, money, and information through a supply chain.

Scheduling

An organization schedules products and services at an established time through the facilities and through equipment with human activities to meet or exceed customer expectations. This process is called scheduling, and it helps an organization increase productivity and reduce cost. Scheduling starts with the aggregate plan to generate a master production schedule that feeds into MRP, and a shop floor schedule is generated. Common performance metrics for scheduling are job flow time, job lateness, make span, and average number of jobs, and they are as follows:

- **Job flow rate:** The amount of time to complete the job after it arrives.
- **Job lateness:** The amount of time a job exceeds its original due date.
- **Make span:** The amount of time to complete a group of jobs from the beginning of the first job to the completion of the last job.
- **Average number of jobs:** Can also be thought of as the work in process.

A good scheduling system can help give an organization a competitive advantage because the right product will be delivered to the customer on time and at the right quantity.

Response Time For Complaints

The response time for complaints should be immediate. A customer that has a defective product or received poor service must be treated with the highest level of respect and deserves a response the same day if at all possible. An unhappy customer will let other customers know that he or she is dissatisfied. This can lead to loss of multiple customers. The rule of thumb should be to contact a customer immediately to respond to a customer complaint. In many cases, customers require that the organization complete some type of problem-solving analysis to show them that the organization understands the problem and actions have been taken to eliminate any other defects that may be in the system; corrective actions should also be put in place to correct the situation and prevent the issue from occurring again. The organization should track the amount of time it takes to respond to a customer complaint.

Product Development

The product development process must be able to produce a product or service within the time line the customer requires. The supply chain will need to be able to develop and supply new products in a timely manner. Most organizations continuously develop new products and services, so the supply chain needs the ability to support the development process. It is necessary to understand the product lifecycle so that organizations can work with the supply chain to stay current on the changes in the product offering. Time to market is a key metric that should be monitored for product development.

Lead Time

The **lead time** is the amount of time between a customer's order and the delivery of the final product or service. It includes the time it takes to receive raw material, components, subassemblies, assemblies, or supplies. The lead time should be understood to accurately plan production or services. This item is one that can offer an organization value by measuring it because a short lead time can be difference in getting a major order from a customer. This metric offers the supply chain a valuable area to target for reduction in time. Lower the lead times translate into better customer service.

Planned Quantity and Time

The supply chain needs to understand what the future prediction is for demand. This is the forecast, and it is used to make informed decisions on resources that are required to meet customer demand. A forecast is not perfect and has an error that is associated with it. The supply chain utilizes this error to make adjustments to the forecast so that it more closely resembles what the demand will be for the product or service. Once the forecast is developed, it is necessary to monitor the forecast. The forecast error should be monitored also.

Forecast error = Actual − Forecast

The forecast approaches can be qualitative and quantitative. A qualitative forecast allows human factors and personal opinions to develop the forecast. The quantitative approach uses data to develop the forecast. Quantitative forecasts are normally more accurate than the qualitative forecast because projections and historical data are used to develop the forecast. An accurate forecast is a better tool for an organization to use so that customer service is met. A successful organization must have customers. Customers require orders to be delivered to them on time and at the right quantity and right quality. A supply chain must serve a market to achieve success. A supply chain must have the appropriate metrics in place to make sure that the market it serves is being supported. The forecast allows planners to plan the appropriate orders that the supply chain must produce to meet the market demand. Execution is a requirement throughout the supply chain so that the customers' wants and needs are realized. Metrics for planned quantity and time are used throughout a supply chain to measure the performance level; they are order fill rate, line item fill rate, on-time delivery rate, number of backorders, value of backorders, return rates, number of warranty returns, and on-time completion rate.

Compliance to Schedule

The scheduling department produces a schedule that the operations utilizes to produce orders for the customer. This schedule is generated from the aggregate plan and MRP. To achieve the appropriate level of customer satisfaction, this schedule requires operations to comply 100%. Organizations normally create a daily metric to measure compliance to the schedule. This is a leading indicator for on-time delivery to the end customer. If an organization is not completing the schedule, then on-time delivery will be impacted negatively.

Demand

Demand is required for an organization to remain viable. A company must sell a product or service to a customer so that it can operate. Demand forecasts are used to give the organization and supply chain a prediction of how much and what kind of product or service needs to be available. The steps in a forecast includes the following items:

- Define the purpose of the forecast.
- Create a time horizon.
- Obtain, clean, and analyze appropriate data.
- Select a forecasting technique.
- Create the forecast.
- Monitor the forecast.

Many organizations utilize time-series based forecasts. This type of forecast utilizes time-series observations to project patterns. These observations are taken at regular intervals. The time-series are categorized as trends, seasonality, cycles, irregular variations, and random variation. There is a technique called averaging where the forecast uses smooth variations in the data. The techniques for averaging are called moving average, weighted moving average, and exponential smoothing. The moving average technique averages the most recent values of the forecast. The weighted moving average technique places a weight on the forecast values, and the most recent values carry a higher weight. The exponential smoothing technique uses a percentage of the forecast error, and it is based on the previous weighted average forecast. Forecast information can be used reactively or proactively. When the data is used reactively, it is used as a view of the future to meet the demand. If it is used proactively, then it is used to influence demand through advertising, pricing, promotions, and or product or services changes. It is critical to share the forecast and demand throughout the supply chain so that the organization can improve quality, customer service, and cost.

DEMAND The quantity of products or services that an organization will require at a defined time period.

Stock Outs

Customers want a product or service at the right time. To remain competitive, the supply chain must have the appropriate products or services available for the customer when the customer wants it. The supply chain cannot allow products or services to be stocked out. If a product or service is stocked out, then customers may turn to another product or service to fulfill their needs. If customers select another product or service to fulfill their needs, then they may never return to the first product or service. It is necessary for organizations to create safety stock to prevent stock outs because stock outs will cause an organization to lose business, and lost business may not return. There are three metrics that can be used to make sure capacity does not cause the organization to have stock outs. Those measures are capacity utilization, design capacity, and effective capacity.

Capacity utilization = actual output rate / capacity × 100%

Design capacity = actual output rate / design capacity × 100%

Effective capacity = actual output rate / effective capacity × 100%

Dashboard

A dashboard of metrics should be visible for the management team to display how the organization is performing. The management team selects the metrics that should be on the dashboard. The dashboard in an automobile has the critical metrics on it so that the driver knows the status of the automobile. The oil pressure, fuel level, RPMs, temperature, and speed are all critical. The dashboard for a supply chain should consist of the key metrics that define the heartbeat of the organizations throughout the supply chain. The managers should work to be proactive in the supply chain by performing preventative actions to keep metrics from going out of control. In an automobile, the oil is changed at a certain frequency prior to it causing problems to the vehicle. The supply chain must do the same. However, if metrics go out of control, the management team must make the appropriate changes to get them back under control.

DISCUSSION QUESTIONS

1. What are leading and lagging indicators, and how can they benefit the performance of the supply chain?

2. What are at least five time based metrics that can be used to control the performance of the supply chain?

3. When should a manager assess the performance of the supply chain?

4. What areas should a manager avoid when creating metrics to assess the performance of the supply chain?

5. How can an organization effectively reduce changeover times throughout the supply chain?

SUMMARY

Measuring the supply chain's performance is necessary so that an organization can control the overall performance and gain a competitive advantage. Customer service that is acceptable allows an organization to meet customers' wants and needs. It is customer service that determines if an organization will gain or lose business. Customer metrics are lagging indicators. Organizations must place a high level focus on the leading metrics that drive the lagging indicators. Indicators such as order completion rates, inventory value, inventory turns, productivity, asset utilization, inventory days, capacity utilization, design capacity, effective capacity, compliance to schedule, planned quantity at a planned time, weeks of supply, and supply chain cost can help an organization maintain a competitive edge in the market. Customer satisfaction is required to maintain customers. Customer satisfaction is achieved with on-time delivery, quality metrics, and cost metrics. The organization should work to build a supply chain that is centered on measuring leading indicators so that the metric categories above will be achieved. At the beginning of this chapter, a young CEO and supply chain manager were given the responsibility to improve the supply chain and eliminate late deliveries. They must evaluate the supply chain and define the key metrics that are required to control the performance of the organization to be successful.

REFERENCES

Burt, D., Petcavage, S., & Pinkerton, R. (2010). *Supply management* (8th ed.). New York, NY: McGraw-Hill Irwin.

Hitt, M. A., Ireland, R. D., & Hoskisson, R. E. (2011). *Strategic management: Competitiveness and globalization, concepts and cases: 2011 custom edition* (9th ed.). Mason, OH: South-Western Cengage Learning.

Stevenson, W. J. (2009). *Operations management* (11th ed.). New York, NY: McGraw-Hill Irwin.

Swink, M., Melnyk, S. A., Cooper, M. B., & Hartley, J. L. (2014*). Managing operations across the supply chain* (2nd ed.). New York, NY: McGraw-Hill Irwin.

CHAPTER 5

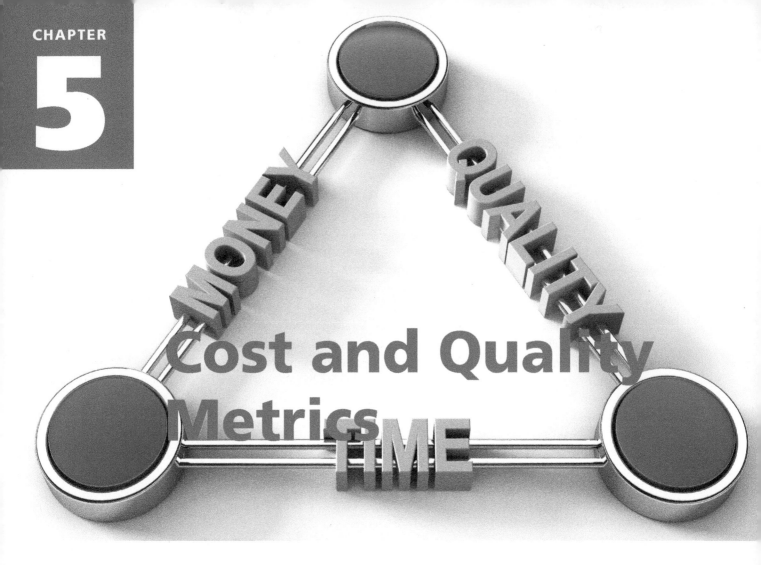

Cost and Quality Metrics

INTRODUCTION

In an effort to maintain and gain market share, a competitive supply chain manages cost and the quality levels effectively. By controlling cost in the supply chain, an organization can offer products or services at competitive prices. Consumers want a competitively-priced product that meets their needs. The areas on which an organization should concentrate to control costs include product costs, supply chain costs, productivity, profitability, sales, inventory, transportation, asset utilization, capacity utilization, and financial metrics. The customer also is looking for a product or service that meet or exceed his or her quality expectations. Quality-based supply chains build a product that is considered reliable and effective to customers. Quality products can build an outstanding brand image for an organization. Once an organization's brand becomes strong and associated with a high-quality product or service, a competitive edge is built for the organization throughout the marketplace. To achieve a quality product or service, the organization must focus on quality dimensions, quality in the functional areas, quality theory, quality planning, cost of quality, customer complaints, internal audits, external audits, and ISO certification. An organization must work to improve quality and costs on an ongoing basis.

COSTS

The goal of an organization is to make money. For an organization to make money, it must control the costs. The cost in the business environment are called operating costs. **Operating costs** are the expenses that a business faces to conduct its operations. The two main types of costs that a business face are fixed and variable costs. Fixed costs also are known as overhead. These costs remain the same regardless of the amount of output that is generated. The fixed costs that an organization incur are salaries, utilities, insurance, fixed asset depreciation, mortgage/rent, accounting costs, legal fees, and membership fees. On the other hand, variable costs vary with the amount of goods that are produced. Variable costs that organizations face are materials, tooling, capital, office supplies, advertising, promotions, telephone, printing, packaging, An organization that is effective will measure each of these cost categories to achieve cost control.

OPERATING COSTS
Expenses associated with conducting business on a day-to-day basis.

Product Costs

Product costs start with the design of the product itself. The product design should go through many phases to achieve a product design that can be manufactured at a competitive cost. The design and redesign of a product or service should be linked to the strategy of the organization. The design of the product must be documented with clear specifications. As the product starts in the design phases, it is necessary to take the customer's wants and needs and create a product or service that matches what the customer wants. It also is necessary to understand the quality requirements as this product is being designed. Cost targets should be considered as well. Effective organizations require that prototypes are built to confirm the design and to validate the quality and cost components for the design. After creating the successful design with validations of the appropriate quality and cost targets, the organization should develop process specification. These specifications will help develop a process and validate that the product or service can be produced effectively. The key measurements for the product cost will be the process steps and process capability. At this stage, the organization needs to confirm the manufacturability and serviceability of the product or service. This means that the organization must be able to make and repair this product or service and achieve a profit while doing it. The organization also should verify that it can meet all legal and ethical requirements because these issues could cost the organization to lose money or destroy its public image.

CHAPTER OBJECTIVES

1. Evaluate the cost- and quality-focused metrics for a supply chain.

2. Assess a supply chain and determine which cost metrics should be in place to evaluate and control the performance level of the supply chain.

3. Assess quality dimensions, quality in the functional areas, quality theory, quality planning, cost of quality, customer complaints, internal audits, and external audits for the supply chain.

4. Evaluate ISO/quality system principles and how these principles help control the quality levels in the supply chain.

KEY TERMS

- gross income (p. 86)
- inventory management (p. 88)
- operating costs (p. 85)
- profit margin (p. 87)
- quality (p. 91)

Total Supply Chain Cost

The total cost of the supply chain includes the cost for all operations and functions associated with the product or service. The supply chain manager should be responsible for making sure the costs throughout the supply chain are being controlled so that the organization can make a profit. Fundamentally, an organization's accounting practices should be sound and should meet General Accepted Accounting Principles (GAAP). These principles are the standards and rules by which accounting departments prepare financial statements. Accounting will keep a detailed record of monetary transactions and historical records. Transactions are recorded twice because the money comes in and then it goes out. Each transaction has a debit in one account and a credit in another account. The account categories are asset, liability, net worth, expense, and revenue. An asset is owned by the company, and it is associated with a dollar value. Liabilities are the debts that the company owes. Net worth is ownership interest, capital stock, and retained earnings. Expenses are the costs to conduct business, and revenue is the income from sales before costs are deducted. The **gross income** for an organization is revenue minus expenses.

GROSS INCOME Revenue minus expenses.

Gross Income = Revenue − Expenses

An organization will measure all these categories to verify that they are compliant with the accounting standards. Additionally, these categories define a company's costs and expenses. Manufacturing organizations and service organizations will utilize these principles.

PRODUCTIVITY

The productivity measure is useful in measuring the performance level of a department, plant, supply chain, and organization. The critical point that should be taken from this measure is that it should be tracked over time, and the realization of performance improvements is the objective. An organization should focus to achieve an upward trend in this performance metric. It is important to chart the performance relative to the area that is being measured. Organizations should not measure productivity of one area relative to another, but they should allow each area to compete against itself. This will drive the areas to improve continuously. Countries with higher productivity levels have higher standards of living. The higher an organization can drive its productivity, the better its competitive edge over its competition. An organization should reach for productivity growth. Productivity growth is computed as follows:

Productivity growth = Current productivity − Previous productivity / Previous productivity × 100

Example: The productivity on an automobile assembly line was 40 in last quarter of 2014. It is measuring at 50 in the first quarter of 2015. What is the productivity growth from fourth quarter of 2014 to the first quarter of 2015?

Productivity growth = 50 − 40 / 40 × 100 = 25%

This metric shows an organization its position on the improvement continual of productivity over time.

PROFITABILITY

Controlling costs in an organization must be fundamental to the organization. An organization achieves confirmation that it is controlling cost by being able to achieve a profit. Profit is the ability of an organization to generate earnings after all the costs have been paid for a certain period of time. Some metrics for measuring profit ratios include profit margin, operating margins, net margins, free cash flow margins, return on assets, and return on equity. These metrics can help an organization and supply chain maintain control over the profitability levels.

Profit Margin

Profit margin is known as gross margin. It is the amount of money an organization makes for each dollar of sales, and this number typically is shown as a percentage. Each node in the supply chain should have measures in place to define profit margins. A company with a high profit margin is a company that makes a premium product that the customer is willing to pay for because the company has a competitive edge in the market.

Profit margin (Gross margin) = Gross profit / Sales × 100

Operating Margin

The measure of how much money a company makes or loses per each dollar of sales represents the operating margins. The operating margin includes the cost of sales plus marketing and other overhead costs. As such, this measure is a good indicator how a company is performing. It is highly recommended that every organization measure this throughout the supply chain.

Operating margin = Operating income or loss / Sales × 100

Net Margins

Net margins is a measure of how much revenue an organization maintain once all costs are paid and any additional income has been included.

Net Margins = Net income or loss / Sales × 100

Free Cash Flow Margins

Free cash flow is a measure of how much of the revenue can be converted to free cash flow.

Free cash flow margin = Free cash flow / Sales × 100

Return on Assets

Return on assets (ROA) is a measure of how well an organization can turn an asset into profits for the organization. This measure is critical to the well-being of an organization. A company must understand the amount of profits that it is generating from its assets.

Return on assets = (Net income + After-tax interest expenses) / Average total assets × 100

Return on Equity

Return on equity (ROE) is a measure of the company's return on the investment by the shareholders.

Return on Equity = Net income / Shareholder's equity × 100

All of these measures can provide an excellent view on where an organization is performing. These measures are shown as a percentage; the higher the percentage, the better the organization is performing.

Return on Capital

This measure is after-tax operating income divided by the value of the invested capital. Return on capital (ROC) is a measure many organizations use to show how well they generate cash flow from the capital in the organization.

Return on capital = After-tax operating income / Invested capital × 100

Lost Sales

A thriving organization should be a growing organization. Growth is extremely important because each product has a life cycle, and once this product goes through the complete cycle, demand diminishes to very small numbers and then eventually to nothing. If an organization is not working to grow the business with a redesigned or new product, then it is putting the future of the company at risk. A company should measure the number of products that it eliminates each year. It also should measure the number of products it adds each year. Other measures in this area are the number of items that are in the development process each year. In summary, those measures are as follows:

- Number products eliminated each year
- Number of products added each year
- Number of items in the development phase
- Percent of development items turned into new products

The primary ways organizations lose sales are based on quality, price, and delivery. Poor quality is a sure way to lose sales. Poor quality will lead the customer to purchase the product from another source. A product that is priced too high will not be successful in the market and the organization can lose sales. If an organization cannot deliver the product when a customer wants it, then the organization may move the product to a supplier that can support its delivery requirements. If a customer cannot purchase your product when they need it, then they may select a product or service from the competitor and may never return to purchase products or services from the original organization.

INVENTORY

INVENTORY MANAGEMENT The oversight of the amount of inventory to carry and how much to order.

Inventory can make a dramatic impact on cost for an organization. The objective of the supply chain is to have the right type, quantity, location, and quality of inventory so that demand can be met effectively at the lowest possible cost. A manager will be required to make inventory decisions and when confronted with these decisions, it is necessary to understand the components of the decisions. **Inventory management** is required to control inventory levels. The components of these decisions are cycle inventory, safety inventory, seasonal inventory, level of product availability, and inventory related metrics. Cycle inventory is the average inventory an organization uses to satisfy demand. Safety inventory is used to protect an organization against an unpredictable process or situations in which demand is greater than the supply. An organization uses seasonal inventory to support predictable demand swings that occur based on regular patterns. The level of product availability is the demand that is supported by product that is in inventory. From a financial perspective, inventory can be measured as follows to successfully control the costs:

- Inventory turns
- Weeks of Supply
- Inventory investment
- Inventory days

- Average inventory
- Safety inventory
- Fill rate
- Fraction of time out of stock
- Obsolete inventory

These metrics can help a company maintain lower inventory levels throughout the supply chain. It is very important to understand the cost of carrying inventory versus being responsive. The amount of inventory an organization carries seems to correlate directly with how well it responds to the customer. An organization must build processes that are predictable and reliable in such a way that inventory levels can be reduced at the lowest possible levels and still be responsive to the customer's needs. Inventory turns is the term that refers to the time inventory is sold within a year. It calculated by finding the cost of goods sold divided by the average inventory. Another critical inventory measure is inventory days. This is a measure of the number of days of inventory that an organization has on hand. Average inventory is an average of the inventory over a time period. Many organizations define an average inventory by month. Safety inventory is another area that an organization can measure to help protect against stock outs at a customer. Fill rate is the number of orders shipped versus the number of orders that were placed on order. It is good to measure stock out time, which is the amount of time a customer was out of an order. The last recommended area to track for inventory is obsolete inventory. This is inventory that you no longer have orders to ship against for this stock.

Inventory turns = Cost of goods sold / Average inventory

Many organizations keep up with the number of weeks of supply that is on hand. This is a basic metric that can be used to help protect the customer against stock outs. An organization also should track and measure how much money it has invested in inventory throughout the supply chain. It is recommended to track the inventory dollars for all the different inventory categories.

TRANSPORTATION

Transportation is required for a business to get product and services through the supply chain. The form of transportation that is used can affect the cost and levels of inventory that are required. Managers have the job of making sure that the correct form of transportation is selected so that responsiveness, location of facilities, and the efficiency of the supply chain are being optimized. The common modes of transportation are air, truck, water, rail, pipeline, Internet, and multimode. Organizations use these modes, in many cases, as multiple modes of transportation. This means that more than one mode is used to get a product from point A to point B. Metrics that can be used to measure the effectiveness and efficiency of transportation are as follows:

- Average inbound transportation cost
- Average income shipment size
- Average inbound transportation cost per shipment
- Average outbound transportation cost
- Average outbound shipment size
- Average outbound transportation cost per shipment
- Fraction transported by mode

The supply chain can use these metrics to help control how effective the transportation modes are throughout the supply chain.

ASSET UTILIZATION

An organization should work to maximize the use of its assets. Asset utilization is a ratio that looks at the total revenue of the organization divided by the total assets in the organization. The higher the ratio the better the performance for this measure. A high ratio indicates that the organization is utilizing its assets more effectively.

Asset utilization = Revenue / Total assets $\times$ 100

CAPACITY UTILIZATION

It is important to understand capacity utilization because it can help an organization meet promises that it makes to the customers. The design capacity equals what the machine was design to produce. If the design capacity is not being met, the organization should understand why a gap exists in capacity utilization. The effective capacity is what the organization is currently producing on the equipment, and it ideally matches the design capacity.

Capacity utilization = Actual output − Potential output / Potential output $\times$ 100

FINANCIAL METRICS

The financial performance of an organization is critical to understand. The management team can affect the performance in a positive manner by making the correct decisions throughout the supply chain. The next step is to monitor the performance through metrics. Several financial metrics such as ROA, ROE, ROC, and profitability were discussed earlier in this chapter. Other financial metrics that an organization should monitor are accounts payable turnover (APT) and cash-to-cash (C2C). These metrics allow an organization to understand key information about transactions. APT is determined by dividing the cost of goods sold by accounts payable. C2C is the measure of when cash enters the process as cost to when it renters the process as revenue that has been collected. A business must have a positive cash flow to be viable in the market place.

An organization that wants to drive the performance in a positive direction must focus on facilities, inventory, transportation, information, sourcing, and price. The facilities are where material is stored, fabricated, and/or assembled. The bulk of the inventory in the supply chain is made up of raw materials, work in process, and finished goods. Transportation is used to move the inventory through the supply chain. Information is essential in every phase of the supply chain and must be accurate, clear, and concise. Sourcing performs the actual work at the different nodes in the supply chain. Price is what an organization charges to offer product and services. These areas are fundamental to the success of the supply chain, and the metrics discussed throughout this chapter can monitor these metrics and show when they are off track.

Cost control in an organization is necessary for the organization. It is recommended that the leadership team defines an approach to review and evaluate the metrics for cost on a regular basis. Organizations that are successful monitor and control metrics in the smallest feasible time-cycle frequency. It is critical to understand issues while they are occurring so that corrective actions can be put in place. Understanding the financial metrics a month after they occurred will not make an immediate impact. This approach is also necessary for improving quality. To be successful in any area of an organization, the monitor and control must occur at the source. This simply means that profitability must be measured on a part-by-part basis as it is being produced. This will allow the organization to define the root causes for the issues and establish the appropriate corrective actions at the time of occurrence. Quality must be produced at the source. An organization will not be successful if it uses mass inspection to control its quality levels. The mass inspection is expensive plus it will not be 100 percent effective.

Quality requires an organization to take a proactive approach. The quality must be built into the product as it is being manufactured. This can be achieved by utilizing some of the latest approaches to quality that will be explained later in this chapter. Quality and cost improvements must be driven by the leadership. The leadership will set the foundation for the organization to be successful. A successful quality culture requires that things are done right the first time. Not producing correctly the first time leads to customer dissatisfaction and higher costs. The leadership team must provide an environment that puts the employees on track to be successful.

Cost and quality metrics are important and should be used to drive the business in the right direction. In successful organizations, quality is listed ahead of cost from a priority standpoint. The employees must understand that quality comes before cost. If the product or service does not meet the customer's wants and needs, then the customer cannot buy the product. Customer satisfaction starts with a quality product or service. The challenge for any organization is making sure that all employees understand the importance of achieving customer satisfaction. The next section of this chapter will focus on quality and how an organization can build a quality system for the supply chain that drives for customer satisfaction. Everything that an organization does should focus on achieving customer satisfaction. A satisfied customer will bring more customers to an organization. A dissatisfied customer will not buy from an organization, and the dissatisfied customer will tell other customers about the company's poor performance and cause the organization to lose business. Customer satisfaction is extremely important to the organization.

QUALITY

Quality is the ability of an organization to produce a product or service that meets or exceeds the customer's expectations consistently. An organization's reputation will be defined by the level of quality that it produces for its customers. Quality is a driver for building brand image. The brand image of an organization defines the organization and will determine if their product or service will be in demand. An organization needs to understand the dimensions of product and service quality. These dimensions of quality will help an organization build quality into the product or service that they offer. An organizations with a strong quality reputation will include quality as part of all the functional areas in the organization. The functional areas will embrace a quality theory that is presented by the gurus of quality.

A strong quality culture will include quality planning in all aspects of the business. While working on the quality plan, it is necessary to include the cost of quality in the plan. It is critical for the management team and all employees to understand each component of the cost of quality so that a proactive approach will be taken on the quality system. By focusing on the cost of quality, the organization must create a culture that produces products and services that meet customer requirements and zero customer complaints should be the target for the organization. Other areas that the organization should focus is performing audits on the quality system. It is also recommended for the organization to obtain some type of certification such as ISO certification. The organization's focus has to be driven by producing a level of quality that the customer expects and demand.

QUALITY The ability of an organization to produce a product or service that meets or exceeds the customer's expectations consistently.

Dimensions of Product Quality

Understanding and achieving acceptable dimensions of product quality are essential to building a product that the customer expects and demand. The dimensions of product quality are performance, conformance, reliability, durability, features, aesthetics, serviceability, and perceived quality. If a product can meet its intended purpose, then the performance is acceptable. Conformance is whether the product meets the specifications. A product that is reliable performs consistently over its useful life. Durability is when the product can withstand extreme conditions, such as cold temperatures and hot temperatures, without failing. The features of the product are attributes that supplement the basic product. Aesthetics are defined by how well the attributes match the customer's preferences. A product that is serviceable can be repaired for routine issues with ease and at an affordable cost. A customer has a view of quality for an organization, and this is considered the perceived quality. This level of quality is defined by the company's reputation and word-of-mouth from other customers. An organization must focus on all these dimensions to ensure that quality is driven into the culture of the organization.

Service Quality Dimensions

Service quality can be measured through many dimensions. An organization should understand the dimensions so that it can achieve an acceptable quality level from its customers. The dimensions of service quality are convenience, consistency, tangibles, responsiveness, empathy, service reliability, and assurance. The customer wants the service to be available and accessible. Therefore, the service must be convenient. A consistent service is required, and this means that the same level of good quality should be repeated. Tangibles are the physical appearances of the supply chain nodes. This includes plants, facilities, equipment, materials, and personnel. The appearance of these items can determine if a customer buys from your organization. The customer expects the organization to respond to their needs in a rapid fashion. An example of rapid response is a visit to a local restaurant at which the customer expects to be have his or her drink order placed within five minutes of arrival.

Customers expect caring individualized attention from the organization. Dependable and accurate service is an expectation of the customer and this is service reliability. The employees of the organization must be able to inspire trust and confidence to the customer during the experience.

Quality in Functional Areas

An organization is built of operations and functional areas. The operations utilize many tools to build the quality into the product. It is necessary for the functional areas to build quality into the processes that support operations. The functional areas that will be discussed are as follows:

- Supply Chain Management
- Engineering
- Operations
- Strategic Management
- Marketing
- Financial/Accounting
- Human resources

Supply chain management must build a supply chain that includes quality at the center. This can be achieved by building a quality system that is built around advanced quality planning. Engineering is the problem solving engine for the organization and must apply these skills to the design products and processes that will deliver an acceptable level of quality. Statistical Process Control (SPC) tools are used in the process that act as the voice of the process. Operations also utilizes a system-thinking approach to build a process that will generate consistent results. The system approach supports strategic management, which establishes a planned course of action to achieve quality requirements. The market also plays a huge role in achieving acceptable quality results. Marketing helps drive the perceived quality view so that the customer views the organization as a positive one. This perception of quality is driven by marketing through price and advertising. The financial team places emphasis on the measurement of the cost of quality. This leads an organization to spend money on quality in the appropriate category. Human resources is responsible for encouraging the organization to empower the associates. When the needs of the organization and its people are aligned, then better quality is produced. Human resources also places high emphasis on job design and structure.

Quality Theory

Employee morale is critical to the success of quality improvement. Quality theory is the model that is used to relate employee morale to quality improvements. For a theory to be effective, it must answer the questions of what, how, why, who, when, and where. An effective theory can be generated by answering these questions. The following quality gurus have generated sound quality theories:

- Deming
- Juran
- Ishikawa
- Feigenbaun
- Crosby
- Taguchi

Deming's philosophy is that poor quality is not the fault of the labor but that poor quality results from poor management of a system of continual improvement. He developed 14 points for management that can help an organization build and deliver excellent quality. The first point is to work towards consistency with the aim of having a competitive business that will provide jobs for people in the community. His second point is to adopt a new philosophy. It is critical for the management team to be willing to change to a new philosophy to build a competitive business. Deming's next point is to cease dependence on mass inspection to meet quality requirements. It is necessary for an organization to build robust designs and processes that work. These processes should be designed such that the quality is built into the product or service. The fourth point is to eliminate the practice of awarding business on price tag alone. An organization must consider quality, delivery, and cost when awarding business. The next point is to improve production and service systems constantly so that quality and productivity improvements decrease costs. The sixth point is to institute training on the job.

Training on the job will help show an employee exactly how the process works with hands-on experience. The next point is to improve leadership. The leadership must be strong and seek to inspire self-improvements that lead to overall company improvements. An organization should have a measurement in place for how much self-improvement has been made by the leadership team each year. The eighth point is to drive out fear so that all employees can work effectively for the organization.

Employees who are fearful will not be open nor will they share information. These employees also will not achieve at the highest possible level and be fully engaged in the organization. It is recommended to measure employee engagement on a quarterly basis through surveys. The next point is to break down barriers between departments. For an organization to be successful, employees must work as a team. Eliminating barriers between departments enables teamwork and collaboration to occur. Deming's next point is to eliminate slogans. The eleventh point is to eliminate work standards on the factory floor. The twelfth point is to eliminate barriers that rob workers of a sense of pride in the quality of their work. When people can be proud of what they are doing, they become engaged and will perform at high levels. The thirteenth point is to institute a vigorous education and self-improvement program. As everyone becomes better educated, the organization becomes better. The last point is to put everyone to work to accomplish the transformation of the company. Deming's philosophy has been helpful to Japan and its automotive industry.

Juran

Juran utilized a trilogy to drive an organization to improved quality. The trilogy includes planning, control, and improvement. In the planning phase, an organization will focus on the operating forces that will provide products and services that meets the customer's expectations. The control phase is focused on achieving control of the process so that the correct measures are in place to achieve the appropriate output. Improvement is a requirement to build and maintain a competitive edge. The organization must improve project by project. Juran utilizes the Pareto law, which indicates that 80 percent of problems are the result only 20 percent of possible causes.

Ishikawa

Training is a fundamental that must be conducted to have a successful work force. Ishikawa philosophy has training at the center. His focus was to train the complete company on quality control. This means that everyone must be involved with quality and performance improvements throughout the organization and the supply chain. Ishikawa also is known for the cause and effect diagram, or fish bone diagram, that is used to help define the root cause for a problem.

Feigenbaun

Feigenbaun's philosophy is based on a three-step process to build quality. The three steps are leadership, quality technology, and organizational improvement. Leadership must be engaged fully with quality improvements that are being developed and implemented. If leadership is onboard with these improvement, the associates will support the quality improvements. Quality technology must fit the organization's strategy. If the quality technology matches the strategy and know-how of the organization, then improved quality levels can be realized. Organizational commitment is a requirement to achieving improved quality levels. The commitment must exist throughout the supply chain and transformation can begin.

Crosby

Crosby's philosophy drives an organization to build zero defects. The philosophy of zero defects utilizes the behavioral and motivational aspects of people to obtain the targeted level of quality. The cost of quality and zero defects are the metrics that can help an organization achieve good quality. Human resources are used to understand how to get the appropriate behaviors from the people and how to motivate people to improve the quality levels.

Taguchi

Taguchi's method looks at the relationship between variables that can be controlled on products or services and the outcomes of the process. This approach adjusts the mean of the process by controlling the variables. An analysis of the relationships are computed mathematically to improve quality. It is critical to create a robust design of the product and process so that variables can control the outcomes clearly.

There are many other quality theories and philosophies that are available for organizations to select from in the global marketplace. For an organization to be successful in quality, it must understand its own culture. The organization should understand its strengths, weaknesses, competencies, structure, and competitors. These are the areas that quantitative measures are used to define. Therefore allowing the organization to build a strong leadership team. Leadership is where quality begins for an organization. The leadership must have a quality focus that is passed on to the employees. Customer focus is at the center of everything.

Quality Planning

Quality planning is required for an organization to have a quality focus. An organization should include as part of its strategy a means to identify, prioritize, and plan for quality improvements. It is recommended that a cross-functional team works together to build the quality plan. The quality plan must keep the customer at the center. There is a tool called quality functional deployment (QFD) that should be fundamental to an organization as the quality plans are being created. QFD is used to translate customer requirements into product and process designs. The first step in QFD is to establish a list of the customer requirements. Next, the organization must develop a list of technical design elements. Once this step is complete, the organization develops a relationship between the customer requirements and the technical design elements. The fourth step is to identify a correlation between the design elements. The next step is to perform a competitive analysis of the customer requirements. The customer requirements then must be prioritized, and the next the organization should prioritize the technical requirements. Once all these steps are complete, a final evaluation must be conducted.

Advanced Quality Planning

A strong quality system will meet requirements that have been set by the Automotive Industry Action Group (AIAG). AIAG has identified that advanced product quality planning (APQP) process should focus in the following areas:
- Failure mode and effects analysis (FMEA)
- Statistical process control (SPC)
- Measurement system analysis (MSA)
- Production part approval process (PPAP)

The FMEA process is used to identify failure modes and the causes and effects for failure modes. It is a proactive approach for an organization to put in place the appropriate controls to decrease risks to the customer. An organization should measure and monitor the number of FMEAs that are in place and regularly update this document to mitigate failure modes. Statistical process control roots go back to the 1920s and Bell

Laboratories. Variation exists in every process. Organizations can use tools like SPC to understand the variation and make changes before the variation leads to substandard products. Variation in a production process falls into two categories—common cause and special cause variation. It is critical for an organization to measure the variation and understand the category into which it falls. Common cause variation is the natural variation that occurs within a process. This type variation can be improved only by changing to a different process. Special cause variation also is known as assignable variation, and it is intermittent and unpredictable. Management must understand the causes of this type variation and eliminate it to protect quality's predictability.

Measurement system analysis identifies the components of variation in the measurement process. This variation can come from the equipment, personnel, procedure, software, and operations. Organizations should measure the repeatability and reproducibility of the measurement equipment. Also, linearity and biasness of the equipment should be measured. These areas will help make sure that the measurement system is capable of measuring the product. Production part approval process (PPAP) is used to make sure that the supply chain can manufacture the product adequately. The first production run goes through the PPAP, which includes providing evidence that the customer design records and specifications are understood completely and being met by the supplier. This process should be measured on all new or changed products.

Quality System

There is an International Organization for Standards (ISO) that have identified critical elements for a quality system. The quality system must have as a starting point a quality policy and quality objectives. The organization should develop a quality manual that addresses some very critical areas. There must be documented procedures on how to carry out the processes that are required by the organization. It is necessary to document how an organization effectively controls its processes, operations, and planning. To be effective, it is also required to keep records to document the quality system. The quality manual must address the following items:

- Customer focus
- Leadership
- Involvement of people
- The process approach
- A systems approach to management
- Continual improvement
- Factual approach to decision making
- Mutually beneficial supplier relationship

Cost of Quality

It is important for an organization to understand the cost of quality and the impact quality has on an organization. Organizations that produces good quality are building a positive brand image and reputation for themselves. Organizations that have a strong brand and good quality reputation can achieve more market share and demand higher prices for its products and services. Good quality also leads to lower liability costs, lower production costs, and higher profits. Organizations should measure all of these metrics to assess their relative positions in the market. On the other hand, organizations that deliver poor quality experience business reductions, lower productivity, higher costs, and higher liability issues. For an organization to control its quality, it should measure the cost of quality (COQ).

Cost of Quality Categories

The COQ is broken down into three categories—prevention costs, appraisal costs, and failure costs. Prevention costs are those costs that prevent an organization from producing poor quality products or services. Examples of prevention costs are training, customer assessments, process controls, quality improvements, and maintenance that prevents producing or delivering poor quality. Appraisal costs are costs that ensure product or service conforms to specifications. Examples of appraisal costs are inspections, tests, calibration of test equipment, and service audits. Failure costs are the costs incurred when a defective product or service is produced or delivered. Failure costs are broken up into two categories—internal failure and external failure. Internal failure is the costs that are incurred to fix problems before the products or services are delivered to the customer. Internal failure costs are broken into two categories—scrap and rework. External failure costs are the costs incurred to fix problems after the products or services have been delivered to the customer. Examples of external failure costs are warranty claims, processing returns, product recalls, and processing customer complaints.

IMPROVEMENTS FOR EACH CATEGORY

The area in which an organization should devote most of its time and money is the prevention category. By putting in place the correct proactive items, an organization can eliminate appraisal, internal failure, and external failure costs. A proactive approach to quality also focuses on building products at the source and reduces appraisal costs. It is recommended that an organization puts quality improvement teams and other proactive approaches in place and leverage these areas to improve quality. It is also recommended that the COQ is measured at least monthly throughout the supply chain so that the management team can control and monitor the quality performance.

Internal Audits

An organization needs for quality to become part of its culture and rooted in every phase of the business. Fundamentally, audits can help root quality in the culture of an organization. An internal audit program is a basic requirement to have a strong quality system and culture. The company should monitor the number of audits performed per month. The organization also should monitor the number of audit findings in each audit and have a system in place to correct the findings. In successful organizations, these audits are performed by certified auditors that the company trains through a certified body. These audits also should be performed throughout the supply chain. The same metrics should be utilized throughout the supply chain.

External Audits

Internal audits are critical for an organization to conduct. The organization also should have external audits performed. These audits can be performed by a third party auditing body or by individuals external to the facility. These independent auditors will have an open view of the facility and offer opportunities that internal audits may not find.

ISO Certification

An excellent method for having external audits performed in the organization is to become ISO-certified. ISO guiding principles, indicated below, are the same items that were identified for a quality system.

- Customer focus
- Leadership
- Involvement of people
- Process approach
- System approach to management
- Continual improvement
- Factual approach to decision making
- Mutually beneficial supplier relationships

Customer Focus

The organization should work to understand the customer's needs and wants by performing research and analysis. The customer's needs and wants must be communicated clearly throughout the supply chain. A system should be in place that manages customer relationships. In the end, the organization must balance the relationships between all stakeholders. This includes the complete supply chain and shareholders. To be successful in managing these relationships, it is necessary for the organization to measure customer and supplier satisfaction throughout the supply chain. It is extremely important to understand the voice of the customer (VOC). The VOC explains the customer's needs, wants, and expectations. There are many ways to obtain this information and an organization should track this information from these sources. The sources to gather the VOC are listed below:

- Comment cards and formal surveys
- Focus groups
- Direct customer contact
- Field intelligence
- Complaints
- Internet and social media monitoring
- Customer visits

Leadership

The leadership must establish a clear vision of where the organization is headed. This vision should inspire employees to be engaged with the organization. The leadership must create an ethical environment that is built on trust. It is also critical to eliminate fear from the environment because employees will not be totally engaged if they are afraid. Successful organizations that engage employees have creative environments that have creative employees. The leadership team must provide adequate resources and training to the employees. People must be inspired, recognized, and encouraged to be the best employees that they can possibly be in the organization.

Involvement of People

People are the most important component of any organization. Organizations must involve people at all levels so that they can give input. It is highly recommended to implement improvement teams in an organization to achieve involvement. It is necessary to allow people to share their ideas freely and help solve problems that the organization may be encountering. Process management is required to control quality levels in the organization. Processes in the manufacturing and service environment should be developed using the mistake-proof approach. This approach is known as *poka-yoke*. The poka-yoke is an automatic device or basic method that will not allow human error to cause issues.

Process Approach

The organization should define a systematic and documented approach for carrying out the processes that will be used to build products and services. This systematic approach should define responsibility and accountability clearly. Additionally, this process approach should evaluate resources, methods, risks, consequences, and other parameters that impact the supply chain. To change results, it is necessary to change the process.

System Approach

A system approach should be utilized to make improvements in the supply chain. The system should be designed to reach objectives effectively and efficiently. The system should utilize capable processes to create the products or services. If the processes are not capable, then the organization must define corrective actions for these processes. To maintain an effective system, the management team must monitor and control the system.

Continual Improvement

Continual improvement should be spread throughout the supply chain. This means that there needs to be a continual improvement champion that monitors and controls this improvement for the complete supply chain. The appropriate level of training is required for the supply chain member, and the tools needed to make these improvements must be provided. A system approach for the product and processes is necessary to make sure that the improvements will be ongoing.

DISCUSSION QUESTIONS

1. What are the product and service dimensions for quality, and how can they benefit the quality performance for a supply chain?

2. What metrics should be used to effectively measure inventory performance through the supply chain, and how can each affect the supply chain?

3. What metrics should be used to measure profitability of an organization?

4. Explain the Cost of Quality (COQ), and discuss which area of COQ an organization should focus on.

5. How can an organization achieve customer satisfaction while introducing a new product?

SUMMARY

A business must control its quality and costs. Quality starts with each individual in an organization. The principles of quality are customer focus, team work, and continuous improvements. An organization that focuses on these principles can build a strong quality culture. A business must focus on the customer and meet the customer's wants and needs. A business cannot be successful if it does not have customers. Quality plays a major role in building customer satisfaction. The organization should work continuously to improve this area by driving and understanding quality dimensions, quality in the functional areas, quality theory, quality planning, cost of quality, customer complaints, internal audits, external audits, and ISO certification. Improved quality also leads to reduced costs.

Controlling the costs of a business is fundamental to it being successful. It is necessary to monitor and control the cost metrics so that an organization stays focused on driving costs lower and improving profits. Customer satisfaction leads to higher profitability for an organization. It is imperative for the organization to improve product costs, supply chain costs, productivity, profitability, sales, inventory, transportation, asset utilization, capacity utilization, and financial metrics. These areas, when improved, will extend the longevity of an organization. It is critical to achieve customer satisfaction because the majority of new business that an organization receives come from the current customer base. It costs five times as much to establish new business from a new customer than from an existing customer. By measuring quality and cost, an organization can control and drive for the appropriate improvements to achieve customer satisfaction.

REFERENCES

Burt, D., Petcavage, S., & Pinkerton, R. (2010). *Supply management* (8th ed.). New York, NY: McGraw-Hill Irwin.

Evans, J. R., & Lindsay, W. M. (2014). *Managing for quality and performance excellence* (9th ed.). Mason, OH : South-Western Cengage Learning.

Hitt, M. A., Ireland, R. D., & Hoskisson, R. E. (2011). *Strategic management: Competitiveness and globalization, concepts and cases: 2011 custom edition* (9th ed.). Mason, OH: South-Western Cengage Learning.

Stevenson, W. J. (2009). *Operations management* (11th ed.). New York, NY: McGraw-Hill Irwin.

Swink, M., Melnyk, S. A., Cooper, M. B., & Hartley, J. L. (2014*). Managing operations across the supply chain* (2nd ed.). New York, NY: McGraw-Hill Irwin.

Domestic Versus International Considerations

Today's global enterprises are under increasing pressure to add value to their international operations. Past notions of **competitive advantage** were largely a series of intangibles that lacked systematic application. Operations management, supply chain management, quality systems, and financial due diligence standards all lacked discipline and rigor. Largely perceived as separate specialties within the enterprise, they lacked coordination and consistency. Attempts at creating value were largely disjointed and had little focus on the strategic direction and goals of the organization. Enter the 21st century. Survival relies on uncompromising value creation throughout all levels of the enterprise and its associated internal management structures. Today, creation of a competitive advantage is not the sole domain of the organizations' visionaries or disciplines, such as marketing, sales, operations, or design engineering. When all is said and done, a competitive advantage embraces two attributes: cost leadership and differentiation. **Cost leadership** is simply having the lowest operating cost in the industry. **Differentiation** is a planned strategy of distinguishing a product and making it more attractive when compared to the competition. The enterprises of today must apply meticulous order and highly functional levels of coordination that focus on strategic goals. This includes upgrades in organizational capability and implementing consistent fundamental processes that are repeatable and strong. Sustaining a robust competitive advantage requires full levels of organization-wide integration, coordination, alignment, and optimization of capability. These are the tangible ingredients that aid in the maturity process of the enterprise from competitive parity to establishing competitive advantage.

COST LEADERSHIP Having the lowest operating cost in the industry.

DIFFERENTIATION A planned strategy of distinguishing a product and making it more attractive when compared to the competition.

COMPETITIVE ADVANTAGE A market position of excellence that is defined by sharp distinctions of superior processes that convert into exceptional goods and services; these goods and services are seen as superior to the competition's goods and services.

DUE DILIGENCE A validation process used to ensure accuracy through the evaluation of various considerations that can lead to a decision.

QUESTIONS TO CONSIDER

Consider the following questions as you discuss this chapter:

1 How does an international operation contribute to the achievement of a firm's competitive advantage in the global market place?

2 What influences do governments of emerging economies have on the development of a competent logistics infrastructure?

3 Why do Incoterms play such an important role in international logistics?

4 What are economies of scale? How can they benefit from international logistics?

ADVANTAGES AND DISADVANTAGES OF INTERNATIONAL OPERATIONS

The global expansion of business operations in recent years was triggered by the lowering and relaxation of trade barriers. Starting with the North American Free Trade Agreement (NAFTA) in 1993, the European Union's

KEY TERMS

- 3PL (p. 108)
- 4PL (p. 108)
- choke point (p. 114)
- competitive advantage (p. 103)
- core competency (p. 107)
- cost leadership (p. 103)
- differentiation (p. 103)
- ERP (p. 104)
- incoterms (p. 105)
- nearshoring (p. 111)
- offshoring (p. 111)
- outsourcing (p. 111)
- transport modes (p. 115)
- value analysis (p. 108)
- value engineering (p. 108)

entry in 1995, the Central American Free Trade Agreement (CAFTA) in 2005, China's accession into the World Trade Organization (WTO) in 2001, Russia coming into the WTO in 2012, and regional trade agreements with South Korea and Vietnam in 1993 and 2012 respectively, these events all lowered the threshold risk for establishing international operations. In early 2015, the United States had 14 trade agreements with 20 countries in place. These multilateral agreements, along with the pending Asia-Pacific trade agreement, also known as the Trans-Pacific Partnership agreement, gave rise to investment options for U.S. companies and their international counterparts.

Prior to the establishment of these trade agreements, a large segment of American business centered on defending manufacturing. It was feared that U.S. manufactures would end up in a manufacturing technology orbit of the emerging Asian manufactures. American businesses sought ways to protect their interests by advocating high tariffs on high tech products to protect their products' niches in the marketplace.

Seeking less expensive methods to export their products, American manufacturers soon began to benefit from NAFTA. NAFTA became the model of future trade agreements where the primary objective was to lower tariffs and minimize all trade barriers.

The political evolution away from trade protectionism to free trade began to take hold and began to lessen the influence of trade-policy critics. Manufacturers entrenched in the camp of protectionism, especially in the high tech industries, soon realized that increased international business had made major inroads in other traditional businesses, such as the textile industry.

The textile industry was, and has been, at the forefront of expanding its operations internationally. Textile took the lead and was on the frontline of developing international operations capabilities. Unlike the antiquated roadmap guiding international expansion, the textile industry focused on technology. With implementation of state of the art manufacturing techniques, automation, and robotics, the industry began rapid operational integration with design capability.

New efficiencies reduced costs, ushering in the establishment and expansion of international operations sites at an accelerated pace. Companies such as Oracle Corporation and SAP SE developed **enterprise resource planning systems (ERP)** with a high level of refinement, enabling automation, transmission, and decision-based data analysis. The impact today of operations is far more effective and efficient than it has ever been. Today, operations like the ones used in the textile industry leverages technology and not the number of workers despite deriving benefits from reduced operating and labor costs. Operations today is all about efficiencies guided by evolving manufacturing principles such as statistical process control and lean manufacturing principles, both elements of lean six sigma principles.

Presently, operations functions remains at high efficiency levels. Success and capability thresholds continue to accelerate to ever higher standards of productivity. Operational dynamics continue to drive efficiencies to unmatched levels. And so how should one take measure of the successes and shortcomings of this revolution?

A good indicator is the converging path that supply chain management and logistics are taking toward blending each process in support of one another. Traditionally, **logistics** was viewed as an activity that added little value to supply chain management. The focus was on cost management and not much else. Initially, logistics methodology focused on physical distribution warehousing, inventory management, and inbound and outbound transportation.

ERP (ENTERPRISE RESOURCE PLANNING)
A comprehensive integrated business software system that synchronizes the entire organization's planning and resource needs.

LOGISTICS Part of supply chain management that plans, implements, and controls the efficient flow and storage of goods, services, and related information between the point of origin and the point of consumption to meet customer requirements.

Contemporary logistic practices concentrate on getting the customer service piece right, achieving cost efficiency across the entire logistics chain, establishing pockets of competitive advantage, and dramatically raising the performance of the organization. Important fundamentals include the following:

- Design and management of transportation networks
- Efficient methodologies that govern the functions of warehousing
- Inventory management
- Materials handling
- Greater visibility of inventory status and order status
- Improving customer service
- Procurement

International logistics is governed by a set of rules that define the responsibility of sellers and buyers. Known as **Incoterms**, these regulations are a set of uniform rules for the transportation of international commercial terms defining the following:

- Costs
- Risks
- Obligations of buyers and sellers

Incoterms is an abbreviation for the International Commercial Terms that are put out by the International Chamber of Commerce (ICC). They deal with the questions related to the delivery of product from the seller to the buyer and include the following:

- Carriage of the product
- Export and import clearances responsibilities
- Who pays for what
- Who bears the risk for the condition of the products at different locations within the transport process

Incoterms must always be used in conjunction with a geographical location (FOB alone is not a recognized Incoterm).

Incoterms do not deal with the following:

- Transfer of title and other property rights
- Payment terms

Updates have been made over the years because of changing trends in shipping, cargo security, and rapid expansion of world trade. The current recognized version is Incoterms 2010.

Examples of expenses addressed by Incoterms are as follows:

- Inland transportation to port and or airport
- Forwarding fees
- Export custom clearance formalities and export duties where applicable
- Origin terminal handling or loading fees
- Consolidation fees
- International freight expenses
- Destination terminal handling or unloading fees
- Import customs formalities, duties taxes, and fees
- Insurance
- Inland transportation to the place of delivery

Incoterms are broken down into four sections, and they are as follows:

- "E" Terms: Departure
  - The seller makes goods that are available at the seller's premises or at another named premise, and these goods are not cleared for export.

INCOTERMS The set of rules governing international logistics defining the responsibility of sellers and buyers.

- There is minimum obligation for the seller with the buyer bearing all costs and risks involved in taking goods from the buyer's premises.
    - An example is ex works.
- ■ "F" Terms: Main carriage unpaid
    - The seller must deliver to a carrier and or place specified by the buyer, and it must be cleared for export.
    - Examples includes FCA (free carrier), FAS (free alongside ship), and FOB (free on board, and this should only be used for sea or inland waterway transport).
- ■ "C" Terms: Main carriage paid
    - The seller must contract for carriage to a specified place (named destination port), and it must be cleared for export.
    - Examples include CFR (cost and freight), CIF (cost, insurance, and freight), CPT (carriage paid to), and CIP (carriage and insurance paid to).
- ■ "D" Terms: Arrival
    - The seller must bear all costs and risks in bringing the goods to a named destination (port or place)
    - Examples include DAF (delivered at frontier), DES (delivered ex ship), DDU (delivered duty paid), DDU (delivered duty unpaid), and DDP (delivered duty paid).

Nowadays, supply chain management has advanced away from the notion of servicing only a specific activity, such as operations management, marketing, strategic procurement, or even logistics. Now, the thought is that supply chain management's role is more accurately defined as a cross-functional set of activities that links all parts of business together.

Operational transactions take place in milliseconds, hardly enough time to digest the consequences of business actions if management makes a mistake. Good intentions aside, a lapse in operational due diligence brings about lasting consequences. Countermeasures are reactive by nature because errors need to be corrected as rapidly as possible. Due to their reactive nature, they are often not well thought out, and the consequences of a reaction can make the situation worse. The intent is to correct the lapse at the local level as quickly as possible. Little thought is given to the organization at large. Due to the high integration level of operations within the rest of the organization, consequences remain hidden, and the effect of recovery actions are not discovered until after a significant cost is inflicted on the organization. Transactional missteps may not be revealed until it is too late to implement effective countermeasures. When implemented, these countermeasures are often not decisive and timely enough; they have a delayed effect in correcting a mistake simply because they do not go far enough in neutralizing a misstep that impacts and affects the organization.

Even so, it is important to review the advantages and disadvantages when establishing international operations because other factors contribute to both. Although there is little doubt that establishing an international operation produces abundant rewards, it also brings a number of inherent risks.

ADVANTAGES OF INTERNATIONAL OPERATIONS
Competitive Advantage

As discussed in the chapter overview, enjoying a competitive advantage means cost leadership and differentiation. Developed by Michael Porter, cost leadership necessitates that enterprise ownership process and cost controls must translate into having the least operational cost in an industry. Operational capability is also a key ingredient of cost leadership. Here, the operation holds process and cost efficiencies enable passing on cost savings to the customer. The efficiency of the operation is refined through means of automation, process controls, state of the art manufacturing techniques, and rigorous cost controls, enhancing efficiency and productivity.

Along with cost leadership, product differentiation is the other critical ingredient when achieving a competitive advantage. Differentiation is a strategy that focuses on exceptional product design in terms of function and quality. Customer perception is enhanced because of a product's unique design and functional qualities, and so the product separates itself from the rest of the competition and is worth the value.

Costco is an example of cost leadership and differentiation. Their strategy focuses on three distinct areas of retailing, and they are as follows:

1. Understand and know the customer.
2. Focus on value, not lower prices.
3. Customer service is not a cost driver; it is an investment.

Costco targets the small business owner who is no different than any other customer. These entrepreneurs have incomes that are above average. They want to buy quality products while keeping their expenditures low. Although not everyone who shops at Costco is an entrepreneur, Costco has remained steadfast in its focus on small, successful business owners. Their monthly publication to the "membership" often gives small businesses advice.

Centering on value and not low price, Costco offers high priced merchandise at a discount. The price range on well-designed and brand name large, flat screen TVs, for example, attract customers. The main driver is technology, not price. Although prices are deemed reasonable, the customer is willing to make the trade-off in return for quality and value.

Although Costco is often criticized for high labor prices, it is not dissuaded because it is willing to pay for outstanding customer service. Its associates make the extra effort to hurry to the other side of the store to pick up a forgotten item or find items the customer is unable to locate or make the customer aware of the latest discounted item. Its checkers are efficient, articulate, courteous, and intelligent and have common sense.

CASE STUDY: COSTCO

Costco's core competency focuses on three areas that differentiate them from the competition. These three areas are as follows:

1. Customer knowledge
2. A focus on value, not low prices
3. Achievement of superior customer service

Log into Costco.com and click on "The Costco Connections" link at the bottom of the home page. Find three examples of each of the three core competencies and explain how each competency is supported by the material in "The Costco Connection" members' magazine.

Global Economics

International operations derive large financial benefits from low-cost country operations (LCCO) investments. Operations are incentivized into developing emerging local manufacturing infrastructures through investments. In return, local direct and indirect costs, such as the cost of capital, taxes, and labor, are significantly reduced. In the absence of a trade agreement, tariff hurdles are diluted and often waived with logistic costs significantly lessened.

All this is in exchange for developing and deploying consistent common processes, tools, and training of the local labor force. The objective is to standardize work processes by leveraging the enterprise's best practices. This brings about the formation of quicker learning cycles and strengthens communication within the organization. As the transformation takes hold, international operations undergo a makeover where they become a source of competitive advantage.

As a result, operations are aligned with the goals and strategies across the enterprise. Implementation of robust tools that support the transformation (global data warehouse, training, change management, and more) are able to withstand rigorous organizational scrutiny. Supporting resources, such as supplier development and **value analysis** or **value engineering** (VA/VE), are replicated organization-wide, embracing common reporting internally and externally.

An example of VA/VE might be when a customer complains that the common nail holding two boards is becoming loose over time. The product manager investigates with engineering why the nail is becoming loose when the board flexes. They discover that this is typically caused by thermal dynamics. After probing how a nail grips wood, engineering came up with a solution. After limited success with several prototype models, they settle on a design of a nail with spiral barbs and straight barbs at the top of the nail. The final hammer blow locks the nail into place. This gives birth to a new product that can be sold at twice the cost of the ordinary nail and is well worth the initial outlay of the production cost.

Low-Cost Labor Force

The most immediate benefit in establishing an international operation is the realization of significant savings due to low-cost labor. Differences in the cost of labor alone creates a competitive advantage, especially when it is sustained by a highly educated and skilled workforce.

Although it is true that the cost of unskilled and skilled labor is rising primarily due to higher standards of living, currency fluctuations, productivity, and increases in wage expenses, low-cost countries still enjoy a significant competitive advantage.

The emerging exception is China. Between 2000 to 2013, labor rates increased at an average rate of 13.9% annually. As the luster of operations in China loses some of its appeal, focus has begun to shift to other low-cost country regions in East Asia. Vietnam and the Philippines, for example, are the latest focus. The global wage advantage that low-cost countries enjoy today will not end anytime soon.

Due diligence and focus on changing macroeconomic circumstances create preconditions that drive organizations into unyielding pursuit of adding value. Companies looking to expand globally tend to chase labor around the world in a relentless search to increase value through reduced labor rates. They understand that cost drivers change over time. Labor is a significant cost driver that does not remain fixed because it changes over time. Internal and external forces act on it, and labor can change in proportion to a change in a company's activities.

VALUE ANALYSIS The application of function analysis techniques to an existing product, process, or procedure to compare customer requirements at the lowest cost, specified performance, and required level of reliability.

VALUE ENGINEERING The application of function analysis techniques during the planning or design stages of a new product before major commitments or investments are made; methodology used to execute advanced product quality planning (APQP).

THIRD PARTY LOGISTICS (3PL) These are companies that contract with shippers to manage their clients' logistics operations. The services they provide include warehousing, management of transportation software, freight bill auditing, and many more logistic elements.

FOURTH PARTY LOGISTICS (4PL) This is a non-asset independent company that brings together the resources, capabilities, and technology of its own organization to other companies, replicating and installing capabilities to design, build, and run supply chain solutions for its clients.

Economies of Scale

Economies of scale are basically when high volume production is achieved at a lower cost. The objective is to reduce the average unit price of production thus increasing product profit margins. This means taking advantage of volume purchases and creating a specialized workforce.

Taking advantage of logistics economies of scale means implementing a transportation management strategy that includes the following:

- Optimization by mode and or carrier
- Global visibility throughout the chain
- Cross unit consolidations
- Operational and cost reporting
- Carrier management
- Accurate freight recovery process

Benefits derived from these actions include the following:

- Reduced freight costs
- Improved logistics productivity
- Logistic financial control
- Improved quality and on-time delivery

Maersk Line, a Danish shipping company, is perhaps the best illustration of benefitting from logistics economies of scale. Maersk has changed the way people look at logistics economies of scale. Maersk redefined container shipping to its current state by inaugurating new, larger container ships.

Countries expanded their deep water ports to accommodate these larger vessels. The primary motivation behind these efforts was to proactively participate in a greater level of economies of scale. Improvements in port infrastructure, such as dredging ports to deeper depths, increasing the number of port gantries, and modernizing the port's equipment, increased port capacities when handling cargo.

Maersk gained a competitive advantage through economies of scale with the introduction of these types of ships. Competitors were forced to order similar sized ships in an effort to contest this advantage. Logistic providers were forced to rethink their competitive strategy by forming alliances that made increased cargo capacity feasible. They now needed partners capable of collecting large volumes of containerized freight. Rapid globalization supported these investments because ship container capacity increased dramatically.

The benefits of using larger and larger container ships are reductions in the per-container cost to transport cargo, optimization of fuel consumption, and ocean voyage time reduction. These gains in efficiencies result in increased generation of logistics productivity.

The focus of economies of scale is not on total production cost but on cost per unit. Typically, as production volumes increase, the average product unit cost drops. As economies of scale drive demand for products higher, an increase in production power and higher material acquisition levels with increased material discounts that the supplier pass on to the enterprise occurs.

Besides purchasing economies of scale, the economies of scale chain is made up of the technical, managerial, financial, and risk economy of scales. All of these items help to make major contributions to the profit of the international operation.

Achieving technical economies of scale means maximizing the capability and efficiency of the operation. This requires investment in state of the art manufacturing techniques such as logistics information flow, inventory tracking, tracking shipments, and ensuring capacity utilization of state of the art equipment. In short, operational efficiency without investment in the most current and modern equipment creates a weak link in the economies of scale chain.

Managerial economies of scale further strengthen the scale chain through the hiring of specialists and subject matter experts. At first glance, this might seem like an added expense. However, specialists bring with them techniques that enhance efficiency beyond the norm. For example, managerial expertise in quality and lean manufacturing techniques improve the overall quality of a product. This activity translates into production increases that have the same level of inputs.

Financial economies of scale concern the leverage of the capital resources of the operation. The operation is able to finance larger amounts of borrowing. Like anyone who borrows money, the banks require collateral. The more collateral, the more there is to finance at lower rates. A large amount of assets allows for lower borrowing rates. Another form of leveraging the operation's capital resources is the raising of equity. Size matters. Larger operations have an easier time raising equity than smaller operations. Service fees for this type financing are considerably less than banks or financial institutions specializing in loans.

Risk economies of scale essentially spread risk over a wide variety of activities. Activities include spreading the risk over a wide assortment of products. Product risks include marketing risk, price risk, lifecycle risks, quality risk, perishable goods inventory risk, on-time delivery of time sensitive inventory risk, such as seasonal products, and safety risk.

Another activity to help spread risk is operating in multiple locations. Natural disasters and catastrophic infrastructure failures in recent years, such as the Japanese tsunami and factory collapses in Bangladesh, illustrate the all too vivid realities of these events.

Nissan and Honda made the speediest recovery in the aftermath of the 2013 Japanese earthquake and tsunami. Collaboration with key suppliers helped their supply chain recover quickly. Their close cooperation stemmed from the fact that they had deep trusting relationships with their supply chains. Both companies maintained unprecedented visibility of their supply chains. An awareness of Japan's susceptibility to natural disasters refined their supply chain's logistics risk strategy. They ensured that their logistics chain were scattered in areas less prone to natural disaster areas.

CASE STUDY: MAERSK LINE

Maersk Lines is the world's largest container shipping company. Their motto is, "Your Promise. Delivered. More than just three words." What are the practical applications and goals behind these mottos?

DISADVANTAGES OF INTERNATIONAL OPERATIONS
Political Instability and Terrorism

The overriding disadvantage of an international operation is the presence of political turmoil. Political instability and economic chaos seems to be the norm rather than the exception. Governments are weak, and they come and go. Attempts to bring order to economic anarchy are remedied by indirect expropriation, such as excessive taxation, capital controls, currency manipulation, and widespread corruption in the form of bribes and permits demanded by government officials. The more direct form of expropriation is the outright nationalization of a foreign operation's assets. Venezuela seized foreign oil assets in 2009. Even the mere threat of seizure sent shock waves through international operation concerns. Another threat, demonstrated by president Mugabe of Zimbabwe's threats to seize the assets of Canadian gold miners in 2013, also had large repercussions.

Governments often change the operating conditions after an international operation has made the investment. The international entity has no recourse because enforcement of the original investment is virtually impossible. Governments ignore international courts of law in the name of national sovereignty. They lack any traditions of law that protect international operations' assets, resulting in all too frequent supply chain disruptions.

Today, international operations procure critical raw materials from all areas of the globe. Political instability can create global disruption and chaos. At times, raw materials are held as ransom as was the case when China began to curtail the export of rare earth materials used in manufacturing the batteries for the Toyota Prius and GM Volt. Regardless of the reasons given, curtailing access to this material was politically motivated. In play were internal dynamic political forces seeking China's self-sufficiency, an action that had military implications.

The unpredictable political environment dismantles any semblance of order, and adoption of a new constitution becomes the convenient remedy. This happened in Venezuela. Instead of stabilizing any remnant of protection of international assets, the new constitution increased political instability. There were massive labor strikes, a series of public protests, and even an attempted coup.

The rise of terrorism has had an enormous impact on global operations. Terrorism is rooted in regional political and sectarian disputes. As terrorists rise in political standing and their influence expands globally, many governments adopt the terrorists' agenda as their own. Any remaining portions of the protection of property rights principles are abandoned.

The key barometer to foreign direct investment (FDI) in operations is political stability considerations. Asia remains at the top of the list of regional continental investments with an inflow of $426 billion in 2013, headed by China, Taiwan, and South Korea. Latin America and Africa saw only small growth while geopolitical tensions in the Middle East and Eastern Ukraine contributed to an FDI outflow.

Intellectual Property

Besides the lowering and relaxation of trade barriers, the rise in the expansion of global operations was also driven by capacity constraints at home. Outsourced products are mature products that are in the decline phase in the product life cycle. The objectives surrounding an **offshoring** strategy are based on extending the life of mature products and squeezing every ounce of profitability out of the product before the product dies. As the product enters the declining stages, the product consumes increasing manufacturing resources. Outmoded technology, inefficient processes, and diminishing material availability become the main drivers to offload these products to an offshore operation.

Despite state of the art investments and ensuring modernity in offshore operations, why would an international operation not want to develop new products at the location? The answer is protection of intellectual property (IP). Whether a

OFFSHORING The process of relocating business processes (this may include, production, or manufacturing) to another country with the intent to reduce costs.

OUTSOURCING A form of a make-or-buy decision where an enterprise chooses to purchase a good or service from a third party that was previously made on-site.

NEARSHORING A form of outsourcing determined by geographical considerations in which business processes are moved to localities that are geographically nearer to the procuring group.

company expands to Brazil, China, India, or Southeast Asia, intellectual property rights are always at risk. Although these countries and regions have statutes and various forms of regulations in place, differences in interpretation of intellectual property rights vary.

The Chinese legal system, for example, is deeply rooted in classical Chinese culture and philosophical traditions such as Confucianism. Chinese legal traditions are very different than English common law conventions. Adherence to Confucian philosophy is based on obedience and conduct, and recognition is seen in the enduring struggle of preserving resources, and this can be rationalized away by copying the master. The individual is responsible for his or her own conduct. Therefore, misbehavior on the part individual is due to a failure of reaching some sort of accommodation or negotiation. It naturally follows then that organizations have little chance to enforce violations of intellectual property rights.

In China, provincial authorities exercise significant authority on the establishment of a local operation. Contracts and agreements covering non-disclosure, IP, and UN based manufacturing human rights principles are signed all day long. Regardless of signed agreements and contracts in place launching the operation, protection from IP violations are not what they seem to be. Chinese authorities insist insertion of a clause that any contracts or agreements are subject to local "applicable laws." Insertion of this clause opens the door to different sets of interpretations that are unfavorable to western traditional enforcement means.

Cyber Security

Critical to an operation's viability is cyber security. In today's world there are increased occurrences of data breaches. It is commonplace to hear of security breaches in government, defense, financial, health, and retail institutions.

Setting up an operation in a low-cost country involves a considerable commitment of resources. It involves wide-ranging cyber security measures that are similar to the home operation and, likewise, comprehensive in nature. Protecting essential data, such as employee communications and client and customer privacy, are indispensable in protecting the durability of the operation. These are fundamental to an operation's effectiveness, profit, and, most important, avoidance of business interruptions.

Data privacy regulations in force in the European Union and the United States do not necessarily carry over to low-cost regions. Illegal access to proprietary data, equipment, and documents are often sanctioned by local authorities in the name of protecting political autonomy. In May 2014, five Chinese hackers were indicted for hacking into major operations, including U.S. Steel, Westinghouse Electric, and Allegheny Technologies. These intrusions occurred over a period of 8 years from 2006 to 2014. A Chinese national was indicted for hacking into Boeing from 2009 to 2013. This individual worked with other hackers (never identified) in trying to steal manufacturing plans for the F-35 and F-22 fighter jets.

The old term "industrial espionage" takes on a more far-reaching undercurrent. These attacks are not only aimed at gaining access to a company's private data but have a larger purpose of uncovering and compromising an organization's infrastructure. Because the offshore operation is part of this infrastructure, its operational strategy is undermined and destabilized. The severity and increasing rate of these attacks have far-reaching consequences and can disrupt continuing operations.

Continuing operations implies levels of efficiency, competitiveness, cost control, and state of the art processes that enhance the quality of the product or the service. With a data breach, all of these fundamentals are compromised. Perhaps the most far reaching is the reputation of the operation. Customer confidence erodes as skepticism increases whether or not the operation is capable of protecting sensitive customer information.

Without constant vigilance, it is far easier today for an operation to lose important information. The situation becomes more acute when the company is unable to discover reasons for underperformance. This is most likely due to an undiscovered data breach not detected until a considerable period of time has passed. With the damage done, most countermeasures are ineffective and have a poor remedy.

Product Quality and Quality Service

International operations experience their share of product and service quality problems. Poor product quality is grounded in the loss of control of the local supply chain. Poor service quality, on the other hand, has its origins in the absence of service quality training that influences the quality of the delivered service. This shortsighted exclusion of service quality training is often deliberate and meant to attain cost savings.

International operations must depend on a supply chain of limited capabilities. Limited capabilities are not only concerned with producing a quality component. Supply chains in low-cost countries do not have consistent and reliable quality assurance systems in place to support an international operation.

A comprehensive quality system consists of corrective actions, preventative actions, records control, safety policies, and raw material or components inspection and certification structures. The local supply chain does not have formal processes in place. The quality of work subcontracted to external sources is by no means assured. There are no provisions in place for verification, storage, reporting, and maintenance of the operation's consigned material, equipment, and tools.

As a consequence, defective product escapes become commonplace. Defective components assembled in the operation interrupts the assembly process and causes major disruptions in the product flow. When a defective product escapes the operations facility and reaches the customer, it may trigger major recalls, costing the operation significant financial setback as well a bad reputation.

An example of things going horribly wrong can be seen with the Mattel toy company massive toy recall in 2007. Nineteen million toys were recalled because their Chinese contractors and subcontractors used lead-based paint and used tiny magnets in a variety of toys. Due to inadequate quality assurance procedures governing manufacturing methods of their contractors in China, Mattel spent $30 million in the recall effort. This reduced their quarterly income by almost 50%. Even though Mattel is one of the best managed companies in the world, this incident showed that even the most well-managed companies are vulnerable to business disruptions because of a due diligence gap.

Repairing defective products consumes valuable operational resources. Although the originating supplier of the defective component replaces the defective component, the operation is still stigmatized and associated as being a source of poor quality.

Deficiencies in poor service quality are due mostly to cost cutting that, in-turn, creates a shortage of financial resources for service quality training programs. The maturity level of service quality is a direct reflection on the operation's responsiveness. Responsiveness is the most important metric in the operations' balanced scorecard. It is a direct indicator of an operation's reliability, integrity, readiness to offer solutions, and overall effectiveness. Customers are quick to abandon products that have virtually no technical support. Second-rate shoddy solutions are simply not acceptable in a world where quality is a given.

With efficiency being the dominant metric, present-day operational pressures divert attention away from acquiring and analyzing service performance data. This results in a scarcity of service quality awareness. Without awareness, service quality becomes unimportant as a viable attribute of the operation. Any improvement efforts are construed as undermining a substandard quality system deemed "good enough."

TYPICAL LOGISTICS CHALLENGES WHEN DEALING WITHIN COUNTRIES' BORDERS

The generally accepted definition of supply chain logistics embraces the planning, implementation, and efficient control of the flow of goods and services throughout the entire supply chain. From its starting point at an operation's facility shipping dock to the point of consumption, this journey is beset by periods of disruptions, delays, and setbacks. These events interrupt the efficient flow of goods and services to their destinations, driving logistic costs beyond planned and tolerable levels.

The leading reasons for growing global operational capabilities are expanding markets, increased sales, improved profits, economies of scale, competitive advantage, and absorption of capacity. What companies often miss in their planning is that the prevailing logistics infrastructure lacks robust components to support an operation's facility.

Logistics involves more than the transport of goods. Supporting infrastructures, such as information and communication, regulation and bureaucracy, energy supplies, and deficiency of trained employees, represent a critical source of underinvestment by the host country. Development of logistic competency is an important planning component and requires the recognition of major structural difficulties. The in-place infrastructure is fragmented and creates all too common **choke points** that reduce leverage and lead to waste in the value chain.

The most common reason for choke points is the lack of resources. One may not have enough time devoted to planning an entire distribution process. Others are attributed to unreliable freight companies, freight shipped to the wrong location, weather and labor problems, and component shortages.

Poor Infrastructure

There are several contributors that add to the difficulties of a poor transportation infrastructure. Beginning with geography and driven by the terrain, lack of adequate roads, bridges, railways, airports, and security slows down the speed and movement of goods. As movement slows, it creates bottlenecks throughout the supply chain. The objective of moving freight as rapidly as possible is to avoid costly storage of goods. This setback offsets one of the major objectives of the supply chain: lowering transit costs through avoidance of warehousing a product. Warehoused products extend transit time and leave the products susceptible to damage.

CHOKE POINT A condition where any number of shortages of material, equipment, services, or incomplete processes affect the completion of an operation.

Movement of material requires equipment that is suited to perform this function efficiently. Often, the equipment is old, underpowered, and poorly maintained. Frequent equipment failures contribute to missed port deliveries. Road transport may worsen the risk because long overland road hauls bring unexpected time delays due to the poor conditions and capacity limitations of the roads. Traffic delays and equipment breakdowns, tolls, and, if crossing a border, differing traffic and control regulations are also problems.

Missed delivery to a rail terminal also carries on-time delivery risks. Rail schedules are unreliable at best. Relying on rail transport in remote regions further adds to risk because equipment maintenance is poor and subject to mechanical failure. Upon arrival at the rail depot, the product may need to be shipped further to a warehouse or port. This additional transport adds time and cost, disturbing delivery timetables.

Like rail transport, shipping routes and timetables are fixed and inflexible. Fuel surcharges, port fees, currency adjustments, and difficulty in tracking goods are all disruptive logistical challenges that are associated with a country's poor logistics infrastructure. Missing a delivery to a port can be an expensive undertaking and bring about costs that are not easy to recover.

Current infrastructure limitations have an effect on product lead times due to the unpredictability in the cycle times of the shipment. This triggers expediting efforts and alternative premium shipping methods that eat into the expected logistic savings.

Laws and Regulations

Government regulation and laws at the national, regional, and local level remains a challenge in most emerging economies today. The regulations tend to be multi-tiered structures that hinder the development of nationwide networks. They may also differ from city to city, further fragmenting and inhibiting the linking of logistic infrastructures.

Dealing with government agencies can be frustrating. They implement day-to-day changes that trigger uncertainty and add complexity. Often, government imposed regulation changes place one agency in direct conflict with another. For example, in 2006 the Ministry of Commerce of China issued new regulations for export processing zones. This put them in direct conflict with China customs because they issued new regulations for bonded logistics parks that support export related handling activities.

Bureaucracy gets in the way, and with the absence of consistent national regulations, inefficiencies are magnified. Inland waterways are a significant means of transport simply because they precede any other modes of modern transportation. Like other modes of transportation, it has its limitations and lack of national regulations. There are often no provisions or guidelines regarding the level of navigational capacity. Despite the increase in air freight, air space is constricted due to military restrictions.

TRANSPORT MODES This is the methods by which a freight is transported. There are three types of transport modes: land (road, rail, and pipeline), water, and air.

Unauthorized and ad-hoc border controls are triggered by corruption, imposition of fees, and customs duties that are difficult to eliminate. Any resistance to payment of these fees simply results in holding the goods hostage. Other border delays are caused by meager infrastructures that create serious shortcomings in the synchronization of border agents' efforts on both sides of the border. Access to adequate power may also be the cause of delay in border crossings. With electricity being one of the fundamental substructures in the logistics industry, shortages often create instances where movement, inspection, and clearing of freight can only proceed during daylight hours.

Even though China has made great strides in eliminating logistics obstacles, the country has difficulty in keeping pace with the demands of swift globalization.

Chinese transport policy remains heavily burdened with regulations; they restrain the dynamics that are inherently present in modern logistics infrastructures. Much work needs to be done in the interconnectivity between modes. This barrier is most visible in air and ports, the most critical points of connectivity. Inland infrastructures lag behind the coastal regions due largely to the rapid development of China's east coast. Inland transportation modes are twenty years behind in development. Although inland investment is increasing rapidly, it will take many years to bring the interior of China to the level of its coast.

Technology

The principle emerging trend as a result of rapid globalization is the growth of e-commerce. In China alone, the e-commerce market size has expanded from $21 billion in 2008 to $300 billion in 2013. With 300 million online shoppers, the logistics challenge is immense. Logistics management is quickly becoming a competitive differentiator with the enormous expansion of e-commerce. Major technological hurdles face logistic providers as they try to tackle growing freight volumes that have no end in sight.

As freight volumes increase, logistic providers require unprecedented operational excellence. Lowest total landed cost is still the standard that most measure the effectiveness of the supply chain by. Despite improvements in the logistics industry, providers still struggle with late deliveries, damaged products, and delivery and collection processes. These processes are outdated, cumbersome, and simply do not work any more. Struggles in the last phases of the logistics chain, such as customer interface, present issues that may be impossible to resolve.

A narrow approach, and likely the last resort to meet this challenge, is technology. The sheer size of global e-commerce calls for highly automated logistics systems. Super computer capabilities are required to process billions of transactions that are finalized in milliseconds. Building internal networks and finding experienced partners or finding partners with in-place networks is one way of leveraging technology. Although logistic technology providers may not be able to achieve logistics success overnight, nonstop integration of applications across the logistic chain is essential. Developing a logistic network means multiple levels of strong relationships throughout the chain must be built up.

The limitations of existing logistics infrastructures are glaring. New business models are needed to meet the inexorable upsurge in demand. New core competencies are required to bring about the seamless interface between technology and the customer. One core competency that is crucial is product tracking. Continuous in-transit product visibility is one primary requirement that ensures critical monitoring of product location in the logistics chain.

Undermining technology advances are energy problems that are commonplace throughout China. Two thirds of China's provinces experience regular blackouts. They have become commonplace and are considered routine. Depending on what city, blackouts sometimes occur in the middle of the workday for periods averaging 2 hours or more. The primary reasons behind the rolling blackouts are price-controls, power consumption due to uncontrolled growth, and an aggressive policy to shift away from fossil fuels. This has an especially crippling effect on the coastal areas because the majority of companies are concentrated along the eastern seaboard. Power starved logistics providers experience normal information and technology gaps, leading to disruptions in communications.

Subnational Logistics

There is another dimension of international trade logistics that is seldom mentioned. Logistic planners tend to design and develop logistic infrastructures from a macro level perspective. Subnational logistics addresses connectivity of provincial and local territories within countries. Little attention is given to subnational logistics and its connectivity to the main corridors of global logistic chains. A robust international logistics infrastructure assumes a strong connection to the local logistics chain. The efficient movement of freight within a country is just as important as the movement of freight between countries.

A sturdy subnational infrastructure is especially important for economies that rely on agricultural exports. For example, where horticulture and fishing industries are vital to the local economy, producers' access to the national and global infrastructures is critical. These products are the livelihoods of farmers who tend to pay higher transport prices because of poorly maintained roads.

In India, for example, 70% of freight movement is transported by road. The roads are poorly maintained and heavily congested. Major highway arteries of India represent only 2% of the road network, yet they carry 40% of the freight. The alternative of moving freight by rail is not feasible because the railroad, a state monopoly, is losing business to roads.

Cross-border cooperation is difficult, at best, especially if the country is land-locked. These countries are dependent on third countries for access to the logistics infrastructure. Transit agreements are non-existent, so there is no integration with world markets. They must cross borders multiple times and unload and reload freight due to differences in customs documentation requirements, politically motivated restrictions, and health and safety regulations. Cross-border movement involves custom clearance and standardized conventions and regulations. The absence of procedural consistency and cross-border in-compatibilities disrupts and slows the flow of goods across borders, resulting in increased cost. Unlike mature global logistics infrastructures, subnational infrastructures lack simplified cross-border clearance mechanisms, and this puts them at a severe disadvantage. They are not able to participate and plug into the global infrastructure.

The consequence of non-participation is a fragmented subnational sector. Negligible coordination efforts facilitate entry of small independent trucking companies with ad-hoc cost structures, inferior equipment, and ill-defined service activities that are burdened with cost inefficiencies. They do not have a perspective of the dynamics of the logistics chain.

Logistics strategy is all about achieving market integration through the reduction of barriers. It is a collection of services with imprecise limitations that are focused on lowering the cost of doing business.

Other Realities

A precondition to achieving a competent logistics infrastructure is the presence of FDI. Most emerging economies have difficulty attracting FDI for a number of reasons. Legacies of bribery and corruption, war, political instability, unstable currencies, lack of logistics training, a poorly educated workforce, and bureaucratic trade regulations, contribute heavily to the stunted development of FDI. The underlying problem is that they are infrastructures in their own right. The absence of these infrastructure substructures creates intractable barriers because the substructures are the preconditions for establishing a competent, functioning logistics infrastructure.

Regulations rooted in cultural and provincial traditions thwart foreign businesses from managing and coordinating distribution. Instead, the government encourages partnering with an assortment of domestic distributors made up of state-owned companies, private exporters, independent entrepreneurs, and family-owned retail outlets, adding to the fragmentation and chaos of the market. These conditions hold back FDI because firms have no desire to invest in financially bottomless and under-developed substructures. Little incentives are in place to overcome delayed delivery of goods at higher costs. This model needs improvement.

Governments do not seem to realize that often they are the source of a region's non-competitiveness. Investments made for developing a capable logistics infrastructure is long-term. Most emerging economies face urgent economic difficulties, requiring resolution for the fear of political instability. Resource limitations and ever mounting economic problems prevent these governments from developing any long-term planning. Chaos ensues, triggering the imposition of taxes, tariffs, "facilitation fees," quotas, and regulations perpetuating corruptive practices.

The majority of emerging economies with legacies of colonialism have never enjoyed extended political stability. After World War II, the colonial powers were no longer able to sustain possessions of overseas colonies. The colonial powers were essentially bankrupt and were forced to grant these nations their independence. Little infrastructure development took place during the colonial period. Newly independent countries in Southeast Asia and Africa were left without any sort of economic infrastructure because their economies were stripped bare. After independence, the focus was not on globalization. Economic necessity forced attention inward. Economic legacies were entrenched in cultural and tribal traditions.

As a result, these countries are deprived of modern economic development practices. They lack a central economic focus and pursue policies that lead to frequent changes in government. The accession of a new government brings a whole new set of programs. Economic development is low in the priority because the political survival of the government is the overriding concern. Lip service is given to the establishment of a market economy while other centers of power promote protectionism.

DISCUSSION QUESTIONS

Consider the following questions as you review this chapter:

1. Discuss the role of logistics in driving value.

2. There are three components in designing a robust global logistics strategy: people, process, and infrastructure. Assign and discuss three attributes of each component.

3. Similar to the logistics discipline, there are three global supply chain strategies that drive capability. People, processes, and infrastructure Assign and discuss three attributes to each component.

4. Achievement of world-class supply chain drives productivity increases across an enterprise. Discuss the requirements to achieve this high level of performance.

SUMMARY

The application of rigorous discipline and coordination are the only means to achieve full supply chain capability. Operations management has undergone two phases of change to reach the strategic position that it enjoys today.

The first phase was largely transactional and tactical in nature. Supply chain management used to be an unfamiliar concept. Procurement and logistics focus was local and regional and was not much beyond this scope. Inconsistent processes and lack of training prevailed. Informal on-the-job training was commonplace. Technology systems to facilitate operational processes, supplier intelligence, and documentation were severely limited and highly variable and inconsistent.

Logistics was known by another name: traffic. The designation of traffic reinforced the concept that procedures were locally developed and often undocumented and outdated. Logistics was considered a stand-alone function relegated to the backwater of the procurement function. Compliance was difficult to measure and often had no connection to the operation. Metrics to gauge the state of the operation were non-existent.

The current phase of logistics is predominately strategic and sustains world-class maturity attributes. Today, operations is in possession of well-documented global processes that are supported by tools and training. Metrics measure outcomes that are highly repeatable and predictable. Global process owners are clearly identified, and processes are highly integrated across the entire enterprise; they are closely interconnected with other enterprise processes. Training and development is well documented and refreshed regularly while personal development is linked to competency. Consistent metrics are defined and measured globally and are aided by modern tools supporting real-time global analysis that are future-action oriented.

REFERENCES

Azzimonti, M., & Sarte, P. G. (2007). Barriers to foreign direct investment under political instability. *Economic Quarterly - Federal Reserve Bank of Richmond, 93*(3), 287–315. Retrieved from http://search.proquest.com/docview/204755669?accountid=26967

Burke, H. (2007) *Mattel recall of lead-tainted Chinese toys cost $30 million.* Retrieved from http://www.bloomberg.com/apps/news?pid=newsarchive&sid=ah7cuhojMidI

Chapman, B., (2014). *Moving operations or functions to a new country? Think long term.* Retrieved from http://deloitte.wsj.com/riskandcompliance/2014/04/30/moving-operations-or- functions-to-a-new-country-think-long-term/

Drikhamer, D. (2007) *India gears up: India's logistics challenge in a nutshell.* Retrieved from http://www.jdmandassociates.com/pdfs/2007_05_SEKO_LT_India_Gears_Up.pf

Goh, M., & Ang, A. (2000). Some logistics realities in Indochina. *International Journal of Physical Distribution & Logistics Management, 30*(10), 887–911. Retrieved from http://search.proquest.com/docview/232586603?accountid=26967

GOV.UK. (2012). *Transport and distribution for international trade – Detailed guidance.* Retrieved from https://www.gov.uk/transport-and-distribution-for-international-trade

Ingersoll, R. (2009). *Global Supply Chain Essentials I* Davidson, NC: Author.

Kearney, A. T. (2014). *China's e-commerce market in 2014-Full report.* Retrieved from https://www.atkearney.com/paper//asset_publisher/dVxv4Hz2h8bS/content/chinas-e-commerce-market-the-logistics-challenges/10192

Knigge, R. (2013). *Freight forwarding and logistics: What the high performers know.* Retrieved from http://www.accenture.com/us-en/outlook/Pages/outlook-online-2013-freight-forwarding-and-logistics-what-high-performers-know.aspx

Kunaka, C. (2011). Logistics in lagging regions: Overcoming local barriers to global connectivity. *World Bank.* Retrieved from http://openknowledge.worldbank.org/handle/10986/2543 License: CC BY 3.0 IGO.

Maersk Line. (n.d.). *Shipping services*. Retrieved from http://www.maerskline.com/en-us/shipping-services/your-promise-delivered/your-promise-delivered/overview

Material Handling & Logistics. (2004). *Ten key challenges for the Chinese logistics industry*. Retrieved from http://mhlnews.com/global-supply-chain/ten-key-challenges-chinese-logistics-industry.

Mentzer, J. T., Stank, T. P., & Esper, T. L. (2008). Supply chain management and its relationship to logistics, marketing, production, and operations management. *Journal of Business Logistics, 29*(1), 31–38. Retrieved from http://search.proquest.com/docview/212664362?accountid=26967

O'Riordan, A. (2013). *Winning in emerging markets: Understanding the barriers*. Retrieved from http://www.accenture.com/us-en/blogs/life-sciences-blog/archive/2013/05/21/winning-in-emerging-markets-understanding-the-barriers.aspx.

Porter, M. E. (1998). *Competitive advantage: creating and sustaining superior performance* (1st ed.) New York, NY: The Free Press.

The Costco Connection. (2015, May). *30*(5). Retrieved from http://www.costcoconnection.com/connection/201505#pg1

Value analysis. (n.d.). Retrieved from http://syque.com/quality_tools/toolbook/Value/value.htm

Walters, R. (2014). Cyber attacks on U.S. companies in 2014. *Heritage Foundation*. Retrieved from http://www.heritage.org/research/reports/2014/10 cyber-attacks-on-us-companies-in-2014

International and Functional Areas of Supply Chain

The international enterprise of the 21st century necessitates maintenance of a wide spectrum of core competencies to sustain the ability to compete on a global basis. There are very few companies left in today's world whose operations are exclusively domestic. Essential to contemporary business strategies are policies that include sourcing and sale of products in international markets. Companies whose business objectives stubbornly cling to strictly domestic trade goals are destined to descend into a state of fixed inflexibility from which there is no recovery. Their fate is to end up with all the other relics of ossified companies not able to adjust to competition emerging from every corner of the globe. Not being affected by international concerns is impossible due to supply chain and customer interface.

Today, the key to competitive participation in worldwide business is putting into practice and synchronizing enduring supply chain management processes. The essence of competitiveness is speed to market, regardless of the length of the supply chain. Upgrades mean considerable investments in management processes. It means reorienting the enterprise from a narrow set of supply chain functional responsibilities, such as materials handling and warehousing, to a wide spectrum of functional areas.

ADDED CHALLENGES WHEN DEALING WITH AN INTERNATIONAL SUPPLY CHAIN

As lowering and reduction of trade barriers increasingly take hold, redesign of the supply chain becomes more important. Supply chain management functions are undergoing a series of fundamental changes, leading to the total makeover of its role in the enterprise. Prior to this transformation, supply chain management concerned itself with mostly local issues that disrupted the flow of products to consumers. Local interruptions, such as supplier bankruptcy, road construction delays, and supplier selection of carriers not bound by a purchase agreement, impacted the flow of product. These disruptions were reasonably manageable because the supply chains were largely local and controllable.

Today, this is far different. Supply chains have extended globally, and any disruption has far reaching implications on the enterprise. Every so often, entire economies are affected. For example, floods in Thailand and the Japanese tsunami in 2011 caused global disruptions in the electronics

QUESTIONS TO CONSIDER

Consider the following questions as you discuss this scenario:

1. How does supply chain volatility affect its ability to respond in an effective manner?

2. How does the enterprise meet competition from emerging economies that do not pay the same wages and benefits?

3. How does the supply chain respond to ever increasing demands to reduce product lead times?

4. What needs to be done to control cost of goods, inventory, and transportation?

KEY TERMS

- bullwhip effect (p. 125)
- center of excellence (COE) (p. 126)
- cross docking (p. 136)
- digital warehouse (p. 139)
- electronic data interchange (p. 129)
- end-to-end supply chain (p. 126)
- enterprise resource planning (ERP) (p. 125)
- excess inventory (p. 124)
- key performance indicator (KPI) (p. 137)
- obsolete inventory (p. 124)
- picking process (p. 125)
- transportation management systems (TMS) (p. 124)

industry, triggering unprecedented stoppages in the automotive industry. The flooding in Thailand caused billions of dollars in property losses and a worldwide disruption in the delivery of hard disk drives to global electronics manufacturers. According to Reuters, nearly 1000 factories in Thailand were closed for extended periods of time, incurring insurers $20 billion in liabilities.

There a number of features that go into the design of a global supply chain. Key attributes such as supply chain flexibility and visibility enhance an enterprise's ability to absorb and insulate the company from unforeseen catastrophic events that could prove costly to the business. So what are these business process improvements? What are the requirements to bring providers, shippers, consumers, and products together? What are the prosperity measures that must be put into place to facilitate uninterrupted global commerce?

Warehousing, Inbound, and Outbound Transportation

Regardless of the industry, the role of supply chains is to move material, goods, and services downstream to the consuming entity in a cost effective manner. Traditionally, this process has been inconsistent and fragmented. This resulted in inconsistent shipping schedules, missed deliveries, and preventable consumer shortages. Logistics became an afterthought because companies sought to cover unpredictable and volatile transportation breaches with inventory. Materials management was merely viewed as a tactical function that was responsible only to ensure availability of inventory and buffer the shortfall of an outmoded and inefficient delivery system. **Excess** and **obsolete** inventories were a result of this, and the accepted strategy to counter uncertainty in demand and supply was hampered. Inventory carrying cost and material lead times increased. A lack of responsiveness to the changing needs of the marketplace resulted in diminished earnings and a deterioration of customer goodwill.

With the ascent of the Internet, supply chain management, like other aspects of business, has undergone a technological revolution. Business-to-business transactions and the rise in e-commerce have radically affected how the supply chain functions. This has created an upsurge in new sets of metrics that determine warehousing and transportation competence.

Access to real-time data has ushered in a new paradigm, enabling analysis, speed, and processing of information at unparalleled levels. It is essential that contemporary supply chain management systems provide for access to real-time data and, more importantly, integrate that data across the entire supply chain. The ability to synchronize data with real-time decision-making capabilities is necessary when acting in response to the dynamics of a changing marketplace.

Not so long ago, warehouse management systems (WMS) and **transportation management systems (TMS)** operated as stand-alone segments of the enterprise. Although each benefited from a period of optimization, lack of coordination between the two resulted in disjointed capabilities.

Companies are discovering how coordination of WMS and TMS results in overall cost savings within the supply chain. The emergence of e-commerce and energetic changes in the demand cycle are forcing companies to ship more frequently in smaller quantities and have shorter lead-times. The development of Internet technology intensifies the need for integration of WMS and TMS.

EXCESS INVENTORY Materials and supplies in excess of demand; these may be inventory items such as raw materials, components, and work in process (WIP).

OBSOLETE INVENTORY Materials and supplies that can no longer be used; this type of inventory is generated by engineering and product changes.

TRANSPORTATION MANAGEMENT SYSTEMS (TMS) A subcategory of supply chain management (SCM) software that is dedicated to transportation functions.

Modern integrated WMS and TMS applications provided by SAP S.E. and Oracle Corporation begin with the handover of incoming orders from the **enterprise resource planning (ERP)** system to the order management function.

The first step to order fulfillment is through the WMS and to gain planning visibility of packaging requirements. This includes types of packaging (boxes, shrink wrap requirements, actual packaging sequences, and others). In parallel, TMS evaluates the most cost effective way to source and ship the orders. This parallel analysis saves time as opposed to performing these functions sequentially. Real-time inventory levels residing in multiple enterprise locations are scrutinized and analyzed. Depending on existing transportation agreements, TMS recommends the most cost effective way to ship the order as well as the facility most suited to fulfill the order. An additional benefit of enterprise wide inventory visibility is that it is now possible to synchronize shipments arriving from multiple locations.

As these orders wind their way through the order fulfillment system, they are routed back through the WMS that then starts the **picking process**. At the same time, the TMS begins the process of scheduling carriers for pickup. Shipping labels and all relevant documentation is generated and stand in ready for application to the freight before it leaves the facility. The TMS tracks the shipment until its arrival at its destination. It performs a special audit function that is used to trigger the payment process. Maintaining visibility of all shipments, the TMS provides for additional data gathering, such as measuring carrier reliability, and leverages this information for use in future carrier rate negotiations.

In an effort to maintain their competitiveness, transportation providers must have the capability to exchange information with the supply chains they serve. Because they are a vital link in the supply chain, transportation providers require full integration in the collection, gathering, and dissemination of data, and this then helps to enhance visibility and maintain competitiveness.

Supply Chain Volatility

The recent economic slowdown has had a far-reaching effect on the supply chain. It changed buying behaviors and lowered the degree of customer loyalty. Customer loyalty is not anywhere near the level that it was prior to the recent economic difficulties. Society is in an age of extensive discounting. On the demand side, consumers are very price conscious. Quality is the primary factor in the final product decision-making process. With a decrease in consumer loyalty, companies are increasingly focusing on strengthening their collaboration with major customers. This helps to minimize the **bullwhip effect** of demand uncertainty and its destabilizing effects.

On the supply side, companies are faced with the challenge of producing accurate forecasts. With market demand being unpredictable, past algorithms that contributed to forecast accuracy no longer apply. The lack of an accurate forecast is the main contributor to supply chain inflexibility.

In response to the global economic slowdown, the supply side idled a portion of their production capacity. This has thrown the supply side into turmoil. Responsiveness, one of the key ingredients of the supply side's balanced scorecard metric, suffered a severe setback due to the inability of the supply side to a ramp up production. The on-time delivery metric worsened the situation because of a lack of responsiveness. This was not the end of it. What was left of consumer loyalty nosedived due to an unreliable supply chain.

ENTERPRISE RESOURCE PLANNING (ERP) An integrated end-to-end suite of business applications that tie together finance, human resources, distribution, manufacturing, service, and supply chain functions.

PICKING PROCESS The process of selecting orders for the release to the warehouse for picking up the product and shipping it to customers; items are pulled from inventory and consolidated for shipment to customers.

BULLWHIP EFFECT A phantom demand created by inaccurate forecasts; this results in increased inventory levels throughout the supply chain as the supply chain reacts by generating more inventory requirements and adding capacity to meet increases in demand.

Volatility is a reality today, and its permanence will continue to manifest itself unless supply chain management comes up with solutions to moderate its impact. Visibility within the supply chain is one way to overcome an unpredictable supply chain. Knowing exactly where products are at any point in the supply chain, for example, leads to proactive and anticipatory actions that moderate the impact of a disruption.

As explained earlier, the enterprise of today buys raw materials from every region of the globe. Locking in the price of raw materials, for example, carries certain levels of risk. Although hedge buying can be risky, it is part of an enterprise's knowledge based centers of excellence (COE). A **center of excellence** is another strategic element of visibility in the supply chain. One of the benefits of visibility is that it brings internal and external control of the supply chain.

End-to-End Supply Chain Risk Management

Modern supply chain management thought is beginning to focus on the study and identification of **end-to-end supply chain** models. This includes identifying new sets of risks. Present supply chains are undergoing shift from upstream and supply side to the downstream and demand side. Today, the customer, not the supply base, is the primary driver of the supply chain.

The severe consequences of supply chain disruptions forces the enterprise to reassess and manage as many inherent risks of each location or node of the supply chain. Supply chain management recognizes the need to identity what these risks are and where they are likely to surface. Efforts are on-going in trying to understand what the risk drivers are, the likelihood that they will manifest themselves, and their effects on the supply chain. Supply chains are getting longer and, as a consequence, are becoming more "fragile".

One method is to create a series of simulations for each node within the supply chain to anticipate the probability of a risk revealing itself; this can be done without exposing the enterprise and the supply chain to damaging consequences. The nodes or the supply chain network consist of suppliers, production points, warehouses, distributors, retailers, and customers. Each node within this network contains or experiences levels of functional risks. These models are quantitative in nature and help when developing possible strategies to lessen the consequence of risk occurrence.

There are several dimensions to a supply chain. Terms such as robust, resilient, agile, and rigid supply chains require definitions. Without differentiation, they are mere abstract concepts. They lack physical description and are poorly understood.

An agile supply chain concerns itself with responsiveness. The word "agile" points to the ability to respond in a quick manner. It implies flexibility, the creation of excess capacity, and the capability to adapt, react, and respond in a suitable and comprehensive way. Management focuses on two main core competencies: creation of excess capacity and designing processes so that products can be manufactured by the smallest possible batch process.

The design of this type of supply chain is aimed at using its means to respond to changes on the demand side of the enterprise. The implication here is that the supply chain has the ability to quickly adapt to the ever-changing dynamics of the demand side of the business. The supply chain aligns itself to the uncertainties associated with the unpredictable and volatile way of customer demands.

CENTER OF EXCELLENCE (COE) A functional team that facilitates the gathering of standards and best practices across the enterprise.

END-TO-END SUPPLY CHAIN A supply chain management practice that specializes in achieving visibility of the entire end-to-end process of planning, sourcing, selecting, acquiring, receiving, paying, and the customer delivery of goods and services.

A robust supply chain has the ability to handle both departure from the functional norm and from disruption. This model defines itself as having the ability to perform its tasks despite the damages inflicted on it. It is immune and preserves its inherent characteristics and takes no notice of dynamic disruptions. It withstands changes and responds to them. The key to its robustness is in the design of the supply chain. The design objective is having the capability to operate across the entire supply chain infrastructure, resulting in performance levels over a wide set of circumstances. It is deliberately integrated into the nodes of the entire chain. It is rooted in the redundancies of the supply chain, so modeling and simulation models are important to its design.

A resilient supply chain has the ability to adapt and quickly right itself to an accidental event. Its design is rooted in contingency planning, enabling quick recovery and restoring control to and normal operations of the supply chain. This model is a blend of agility and robustness. Its main feature is the ability to recover quickly from a disruptive event and restore normal operations. Sustaining supply chain operations or bringing about a newly established condition is key in this model. Resiliency implies enduring, constant, and adaptable attributes of the supply chain. Its ability to recover quickly from disruptions and its ability to cope with change are its key characteristics.

A rigid supply chain is the direct opposite of a resilient supply chain. This supply chain model does not use the resources at its disposal to deal with change. It is unable to respond to market changes. This model is antiquated and is typically highly vertically integrated. It adheres to rigid inputs and assumes that demand, cost, and service requirements are fixed; therefore, it is not able to persevere the volatility of demand. It was designed purely to achieve cost reduction and has little chance of achieving any sort of dexterity in bringing new products to market.

These supply chain models have their upsides as well as downsides. Risk managers must be aware of the differences in managing an international supply chain versus a domestic supply chain. Risk levels differ in matter of degree because there is a greater propensity of things going wrong in the international supply chain. They are difficult to predict, and the costs associated with mitigating them is expensive. Anticipating these potential risks are challenging and difficult.

Technology is critical. Global alignment and integration of systems, largely through standardization, enable rapid data exchange. Development of technology know-how is key when gaining end-to-end supply chain and demand visibility. Technology is an enabler that creates seamless interfaces that permit the supply chain to function efficiently.

The presence of technology enables continuous monitoring of the supply chain. Sellers and shippers need to know where their goods are at all times. An efficient supply chain is a competitive advantage, and its utilization comes from a strategic perspective. Technology is the prime risk-mitigating factor across the entire chain, regardless of its length.

For example, having visibility of port congestion gives insight into offloading risks. The enterprise can respond by diverting the shipment to another port. There would also be time to re-orient its domestic transportation providers to the alternate port to collect the goods and transport them to their eventual destinations.

The international supply chain is vulnerable to information scarcity. North America and Europe have reached high levels of maturity in the acquisition and management of electronic information flow. Asia, South America, and Africa, on the other hand, are not at comparable levels. Lack of accurate information flow in less developed, and emerging economies come with an increased risk and place limits on the flexibility of the chain. The challenge within contemporary supply chains is the acquisition of data as opposed to efficient movement of goods. Efficient movement of goods is the result of managing information.

For example, end-to-end supply chains from China to the U. S. inevitably suffer from visibility gaps associated with the complexity of the transfer of goods. Numerous handoffs can be one variable that can create complexities diminishing and undermining integrated systems that are designed to synchronize movement of goods.

One mitigating option is to outsource the logistics function to providers whose core competency is managing complex global supply chains. Third- and fourth-party logistic providers (3PL, 4PL) specialize in cross-border trade and are equipped with systems and management expertise to keep the supply chain moving. Their overseas presence and partnerships with in-country logistics providers gives them access to ever-changing global shipping issues.

Alan Gershenhorn, Vice President of Global Transportation and Shared Services at UPS Supply Chain Solutions, offers six characteristics of companies that successfully manage global supply chains. They are as follows:

- They act as 'thought leaders' who seek and find more efficiency in the supply chain.
- They maintain global capabilities and partnerships to maximize service reach and expertise.
- They utilize integrated systems to coordinate activities throughout the entire supply chain from raw materials and components to the end-consumer.
- They incorporate visibility tools to both track product movements and obtain information with which to make financial decisions, serve customers, and respond quickly to competitive threats, cut costs, and speed delivery.
- They adapt to new security requirements and provide guidance to their partners to comply with new regulations.
- They encourage the opening of more world economies to improve trade practices.

Which supply chain model is best suited to respond to international vulnerabilities based on risk? Four models were discussed: agile, robust, resilient, and the rigid supply chain types. A brief review of each might be helpful.

The agile supply chain is the responsive supply chain model. It aligns itself to the uncertainties associated with the unpredictable and volatile nature of customer demands. This model is aimed at using its means to respond to changes on the demand side of the enterprise.

The robust supply chain resists change rather than responding to it. It is immune and preserves its inherent characteristics and takes no notice of dynamic disruptions. The attribute most noticeable in this model is that it has the capability to sustain operations when a disruptive event occurs.

The resilient supply chain has the ability to manage change. Contingency planning enables quick recovery from a disruptive event and restores control to and normal operations of the supply chain.

The rigid model is not able to respond to market changes. It cannot keep up with the volatility of demand. Its main objective is to undertake cost reduction and has little chance of achieving any sort of flexibility in new product introductions.

Supply Chain Model Recommendation

The international supply chain of today is beleaguered with a number of vulnerabilities. From natural disasters, government policies, terrorism, and outsourcing to volatile locations. Regardless of the extensiveness of the disruption, whether affecting a major customer, a supplier, a subcontractor, or labor actions, a break of a single supply chain link can inflict serious damage to manufacturers and a whole range of industries. Although the majority of manufacturers have risk mitigation strategies in place to manage minor disruptions, recent natural disasters like the Japanese tsunami and flooding in Thailand were either unnoticed or thought to be unimportant. Political events in Egypt and Ukraine severed vital supply chain actions when the flow of goods simply stopped because of catastrophic effects on those countries' economic infrastructures.

Today's market conditions are significantly different from the recent past. Manufacturers are offering increasing levels of product variety and customization. In response to customer demand, manufacturers must take timely actions as a means to achieve a critical competitive advantage. Manufacturers are streamlining their processes in response to the volatility and unpredictability of demand.

A common mistake many organizations make is that responsiveness is confined to external requirements. Internal response levels to an organization's inside requirements changes are directly linked and just as important. Examples of internal disruptions might be machine breakdown, supplier problems, internal supply chain disruptions, and inefficient manufacturing processes. Without internal risk mitigation strategies, the supply chain is directly affected by disruptions because product flows are delayed and interrupted. Contingency planning is a crucial element that plays an important role in refining the organization's internal responsiveness threshold.

Responsiveness comes in other forms that should not be minimized. As market volatility becomes more the norm rather than the exception, deciphering product and volume mix forecasts remains challenging at best. The maturity and accurateness of the forecast is directly related to delivery responsiveness. Without accurate forecasts, the manufacturer is vulnerable to component delivery disruptions. This directly affects the short-term, medium-term, and long-term responsiveness perspectives of the supply chain.

It is for this rationale that the agile supply chain model is suggested. The main driver of this supply chain model is the competitive advantage. It has the capability and capacity to sustain unplanned and unpredictable demand in excess of a customer's forecast and at reduced lead times. The agile supply chain is sensitive to real market demand. This model is directly plugged into the customer base so is demand driven rather than forecast driven.

The real-time technology flow between the agile supply chain and its suppliers makes it nearly a virtual supply chain. **Electronic data interchange (EDI)** and the rapid development of the Internet allow buyers and suppliers to share real-time information. High levels of collaboration allow both partners to act on real demand rather than an elaborate series of information translation actions that are subject to data errors and inconsistencies. Redefinition of the relationships between organizations by sharing risks and cost are equitably reinforced and rewarded.

Process integration is undergirded by shared information and system commonality. Definitions of core competencies are sharply delineated as non-competence products and services are outsourced. Partnering with third-party logistic providers

ELECTRONIC DATA INTERCHANGE Computer-to-computer communications exchanging business documents in a standardized format (purchase orders, invoices, advanced ship notices).

is a good example of a non-competent outsourced service. Trust and greater reliance on the supply base is the common thread that makes this model the most suitable to deal with the new realities of global operations.

The agile supply chain is also designed to meet ever-increasing customer demand, especially those who live in disorderly political, geopolitical, and economic environments. Their demand for product flexibility, along with increasingly reduced lead-time demands, are no different from consumers who reside in more traditional worldwide consuming regions. They want a high quality at a low price.

The global supply chain has evolved into a global linkage of suppliers. Companies are no longer stand-alone entities. They have redefined themselves as a global supply chain that uses the supply chain network as a competitive advantage. The supply chain converts into the demand chain. All actions, movements, and product manufacturing is in response to known demand.

The traditional competitive advantage referred to one company competing against another. Today, it is the competition between supply chains that defines the true nature of a competitive advantage.

CASE STUDY

In January 2015, Target announced that it was abandoning its Canadian operations after opening 124 stores in 2013. Target blamed the shuttering of 133 stores on deeply flawed supply chain and logistics infrastructures.

In contrast, Nordstrom's Canadian entry took a different approach, and the company saw far different results. Compared to Target's approach, Nordstrom's Canadian migration was very successful.

Although both retailers enjoyed a legacy of excellence throughout their operational history, the results of their actions turned out considerably different. Compare and contrast the approaches of both enterprises and the consequences of their actions.

WHAT ARE THE DIFFERENT FUNCTIONAL AREAS WITHIN THE LOGISTICS FUNCTION?

A number of functional areas within the international logistics field are in different stages of development. Logistics functional areas exist to increase global connectivity, and massive investments in their development are key to establishing an ongoing competitiveness of emerging economies.

A review of their state of maturity and significance of their presence might be helpful. These functional areas consist of the following:

- Over the road (OTR) and less than truckload (LTL)
- Ocean freight
- Inland waterways
- Railroad
- Pipeline
- Digital
- Warehousing

Each one contributes to the delivery of goods and services. They are essential parts of a structure that sustains the material flow from manufacturer to consumer. Each contains components of efficiencies; however, they also suffer from a range of ineffectiveness. Their growth or lack thereof is tied to a number reasons.

Over the Road (OTR)

The backbone of the logistics infrastructure is the road network connecting every locale and region of the country to e-commerce and export outlets. Contrasting levels of maturity restrict this prevalent mode of transport that suppliers use to get their products to the market. Roads indirectly contribute to a country's economic development. Their layout and reach are essential.

Two of the world's rising e-commerce and export powers are China and India. Vast quantities of goods are transported daily via OTR to intermodal connecting points. The inefficient functions of these connecting points are directly influenced by underdeveloped OTR infrastructures.

In China, for example, there is a marked difference between highways serving the big coastal cities and the rural roads. Although big city highways are very good, the rural roads are small, narrow, and in very poor condition. This contributes to the costly and cumbersome flow of goods as they make their way through a number of warehouses to the ports for export.

Despite the fact that China has made enormous strides in improving their road infrastructure in the last 15 years, the focus has largely been on exports. With the exponential rise in e-commerce driven by consumption at home, little attention has been given to investing in a means of transport that is critical to e-commerce transactions.

China's export levels are eroding, and e-commerce customers have little tolerance of logistics bottlenecks because it has the potential to choke off this growth sector. Unlike industrial customers, e-commerce customers demand higher levels of customer service at low prices.

Most warehouse facilities are out of date and experience serious automation and robotic shortcomings. Although labor is inexpensive, the manual handling impacts the flow of goods. Disposition of freight to its next destination is inefficient and costly. In-transit goods are transferred as many as a dozen times from truck to truck in their cross-country passage. Cargo hubs that serve as links to railroads are almost non-existent. Freight trucks are run-down, old, and overloaded, losing significant percentages of their load either through damage or outright falling off the truck when heading to the terminus. Many of them are unable to arrange for return cargo on more than a third of their passage.

Trucking operations are fragmented. There are over 700,000 trucking companies in place, the majority of them one-man outfits. Fierce competition on price barely makes the trucks profitable. As a result, there are no means to modernize their trucking fleets, and this, in turn, keeps them from attaining economies of scale.

Local protectionism and corruption present severe hurdles to the operators. Besides scant access to equipment, local operators are burdened with an imposition of taxes and regulations, requiring special licenses to operate. Excessive road tolls and regulations preventing trucks from entering urban areas compels the trucks to offload their freight onto smaller vehicles, adding another unnecessary handoff.

Opportunities for international firms like FedEx and UPS are severely restricted due to limited licensing for domestic delivery. Foreign logistics operations are weighed down by high costs, making it difficult to compete against competitors.

The road infrastructure in India is far less developed than China. India is decades behind China in regards to bringing their road infrastructure up-to-date. Quick and efficient transport of goods from inland facilities to India's warehouses and ports is far below China. India's roads are typically one or two lanes. There are no lane dividers, and India's drivers see any line dividing a street as "reference only." India's freight trucks are designed to navigate their way through slow traffic and, as a result, are underpowered. These underpowered trucks are restricted in their speed when they drive on any good road or moderate sized highway. Generally, top speeds do not exceed 30 km/hr (15 mph). With India's vast rural population, access to all weather roads is virtually non-existent during the monsoon season.

India's economic struggles and diminished gross domestic growth (GDP) created decades of underinvestment in India's road infrastructure. As a result, transportation of goods takes an inordinate amount of time. Roads are not expanding and are unable to keep pace with logistics demands. Transportation providers face endless road congestion, driving costs higher.

Existing highways are not designed to handle the pressure created by large vehicles. India's national highways amount to only 1.6% of the total Indian network. They are burdened with 40% of road-based traffic. This makes it the most critical segment of the road sector.

A McKinsey study concludes that transportation costs by road in India are 30% higher than in the United States. Overloaded trucks and oversized cargoes contend with heavy congestion and move without any sort of regulation. Multiple checkpoints, heavy tolls, vehicle inspections, and imposition of special tax collection all delay the transit of goods.

Government efforts at bringing the road infrastructure to acceptable functional levels have come up short due to corruption and heavy bureaucracy. Private sector participation is being encouraged with limited success, and this is partly due to the worldwide economic slowdown.

The tasks ahead are enormous because the budget to merely maintain the road infrastructure is immense. This expenditure excludes any monies set aside for new development.

Less Than Truckload (LTL)

A subcategory of OTR is less-than-truckload (LTL) shipping. LTL gives shippers added flexibility due to its relatively low cost. A LTL carrier enables the movement of goods from many different customers all on one truck. A number of vehicles collect freight from a local or regional area on a daily basis. The freight is then offloaded and consolidated at a central terminal. Each product shipment is weighed and rated, allowing generation of customer invoices. Individual shipments are then loaded onto various outbound transports that contain goods from other customers departing to the same geographic area. The outbound transports deliver their load to regional terminals where the goods are offloaded. The shipments are sorted and placed on local delivery vehicles that then deliver the goods to their final destinations.

The main advantage of using a LTL shipping method is cost. Compared to parcel carriers, the cost of shipping a product using the LTL shipping method is significantly lower. LTL carriers compete with small parcel carriers who limit acceptance of shipments between 70 and 100 pounds. Due to economies of scale, the LTL carriers are able to offer lower rates per pound than parcel carriers.

Ocean Freight

The capability of efficiently transporting goods via ocean freight has been solely achievable with development of port capacity that is supported by sustained investments in maritime infrastructure.

China and East Asia have been experiencing an on-going harbor construction boom for the past 15 to 20 years. Chinese ports present a formidable competitive challenge to other non-China Asia seaports. In response, the port of Busan in South Korea, the fifth largest port in the world in terms of tonnage, doubled its capacity in 2011. As China develops the port of Shanghai, South Korea differentiates itself by highlighting their superior efficiency and competitive pricing.

Seaports are a country's lifeline. The objective of port investment is to lower transportation costs. Carriers are building ever-larger container ships to lower their costs. To accommodate these large ships, global terminal expansion is occurring at an accelerated pace.

There are basically three long-distance ocean routes from Asia: the North America Pacific Coast route, the North America East Coast route, and the European route. Increasingly, larger vessels sail these routes, taking maximum advantage of economies of scale. Freight rates are continuously decreasing because these three routes occupy significant import and substantial export tons of container departures and arrivals.

Ocean freight services remains one of the most requested, cost efficient, and most economical means to overcome long distances. Sea transports call on harbors whose offloading efficiencies are supported by the best of infrastructures. It permits the greatest amount flexibility by shipping the greatest quantity of materials to somewhere with a large storage capacity.

In terms of effectiveness, ocean vessel transport is the most efficient mode of transport. For example, on a single voyage a container ship is capable of transporting 2000 to 11,000 containers. Compared to railroad transport, many miles of rail cars and hundreds of trucks would be required to fit all the goods on one large container ship.

Sea traffic connects countries, markets, businesses, and consumers, permitting them to buy goods at unprecedented scales. Today, the ocean transport industry represents roughly one-third of the total value of worldwide trade. From a global enterprise perspective, the industry creates millions of jobs and makes significant contributions to global gross domestic product (GDP). Because ocean transport is vital to global economic prosperity, it contributes to international stability and security.

Inland Waterways

The practicability of the use of inland waterway transport (IWT) varies from country to country. The discipline of logistics concerns itself with the performance or price-quality ratio of each transport mode. Because cost, speed, and reliability are critical factors, each transport mode's competitive position is determined by the price-quality ratio metric.

Inland waterway transport has reached a mature competitive stature in Europe, with Belgium, Finland, France, Germany, the Netherlands, and Poland having the largest waterway networks. These waterway networks represent 81% of the total EU waterways.

The governments of China, India, and Brazil have fundamentally different strategic visions regarding IWT. Each country is at a different stage of developing their IWT strategy. All three nations recognize the need for a clear policy; however, developmental motivations differ in each country.

China alone has seen significant annual increases of IWT tonnage, ranging from 9% to 12%. Growth in India has been less than 1% in recent times, while Brazil's expected growth is projected to increase from 13% in 2005 to 29% in 2025.

China has a clear policy to stimulate IWT and has an objective to link rail and seaports. The government sees IWT as a clear alternative to increasing overcrowded and congested roads. The main commodities transported today by IWT are building materials, (34%), metals and ores (19%), and coal and coke (17%). The volume displacement of these commodities is enormous, and road transport is simply not feasible. River barges are perfectly suited for the transport of these materials.

The Chinese inland waterway sector has experienced an enormous increase in volumes of these commodities, especially on their two main river systems. The Yangtze and Pearl rivers, China's two main rivers, are benefitting from upgrades of existing ports, as well as construction of new ports.

Brazil's approach is much different than China's approach. Despite the country's extended system of inland waterways, ITW is primarily limited to agricultural products. Although the government recognizes that ITW development is essential to global competitiveness, its use of the waterways is limited commercially. This is largely due to an oversight in the recognition of the need to build ship locks. Priority has been given to the construction of hydroelectric dams without integrating ship locks, and this holds back the development of inland shipping. Although IWT is recognized as a promising mode for freight transport, Brazil is considering the removal of environmental barriers and bringing its environmental policies more into balance to accommodate inland waterway development.

India, no different than Brazil and China, is experiencing growing freight transport volumes. The Inland Waterways Authority of India (IWAI) is actively promoting policies that will stimulate investments into IWT on the Ganges and Brahmaputra. These efforts are being generally ignored by the private sector as demonstrated by the lack of interest from shippers. This comes as no surprise because the central government has neglected the inland waterway system for many years. The necessary funds for any sort of improvement of the waterways were simply not available. India has not promoted the economic viability of IWT.

The private sector has been reluctant to invest or participate in government efforts to promote the waterway sector because of global economic uncertainties. Confidence in the Indian government is low because of their long record of inaction.

Railroads: Dry Ports

The level of intraregional exports and imports are on the increase in Asia. In the early stages of transport development, not much thought was given to the future integration of roads and railroads. Multimodal and intermodal transport operates through several modes of transport to deliver goods from origin to destination.

There are three attributes that make development of intermodalism possible: transport links, transport node, and providing competent transport services. One of the most essential of these transport nodes are railway networks. In Asia, there are twelve landlocked countries that depend on efficient rail transport.

Today, extensive investments are taking place in the development of road and rail systems. One area that has undergone little development is inland dry port terminals (IDPT), and these terminals are critical for efficient rail transport. An IDPT is an intermodal facility that connects remote regions of a country to seaports via rail. IDPT's provide for the temporary storage and control of freight containers, general bulk cargoes that crisscross the IDPT by any mode of transport, including railways, roads, airports, and inland waterways. In addition, they provide custom services, import and export cargo inspection, warehousing, container parking, repair facilities, quarantine measures, and customs documentation services. The link to railway operations makes the IDPT a fully integrative part of the entire logistics chain.

Before the Asian inland dry ports become fully operative, major upgrades are required. Although China and India have extensive railway networks, much work needs to be done to bring these railway systems into a competitive state.

This is especially true of the landlocked countries because rail is considered the best mode of transport between seaports and dry ports. Quality is the biggest difficulty affecting railroad operations. Quality and service improvements like punctuality must be achieved to attract greater shares of freight. A complex set of interrelated parameters must occur to ensure efficient and cost effective rail transport.

Asia's landlocked countries are beset by a number of difficulties as their goods make their way to a neighboring country's seaport. These countries often have to contend with physical limitations as they transport their freight. For example, the number of railroad cars of incoming trains often exceeds the length of available track for offloading. As a result, the train has to be de-coupled over two or more tracks as freight is transshipped. Often, the number of incoming trains exceeds the number of transshipment tracks. This means that after unloading, the train has to be moved to another parking track to make room for other incoming trains. In the meantime, the unloaded freight is moved onto trucks or unprotected storage spaces. From there, they await customs inspections and are then assigned further transshipment. The average wait time for freight to cross a border is 2 to 3 days.

One other issue contributing to cost and freight delays is the lack of standardization of railroad track gauge. A railroad track gauge is the width of the inside faces of the running rails. Approximately 60% of the world's railway tracks are of the standard size adopted from the British. This leaves 40% with a wide variation of railway gauges that are non-standard. In some instances, deviation from the standard was caused by deliberate political policies. Many nations based their construction of track width on the "defensive use of gauge" to prevent unwanted interference from neighboring powers. Another reason for going off the standard was that most major railroads were built by private companies and people who paid no attention to gauging.

This is the case in many Asian countries. Different gauges at border crossings prevent the trains from passing through. The freight has to be transferred across borders in separate operations from one railroad car with one gauge to another of a different gauge. Manual labor and lack of proper offloading equipment contribute to further slowing of the transport process. Several countries operate railroads on two or more different track gauges. Pakistan operates on three while India operates on four.

Dry ports are an important element of the railway infrastructure. They facilitate international trade and are strategic inland way stations that help in intermodal freight movements from a country's remote regions. This enables transportation to and from seaports by rail with roads used for collection and distribution.

Bonded Warehousing

A warehouse is not simply a place to store goods; this is only one function that warehousing offers. Among other things, warehousing provides a means to reduce cycle times, lower inventory levels, and most importantly in times of uncertain demand, improve customer service. Warehousing provides a means of product availability to ensure that the product is there at the right place and at the right time. A warehouse adds value through order consolidation, assembly services, product mixing, and **cross docking**. They provide economies of scale through central location and storage capacity.

The same holds true of bonded warehousing. These types of warehouses are secure buildings or areas that accommodate and store dutiable products. As goods enter the warehouse, the stocking facility's owner incurs a liability as the goods stored are put under a warehouse bond. The purpose of this type of warehouse is to provide supervision, management, and security prior to payment of duty. When the goods are removed, duty becomes payable. Bonded warehouse is capable of giving different kinds of value. Some of the permitted activities include the following:

- Sorting
- Remarking
- Cleaning
- Repacking
- Relabeling
- Assembly
- Inventory management

These types of warehouses are made available to traders as their goods are transiting through a seaport for export. Most are administered by private enterprises that are authorized by local customs authorities. They are subject to regular inspections and scrutiny to ensure that no material bleeds out of the facility without payment of customs duties.

Goods that are imported and stored in bonded warehouses are exempted from import and export duties, provided that they are used in the manufacturing and assembly of export goods and purposes only.

Bonded warehouses have additional benefits associated with their use. Storage can be indeterminate. An importer can choose to delay the release of the goods until demand increases. This contributes to cash management because an increase in demand is usually associated with increased revenues. A bonded warehouse also provides security, especially if the goods are subject to restrictions. The importer or exporter is given time to store restricted items until such time as they can be moved somewhere else or special approval to import or export the goods out of the country is given.

Pipeline

Pipelines are the most convenient and efficient way to transport enormous volumes of liquids over long distances, regardless of terrain. Pipelines may run above ground or below the surface. They also have the option of being located under water. They are a limited mode of transport in that they are unidirectional. Once a pipeline is laid, it is not flexible because it can only be used for limited fixed points. The capacity of the pipeline cannot be increased beyond its capacity design.

The major commodity moved along a pipeline is oil. Other commodities include natural gas and chemicals. Chemicals such as anhydrous ammonia (fertilizer), propylene (industrial detergents), and ethylene (antifreeze) are common chemicals sent through the pipeline to a destination. Pipelines also transport solids in the form of slurry. For example, coal is broken up and suspended in a liquid and transported as slurry. When the slurry reaches its destination, the liquids are removed, leaving the solid coal. Slurry as a means of transport is mostly conveyed to utility companies that generate electricity.

On average, a pipeline transports three million barrels of oil every day. This is the equivalent of 15,000 oil tanker trucks or 4,200 rail cars. Pipelines are the most cost-effective form of transportation. They consume significantly less energy than truck or rail operations.

Despite environmental concerns, pipelines are a safe mode of transport. Although there have been incidents of pipeline spillage, the industry has made remarkable improvements in safety during the last 15 years. Regular inspections that detect corrosion, flawed pipe material, and X-ray of pipe seam welds are routine. Inline inspection technology has made significant gains in recent times. The technology is capable of detecting any sort of spillage immediately after a breach of the pipeline has occurred. Pipeline operators are also raising awareness levels of pipeline vulnerabilities by educating third party excavators who might accidentally damage the pipeline.

Digital Logistics

Society has entered into a new era in logistic operations and strategy. The communications revolution, driven by the ascendency of the Internet, fundamentally changed the way companies shape logistic strategies, processes, and systems. Companies today are embracing new paradigms that have reduced operating costs by millions, accomplished superior supply chain integration, and enriched market power through customer-focused order fulfillment strategies.

Today, more and more companies are promoting and amplifying the importance of logistics to the highest levels of corporate strategy. The new wave in logistic practices focuses on an enterprise's ability to respond to dynamic demand-driven supply chains, thereby enhancing the **key performance indicators (KPI)** of cost reduction, increased profitability, and growth.

In previous eras, logistics practices were tactical and short sighted. Logistics was considered an afterthought and was banished to the backwater of the enterprise. Contemporary logistics strategy is far-reaching and complementary to global enterprise strategies. The use of new technologies, such as gaining visibility from operations planning and execution to increasing customer satisfaction and retention by means of real-time performance monitoring and management, gives millions of dollars of value. A new generation of Web-based applications that enable collaboration through software development provides visibility across the entire enterprise and the global supply chain. These new applications are closely integrated with warehouse and transportation systems, and they are leading to new order fulfillment process models.

Companies failing to adopt the new logistics' order find themselves at a severe disadvantage that is becoming exceedingly hard to overcome. An example of a company falling short is cosmetics firm Avon's failed implementation of a new management order system. Part of the problem was that the multi-year software project was difficult to implement because of "user friendly" issues. The main reason why the project was abandoned was because Avon's business model is based on direct

KEY PERFORMANCE INDICATOR (KPI) A measurable value indicating a company's effectiveness in achieving its business objectives.

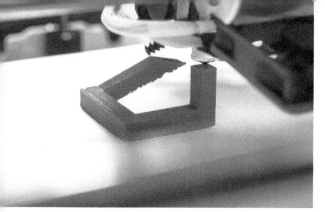

sales. Implementation of the new order management system turned out to be a misalignment of sales strategies. Avon's leadership misjudged the compatibility of the software with an indirect and independent sales force that was not direct employees of the company. The company was forced to write down a loss of between $100 million and $125 million.

Interaction and cooperation in the processing of enormous amounts of data with new logistics function prototypes will have a significant impact on future logistic functions. Data streams flowing from the integrated supply chain to the logistics providers will overcome logistics market fragmentation and permit the establishment of global logistics super grids.

Super grid logistics will produce the next generation of logistics providers. Their primary focus will be on the rapid synchronization of global supply chain networks that integrate groups of production companies and logistics providers. Utilization of hyper collections of data increases transparency, augments resource consumption, raises the level of process quality and performance, and makes anticipatory logistics a reality. Fueled by large data based predictive algorithms, anticipatory logistics assist logistic providers in considerably increasing process efficiency by accelerating delivery time and boosting network utilization capacity.

The emergence of three-dimensional (3-D) printing is adding a tier of complexity to the logistics industry. New flows of manufactured material and products produced by the 3-D printing process require that logistics blend processes that facilitate smooth product flow. Fabrication of 3-D products will open up new opportunities for logistic providers to grow their value chains through the assimilation of 3-D production capabilities to their end-to-end logistic services.

Additive manufacturing (AM) or 3-D printing is the process of adding layers of material to make three-dimensional solid objects. The 3-D printers in use today are capable of producing complex components, fully functional tools, and large scale products, and the printers are making these goods with increased precision and improved resolution while wasting less material.

With the emergence of this technology, new industries will appear. Some firms will supplant entire traditional manufacturing with AM. Others will replace selected product components. Whatever the case, distribution and warehousing will undergo profound changes as companies fabricate, outsource, and relocate near airports or hubs instead of storing their products in warehouses. It is conceivable that logistics providers will inaugurate their own hubs, warehouses, and fulfillment centers by introducing and distributing 3D models. This creates a new competitive segment in the industry.

CASE STUDY

Even the most mature and sophisticated logistics infrastructures can fall short in terms of responsiveness. In the wake of Hurricane Katrina in 2005, vast stretches of the Gulf coast were without basic survival necessities. The Federal Emergency Management Administration (FEMA) responded poorly when bringing supplies to the victims of the storm. Aside from politics, what logistics issues contributed to FEMA's mediocre response?

Benefits accrued to the logistics providers include participation in new industries, requiring reorganization of complex fragmented supply chains for raw materials and end products. They will be in the forefront of **digital warehousing** and 3D fabrication and will be able to transform into a trusted service provider for secure data hosting and exchange (online capability, aftermarket capability in providing spare parts).

A large percentage of goods previously outsourced to China and other Asian nations, for example, would revert to their manufacturing origins. This "near-sourcing" of products to North America and Europe reduces air cargo volumes and shipping costs. As 3-D printing technology and capabilities expand, mass customization becomes much less expensive, and the need to keep large inventories is no longer necessary, thereby lowering inventory liabilities.

The profile of future logistics companies will resemble the 4PLs. Business competencies will center on software development, delivery services, relationship management, intellectual knowhow, and contract management.

Today, approximately 30% of finished products contain 3-D components. By 2016, this number is expected to rise to 50%, and by 2020, 3D content levels will be at 80%.

Additive manufacturing will have the biggest impact on global supply chains and logistics. The rapid expansion of globalization has been principally driven by low labor costs. This generated remarkable growth in low cost country freight transport to North America and Europe. This balance between labor and transportation will begin to regress as a new wave of globalization takes hold. The new global business model will be undergirded by local 3-D production whose core competency will be speed, quality, and customization. This will lead to decreased shipping volumes between the low cost countries and the wealthy countries.

The world's largest logistics enterprises have already taken notice of this trend. In response to their vulnerabilities, they are actively developing new business models to deal with new types of organizations that will leapfrog them.

DIGITAL WAREHOUSE A storage architecture designed to secure and hold massive amounts of data extracted from transaction systems, operational data stores, and external sources.

DISCUSSION QUESTIONS

1. What does a world-class supply chain look like?

2. Why do people, processes, and infrastructure drive global supply chain capabilities?

3. What are the differences between direct and indirect logistics?

4. Why is global visibility throughout the supply chain critical to an enterprises' transportation management strategy?

SUMMARY

Global economic changes and shifts in the patterns of trade will have monumental impacts on global supply chains. Society is in the midst of growth patterns that are changing the logistics landscape. For a number of years, the logistics industry has been driven by exports from Asia to North America and from Asia to Europe. Soon, this will no longer be the case because trade will come from other places. The emergence of global megacities will power unprecedented economic and infrastructure changes. The presence of a full-bodied infrastructure will be the main determining factor for growth.

Meeting consumer demands from multiple locations with multiple modes of transport at all times involves an agile supply chain that easily adjusts to unpredictable changes and conditions. Having visibility of the entire supply chain is critical and achieves true demand-driven planning processes that can bring efficient responses to changeability in sourcing, supply, capacity, and demand.

REFERENCES

Ballis, A., & Golias, J. (2002). *Comparative evaluation of existing and innovate railroad freight transport terminals. Transportation research part A: Policy and practice*. Retrieved from http://www.worldtransitresearch.info/research/2100/

Banham, R. (n.d.). *Political risk and the supply chain*. Retrieved from http://www.rmmagazine.com/2014/06/01/political-risk-and-the-supply-chain/

Bubner, N., Bubner, N., Helbig, R., & Jeske, M. (2014). *Logistics trend radar*. Retrieved from http://www.dhl.com/content/dam/downloads/g0/about_us/logistics_insights/DHL_Logistics-TrendRadar_2014.pdf

Canadian Energy Pipeline Association. (2015). *Why pipelines are needed*. Retrieved from http://www.cepa.com/about-pipelines/why-pipelines

Chand, S. (2015). *Warehousing: Function, benefits and types of warehousing*. Retrieved from http://www.yourarticlelibrary.com/marketing/marketing-management/warehousing-function-benefits-and-types-of-warehousing/27952/

Chopra, S., & Sodhi, M. (2004). *Managing risk to avoid supply-chain breakdown*. Retrieved from http://sloanreview.mit.edu/article/managing-risk-to-avoid-supplychain-breakdown/

Fitzgerald, D. (2013). *Avon to halt rollout of new order management system*. Retrieved from http://www.wsj.com/articles/SB10001424052702303932504579251941619018078

Gershenhorn, A. (2004). *The making of a successful supply chain*. Retrieved from http://search.proquest.com.proxy.cecybrary.com/abicomplete/docview/228233312/33C9A3FA6B3E4A9APQ/1?accountid=26967

Ghegan, D. (2014). *Advantages of a bonded warehouse*. Retrieved from http://www.bondedservice.com/2014/07/advantages-bonded-warehouse/

Hanaoka, S., & Regmi, M. (2011). *Promoting international freight transport through the development of dry ports in Asia: An environmental perspective*. Retrieved from http://www.sciencedirect.com/science/article/pii/S0386111211000148

Holland, J. (2005). *Calculating risks in the Chinese logistics market*. Retrieved from http://search.proquest.com.proxy.cecybrary.com/docview/228322060?accountid=26967

iContainers. (2014). *5 benefits of ocean freight*. Retrieved from http://www.icontainers.com/us/2014/10/24/5-benefits-ocean-freight/

Khalid, N. (2006). *China's port development and shipping competition in East Asia*. Retrieved from http://www.japanfocus.org/-Nazery-Khalid/1649/article.pdf

Lamberti, M., Costello, M., & Getz, K. (2012). *Global supply chain management*. Retrieved from http://search.proquest.com/docview/1081340862?accountid=26967

Lee, H. (2004) *The triple-a supply chain*. Retrieved from https://hbr.org/2004/10/the-triple-a-supply-chain

Lohrey, J. (2015). *The importance of warehousing in a logistics system*. Retrieved from http://smallbusiness.chron.com/importance-warehousing-logistics-system-74825.html

Lummus, R., Melnyk, S., Vokurka, R., Burns, L., & Sandor, J. (2007). *Getting ready for tomorrow's supply chain*. Retrieved from http://search.proquest.com/docview/221200125?accountid=26967

MacDonald, A. (2006). *The difference between managing a global vs. domestic supply chain is a matter of degree*. Retrieved from http://connection.ebscohost.com/c/articles/23587854/difference-between-managing-global-vs-domestic-supply-chain-matter-degree

Manners-Bell, J., & Lyon K. (2014). *The implications of 3D Printing for the global logistics industry*. Retrieved from http://www.supplychain247.com/article/the_implications_of_3d_printing_for_the_global_logistics_industry

Mason, S., Ribera, M., Farris, J., & Kirk, R. (n.d.). Retrieved from http://citeseerx.ist.psu.edu/viewdoc/download?doi=10.1.1.19.3516&rep=rep1&type=pdf

Mizutani, M., Tsuchiya, K., Takuma, F., & Ohashi, T. (2005). *Estimation of the economic benefits of port development on international maritime market by partial equilibrium model and scge model*. Retrieved from http://www.easts.info/on-line/journal_06/892.pdf

Murray, M. (n.d.). *Less than truckload (LTL)*. Retrieved from http://logistics.about.com/od/supplychainmodels/a/LTL_Carriers.htm

Nabben, H. (2014). *12 trends that are shaping the future of logistics*. Retrieved from http://blog.damco.com/2014/07/14/12-trends-that-are-shaping-the-future-of-logistics/

Pearson, M. (2012). *The dynamic supply chain*. Retrieved from http://www.industryweek.com/articles/the_dynamic_supply_chain_26771.aspx

Perez, H. D. (2013). *Supply chain strategies: Which one hits the mark?* Retrieved from http://www.supplychainquarterly.com/print/20130306-supply-chain-strategies-which-one-hits-the-mark/

RedPrairie. (2002). *The new era of digital logistics*. Retrieved from http://www.idii.com/wp/rpNewEraDigitalLogistics.pdf

Reichhart, A., & Holweg, M. (2007). *Creating the customer-responsive supply chain: A reconciliation of concepts*. Retrieved from http://search.proquest.com.proxy.cecybrary.com/abicomplete/publication/publications_36644?accountid=26967

Reuters. (2014). *China to establish $40 billion Silk Road infrastructure fund*. Retrieved from http://www.reuters.com/article/2014/11/08/us-china-diplomacy-idUSKBN0IS0BQ20141108

Runckel, C. (n.d.). *Infrastructure India: A long road ahead*. Retrieved from http://www.business-in-asia.com/asia/infrastructure_india.html#transport

Rutkowski, R. (2015). *Transportation and logistics*. Retrieved from http://www.accenture.com/Microsites/supplywatch/articles/archive/issue1/Pages/transportation-and-logistics.aspx

Storey, J., Emberson, C., Godsell, J., & Harrison, A. (2006). *Supply chain management: Theory, practice and future challenges*. Retrieved from http://search.proquest.com.proxy.cecybrary.com/abicomplete/docview/232328680/88E281B5A7214C0BPQ/1?accountid=26967

Supply Chain Digest. (2010). *Supply chain news: The five challenges of today's global supply chains*. Retrieved from http://www.scdigest.com/ASSETS/ON_TARGET/10-08-12-3.php

Takach, J. (2010). *Five priorities for supply chain success*. Retrieved from http://search.proquest.com.proxy.cecybrary.com/abicomplete/docview/903552548/7789BB25B9554DEFPQ/1?accountid=26967

The Economist. (2014). *The flow of things*. Retrieved from http://www.economist.com/news/china/21606899-export-superpower-china-suffers-surprisingly-inefficient-logistics-flow-things

Vermont Agency of Commerce and Community Development. (n.d.). *About bonded warehouses*. Retrieved from http://accd.vermont.gov/sites/accd/files/Documents/business/vgtp/AboutCustomsBondedWarehouses.pdf

World Bank. (2015). *Good practices in the inland waterways sector: Project PLATINA*. Retrieved from http://www.ppiaf.org/freighttoolkit/case-study/good-practices-inland-waterways-sector-project-platina

World Bank. (2015). *Increasing the use of inland waterways in the modal share – in China, India and Brazil*. Retrieved from http://www.ppiaf.org/freighttoolkit/case-study/increasing-use-inland-waterways-modal-share-%E2%80%93-china-india-brazil

World Bank. (2015). *Intermodal freight systems*. Retrieved from http://www.ppiaf.org/freighttoolkit/knowledge-map/road/intermodal-freight-systems

World Bank. (2015). *National plan for logistics and transport in Brazil*. Retrieved from http://www.ppiaf.org/freighttoolkit/case-study/national-plan-logistics-transport-brazil

World Shipping Council. (2015). *Benefits of liner shipping*. Retrieved from http://www.worldshipping.org/benefits-of-liner-shipping

Zigiaris, S. (2000). *Supply chain management*. Retrieved from www.adi.pt/docs/innoregio_supp_management.pdf

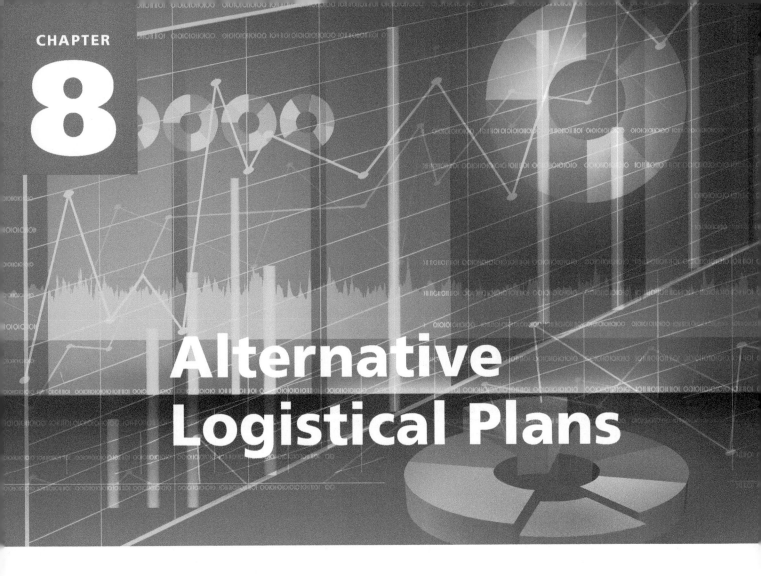

CHAPTER 8

Alternative Logistical Plans

QUALITATIVE AND QUANTITATIVE ASSESSMENT FUNDAMENTALS

Introduction

Chapter 8 will provide an overview of alternative logistical plans; the chapter has a focus on qualitative and quantitative assessment fundamentals that support supply chain management decision making. The decisions impact facilities, sourcing, pricing, inventory, transportation, distribution, order fulfillment, information systems, and sustainment. The chapter is organized to three sections.

Section 1

Logistical plans and decision making. Logistical planning and supply chain management decision making will be discussed. Qualitative and quantitative analysis along with the theory of constraints will be reviewed to provide an overview of key fundamentals that support alternative logistical plans.

Section 2

Logistical analysis and methodology. Fundamental approaches to determine a proper course of action with logistical plans will be presented using qualitative and quantitative data. Four analytical methodology examples will provide a basis for effective assessment of alternative logistical plans. The four methodologies are as follows:

- **Comparative analysis:** Measures two or more comparable alternatives
- **Cost–benefit analysis:** Quantifies costs and benefits
- **Gap analysis:** Identifies the current and desired state
- **Benchmarking analysis:** Evaluates company performance

Section 3: Alternative logistical plan cost centers. Cost center examples will be presented to provide alternate logistics planning requirements to support decision making based on timely, relevant, and actionable planning data. The following cost center examples will focus on operational cost savings and key logistical drivers that impact supply chain management efficiency and responsiveness:

- **Facilities:** Physical location of supply chain operations
- **Sourcing:** Procurement of materials and services
- **Pricing:** Amount established to buy and or sell goods and services
- **Inventory:** Receipt, storage, and issue of stock
- **Transportation:** Movement of physical goods
- **Distribution:** Warehouse and network operations for storage and shipping
- **Order fulfillment:** Right product, right price, right quantity, and right place
- **Information systems:** Automated data, reporting, and analysis
- **Sustainment:** Company commitment to business and community needs

LOGISTIC PLANNING AND DECISION MAKING
Planning

PLANNING Requires a broad range of skills and the understanding of resource management.

Planning requires a broad range of skills. What is central to logistical planning skills is the understanding of resource management. Identifying the long-, short-, and near-term planning requirements and matching efficiency, cost, and quality of operational capacity helps to support logistical planning and implementation.

The keys for a planning team is to involve the implementation team early in the plan process. An understanding of basic planning skills will have a major impact on successful logistics planning. The ideal planning fundamental is to "keep it simple" and "plan the work and work the plan"

1. List five factors of basic planning.

2. Describe four types of analytical methodologies for decision making.

3. Define nine major logistical functions impacting supply chain management.

KEY TERMS

- benchmarking (p. 152)
- certainty (p. 146)
- comparative analysis (p. 149)
- decision theory (p. 144)
- forecasting (p. 146)
- gap analysis (p. 151)
- learning curve (p. 148)
- linear analysis (p. 148)
- planning (p. 143)
- queuing (p. 148)
- theory of constraint (p. 144)
- time series (p. 147)
- trend analysis (p. 147)
- uncertainty (p. 146)

for all involved; but there is some exceptions for the tax accountants and managerial finance analysts who can crunch the numbers for financial reporting and senior comp controllers. Logistics planning involves front office corporate strategic goals, middle management operational objectives, and shop floor tactical action plans.

The following are basic planning factors:
- Define plan requirements and scope
- Identify plan capacity
- List plan goals, objectives and action plans
- Establish long-, short-, and near-term scheduling
- Build planning and implementation team

Decision Making

The best supply chain logistics solution in a decision-making action should be based on best value where the lowest cost is not the deciding factor. Having a best value policy with a sustained decision-making process to analyze the environmental, social, and economic impact of a major or minor decision will increase supply chain logistic performance. Best value places an emphasis on evaluating factors in addition to the price of an item or acquisition cost for equipment, facilities, or systems. Best value is also a process used in competitive negotiated contracting to select an offer that is advantageous to the company. The process includes evaluation and comparative factors in addition to price and cost. To make a best value decision, a company should ensure that the decision has a rational basis that is consistent with stated evaluation criteria and that it takes into consideration whether or not key benefits are worth a price premium.

The following best value procurement guidelines support a supply chain logistic decision-making approach:
- Evaluate and compare factors against evaluation criteria.
- Price and cost is an evaluation factor.
- Supplier past performance is an evaluation factor.
- Contract solicitation will be a best value decision.
- Relevant supplier information will only be used to evaluate proposals.
- Ensure consistency with procurement objectives and processes.

Decision Theory

Decision theory is a systematic approach to conditions of uncertainty by designing a decision matrix chart of rows, columns, and entries and then applying moving averages, exponential smoothing, and regression statistical methods. Part of decision theory is the role of expected value of each action and picking the best one. Expected value provides the rational means for selecting the best course of action and is defined as the weighted means using the probabilities as weights.

Theory of Constraints

The **theory of constraint** is based on the premise that every system has one or more limiting factors that prevents it from attaining a specified goal. This can be applied to supply chain logistics decision making in that there can be a positive outcome with an alternative course of action plan; however, keep in mind the need to identify any and all possible constraints from a new course of action. The theory of constraints focuses on identification of the constraint or bottleneck and developing a process to lessen the impact.

For example, consider the following example. A northeast shipper signs a new lucrative distribution contract for a customer demand of 40,000 finished units a day but can only ship 20,000 finished goods a day due to the size of the current private truck fleet. This constraint, or bottleneck, can be limited by partnering with a third party logistics provider (3PL) who can ship the other 20,000 finished goods a day.

Qualitative Analysis

To define a qualitative approach is to understand the data collection and analysis requirements. Qualitative research requires management openness, employee based experience, and good data taken from the shop floor to the corporate boardroom. Qualitative analysis must take into account rigid historical or traditional beliefs that can be incorrect or behind the times.

Qualitative data describes characteristics and puts pieces of data together to create a big picture or meaning but does not measure the attributes or properties. Qualitative analysis focuses on the examination of the non-measureable data collected from one or many sources. It is important to know that qualitative data can be turned into statistical data. Overall, qualitative analysis begins with specifics and then moves to the general with a conclusion to support decision making. Employee morale and supplier relationships can be examples of qualitative characteristics.

A qualitative approach can be used with a SWOT (strengths, weaknesses, opportunities and threats) analysis. SWOT is a form of gap analysis that identifies the current and desired state. The simple approach is to have document feedback from a group or team on the four key SWOT elements to establish a baseline of the current state. Strengths can be the core competencies of the business and what is being done well. Weaknesses are areas for improvement. Opportunities need to be realistic, and threats are factors that can misalign efforts. The focus is participation and the collection of bits of data to form a recommendation and how to proceed in the future.

Consider the following example. A warehouse company has a difficult time keeping junior and senior forklift operators due to the demands of sitting all day while operating the forklift. Management decides to have the forklift operators switch job roles with the warehouse clerks for 2 hours a day. This decision provides job enhancement by increasing the overall skill set of operators and clerks and gives time off the forklifts.

Quantitative Analysis

Defining a quantitative approach is understanding the data collection and analysis requirements for quantitative analysis. Quantitative research requires openness by management, objectivity, conciseness, replication, math formulas, and can have a cause and effect relationship on theory based probabilities. Quantitative data is subject to statistical formulas and defines data that is compared to qualitative data that describes other data. Quantitative analysis looks at measurable and verifiable data such pricing, operational costs, and customer demand. Quantitative analysis directly impacts supply chain logistics planning and decision making, and the common response of "show me the numbers" or "run the numbers" is the management signal to say a quantitative review is required before a preliminary or final decision can be made.

Consider the following example. A warehouse company is thinking of raising the hourly rate for junior and senior warehouse forklift drives by $3.00 dollars. There are five forklift operators working 40 hours per week, and management determines the increase to be $600 dollars ($600 = 5 drivers × 40 hours × $3).

Use of a quantitative process, called forecasting and supporting statistical methods, can identify customer demand, and this is central to establishing a supply chain logistics plan where inbound sourcing from suppliers matches outbound demand from customers for goods or services. Below are quantitative methods for decision making that will impact logistical supply chain requirements.

Note: The actual calculations required for the quantitative methods identified will not be explained in detailed formulas. Detailed forecast formulas require a student to complete a business statistics course.

Quantitative Methods

These data measurement methods are used for logistic supply chain analytical decision making by managers. Actionable supply and demand data from quantitative methods support supply chain key performance indicators and metrics. Successful supply chain management companies strive to have operational efficient and responsive actions to meet changing customer demand. Forecasting customer demand provides a basis for understanding a key quantitative business function to measure and predict material supply and customer demand. Customer demand for goods and services drives service and production labor or material requirements. Forecasting, demand, and trend analysis, along with the other quantitative methods below, provide managers with measured data so that the managers can make good decisions for effective planning and for the operational efficiencies impacting supply chain logistics.

Decision Making and Uncertainty

UNCERTAINTY Risk.
CERTAINTY One event and one outcome.

Decisions are made under certainty and uncertainty. **Uncertainty** can be defined as risk. **Certainty** can be defined as one event and one outcome. Uncertainty can have several events due to one action, and these events can have different probabilities of occurrence. Three statistical methods for uncertainty measurement are expected value (rational course of action), standard deviation (higher the standard higher the risk), and coefficient of variation (relative risk).

Forecasting Analysis

FORECASTING A systematic approach using statistical methods and workforce judgements (experience and knowledge) to project future service and production supply requirements to meet customer demands for services and products.

Forecasting is a systematic approach using statistical methods and workforce judgments (experience and knowledge) to project future service and production supply requirements to meet customer demands for services and products. Ineffective forecasting can result in efficient inventory volumes that do not support time-phased production material scheduling for goods or customer services in the front or back office operations. Accurate forecasting is needed within organizational functions and must include human resources, accounting, finance, marketing, distribution, and operations management. Overall, forecasting allows managers to make decisions under conditions of certainty and uncertainty (risk). Use of forecasting methods help to determine the probable future occurrence of a supply and demand course of action.

Demand Analysis

Implementation of enterprise resource planning (ERP) applications from Oracle and SAP provide the software to integrate business functions into a single demand plan. The forecasting of customer demand sets in motion backward planning that helps to establish supply baselines for inventory levels and production material schedules. Short- and long-term forecasting helps managers plan capacity for a future requirement by using proven forecasting techniques that provide stable and consistent data to support decision making for supply chain management.

Trend Analysis

Trend analysis is a measure of increasing or decreasing observations for a given time period. It is simple to read a graph with an x- and y-axis; this can provide the management analytics for effective decision making. Observations, for example, can be cost or volume over a 12-month period. A trend line can have a positive or negative display of collected data points. You can also have a trend line that is trending down or trending up. Important with trend analysis is having the right people interpret the data for effective analysis. Linear trending is in a semi-straight line format, and sloping up or down displays a consistent pattern of data points. Non-linear sloping line can have a semi-sharp curve sloping up or down, indicating a sudden inconsistent pattern in data points. Seasonal patterns, cyclical patterns, and unexplained variations will cause trend lines.

TREND ANALYSIS A measure of increasing or decreasing observations for a given time period.

Forecast Accuracy Analysis

All forecasts can have errors. This is why it is important to use a variety of judgment and quantitative forecasting techniques. Statistical methods are not always an effective way to measure events such as product or service promotions or unplanned occurrences in the market. The selection of forecasting methods combined with managerial input can reduce forecast error accuracy. It also important to understand that management bias can cause misinterpretation of the forecasted statistical data. Three common measures for forecasting accuracy are mean square error (MSE), mean absolute deviation (MAD), and mean absolute percentage error (MAPE). MAPE is the average of the percentage error for each forecast value in a time series. MSE is the most popular, but MAPE uses a percentage and is the easiest to interpret. A **time series** is a set of observations measured at successive points in time or over successive periods of time. An example of a time series can be the monthly volume of sales for a product

TIME SERIES A set of observations measured at successive points in time or over successive periods of time.

Moving Average

Moving average works best for short-term planning and when demand is relatively stable. Basically, moving average works by taking the average of three periods of inventory volume and forecasting the inventory volume in the fourth period. Each point of a moving average of a time series is the arithmetic or weighted average of a consecutive points of a series where the number of data points is chosen so that the effects of seasonal or irregularity or both are eliminated. Moving average can be used for inventory control of low volume items. A minimum of 2 years of historical data is required for accurate forecasting.

Single Exponential Smoothing (SES)

With SES, the new forecast is equal to the old forecast plus some proportion of the past forecasting error. SES methods do not try to include trend or seasonal impacts to demand. SES forecasts are based on averages using and weighing (more emphasis) the more current actual demand instead of older demand data (historical data).

Regression Analysis

Regression analysis has wide application for supply and demand analysis. Relationships are primarily analyzed statistically, and the method uses the one of least squares. Linear regression analysis defines the numerical relationship between a single dependent variable and one independent variable. Multiple linear regressions have more than one independent variable.

Linear Analysis

Linear analysis is concerned with optimal allocation of limited resources among competitive activities. Two important parts of linear analysis is the objective function and constraints. An example can be finding the right mix of material and production. The objective function is to minimize production costs and the constraints are production requirements, inventory levels, production capacity, and labor. Key to formulating the analysis is defining the decision variables trying to be solved.

Learning Curve

The **learning curve** states that labor hours decrease as labor operations are repeated. As the output doubles, the labor rate will be reduced by 20%. With a reduction of 20% labor, the learning curve would be stated as 80%. Another way is to say as production quantities double, the average time needed per unit is reduced by 20% from the previous time.

Inventory Planning and Control

The purpose of this method is to obtain optimal inventory levels while minimizing purchase order, inventory carrying, and stock shortage costs. Establishing safety stock levels, along with stock reorder points and stock reorder quantities, minimizes overall inventory costs and are key processes of the economic order quantity (EOQ) model. The EOQ model works best when lead time and demand are constant, and this works for many organizations that run inventory operations with known certainty for supply and demand.

Queuing Models

Queuing is standing in line or waiting for services. The focus is the cost of delayed time by customers or businesses. Another cost is that of providing extra service facilities or customer representatives. Examples can be medical clinics or car washes. Three key organizational factors to apply statistical analytics can be the organization's experience with daily volume of customers, the potential for large arrival of customers at one time and the costs of waiting, and the rate of service provided to the customer. A single channel exponential service time model uses a mean arrival rate and mean service rate that can establish costing data for management analysis and decision making.

LOGISTIC ANALYSIS AND METHODOLOGY

Four methods of analysis will be applied to alternative logistical planning in this section of Chapter 8. It will help to provide an overview of qualitative and quantitative data analysis. The four methods are comparative analysis, cost–benefit analysis, gap analysis, and benchmarking analysis.

Comparative Analysis

Comparative analysis is a technique that looks at an item-by-item comparison of two or more comparable alternatives or processes. Sometimes known as comparability analysis of items like products and systems, this analytical method can detect supply chain management trends and results.

COMPARATIVE ANALYSIS A technique that looks at an item-by-item comparison of two or more comparable alternatives or processes.

Comparative analysis can be demonstrated by the use of planned and actual results. What was planned and what actually happened can provide managers with a comparative result to support decision making and analysis. The comparative result is displayed in the form of a percentage change. The percentage change indicates an increase or decrease in the actual results when compared to what was planned for a given time period of a year, month, week, or day.

The comparative analysis example below uses qualitative and quantitative analyses to solve a problem by forecasting customer demand accuracy.

Problem: Inconsistent forecasting of customer demand for a finished product.

Qualitative analysis: The forecasting of customer demand has been inconsistent for two of the last 3 years. The comparative analysis below for years 1 and 2 were a result of high employee turnover and lack of training in the customer demand planning team. In year 3, management implemented a training program and gave higher wages, and this resulted in no employee turnover.

Quantitative analysis: Below is a table of quantitative values to support decision making. In year 1, the company planned to sell 100 units but actually sold 60 for a decrease of 40%. The decrease of 40% is a result of a forecasting error in customer demand. Year 2 had an increase of 18%, and year three had no percentage change.

YEAR	PLANNED	ACTUAL	PERCENTAGE CHANGE	INCREASE/ DECREASE
1	100	60	40%	Decrease
2	110	130	18%	Increase
3	120	120	0%	None
Formula				
P − A = X then X / P = % Change	100 − 60 = 40 then 40 / 100 = 40%			

FIGURE 8.1 Quantitative-Comparative Analysis

Summary: Customer demand forecasting in year 3 had a 0 accuracy error rate, and this was attributed to training and wage increases.

Cost–Benefit Analysis

Cost–benefit analysis supports quantifying the costs and benefits of a decision by management within a given time period. This analysis is a straightforward tool to determine the validity of a project or can be used to jump start a course of action that requires decision making. The results can be expressed in the form of a payback period, the time it takes for the benefit (savings) to pay back the cost. Cost–benefit analysis can be used for quick calculations to determine if the course of action is even doable. Use of net present value and internal rate of return are more appropriate for large sums of money decisions.

Four basic steps are required for cost–benefit analysis, and they are as follows:
1. Socialize and brainstorm costs and benefits.
2. Establish a money value to costs.
3. Establish a money value to benefits.
4. Compare costs to benefits.

Cost–benefit analysis, sometimes known as feasibility studies, can get management attention for a process change that will generate a savings (benefit) from current operational costs. The forecasted benefit coupled with a payback timeline can provide a manager with actionable data to support a change.

The cost–benefit example below uses qualitative and quantitative analysis to solve an inventory stocking problem.

Problem: Inventory personnel do not place "just received" maintenance, repair, and operations (MRO) stock into required stock bins in a timely manner, causing stock to be unavailable. These stock outs have decreased production equipment reliability.

Qualitative analysis: A new process is implemented using bar coding capability to alert the inventory supervisor that "just received" MRO stock is sitting on the loading dock. The bar coding labeling enables the stock to be automatically scanned, and the location of the stock is identified.

Quantitative analysis: Below is a table displaying quantitative values to support analytics decision making. Cost to implement the bar coding system for MRO stock cost 120k with a savings benefit of 60k the first year and 60k the second year. The payback is 2 years.

PROCESS	YEAR	COST	BENEFIT	PAYBACK
New	1	120k	60k	
New	2	0	60k	2 years
Total		120k	120k	
Formula				
Payback = cost / benefit		2 years = 120 / 60		

FIGURE 8.2 Quantitative Cost–Benefit Analysis

Summary: The capability to reduce MRO stock outs using a bar coding system for stock location has a savings of 60k per year with a payback in 2 years. The savings is attributed to an increase in production equipment reliability.

Gap Analysis

Gap analysis is a technique to determine what is required to move from a current state to a desired state. Gap analysis is sometimes called a needs analysis or needs assessment. Gap analysis consists of the factors needed to meet future requirements, such as system attributes, reporting capabilities, personnel competencies, or supply chain performance metrics. After the present situation of factors is documented, there is a second listing of factors that must be completed to achieve future requirements. The "what is" and "what needs to be" are tallied up and the gap is highlighted. The gap is basically the difference between the existing list and need to be filled list.

Gap analysis allows managers to reflect on requirements to move from a current state to a desired state and is displayed in the quantitative table and qualitative narrative below.

> **Problem:** The current transportation management system lacks an upgraded applications package, causing an increase in manual processes to support customer demand for delivery services.
>
> **Qualitative analysis:** The qualitative values for the purchase of an advanced systems application package includes an increased customer service efficiency and promotes job enhancement for logistics personnel who are managing inbound and outbound deliveries. Personnel will do less manual processing with the new application package, and it will allow more time for improving customer service.
>
> **Transportation management system:** The current system has 10 applications, and the required end state or desired state is 15 applications.
>
> **Gap analysis:** The gap or delta for the required applications is five.
>
> **System cost:** The total cost of the current system is 50k, and the desired system is 150k.
>
> **Manual processing costs by personnel:** The current system has higher manual operational processing costs at 250k. The desired system has less manual operational processing costs at 100k due to the five applications added to the desired system.
>
> **Gap cost savings:** Closing the gap of five applications would have a savings of 50k.

Below is a table displaying quantitative values for analytics business decision making.

SYSTEMS	APPLICATIONS	GAP ANALYSIS	SYSTEM COST	PROCESSING COSTS	GAP COST ANALYSIS
Current	10	5	50k	250k	300k
Desired	15	0	150k	100k	250k
Total		5			50k Savings
Formula					
Gap Analysis = Desired − Current		5 = 15 − 10			

FIGURE 8.3 Quantitative Gap Analysis

GAP ANALYSIS A technique to determine what is required to move from a current state to a desired state.

Summary: Gap analysis consists of factors needed to meet future requirements, such as system applications, reporting capabilities, personnel competencies, or supply chain performance metrics. The gap analysis example here demonstrated the gap between current and required system applications. The gap analysis allows managers to base decisions on a documented list of operational needs for increased efficiency and responsiveness. The end result is a decrease in manual processes, an increase in customer service, and an overall savings of 50k.

Benchmarking Analysis

Benchmarking is an analytical process a company can use to evaluate its performance against the performance of another company or industry standard. This is a specialized form of gap analysis and requires a company to accurately measure its own performance standards and goals. Below is a basic benchmarking analysis example.

Problem: An auto parts supply company wants to evaluate its inventory carrying costs against an industry market leader. The concern is the warehouse facility costs associated with the basic inventory functions of receiving, storage, issuing, and shipping.

Qualitative analysis: The cost of carrying inventory can and will be different from company to company. Most companies will determine inventory carry costs by summing up personnel wages, looking at the handling of inventory stock, analyzing the facility space utilization requirements, and determining the money spent for stock sitting on the shelf. Other cost considerations are stock deterioration and obsolescence.

Quantitative analysis: Most inventory carry costs are computed for a year and are expressed as a percentage of the cost of the inventory items. This auto supply company has inventory carry costs at 10% with a total cost of inventory on the shelf at 300k per year. The company spends 30k per year in inventory carry costs. The market competitor spends 5% for inventory carry costs, or 15k per year, while maintaining the same cost of inventory at 300k per year.

Summary: The auto supply company has determined that the warehouse facility costs (rent, security, utilities, and insurance) are 20k per year and make up 66% of inventory carry costs (20k / 30k = 66%). There is a need for the company to lower inventory carry costs to be competitive with the industry market leader, and to do this, finding a less costly warehouse facility is required.

ALTERNATIVE LOGISTICAL PLANS

The following supply chain logistic cost centers will provide an illustrated decision-making process to evaluate an alternative logistics plans (ALP) that is based on qualitative and quantitative factors that can impact a best value course of action. The ALP focus will be on lowering operating costs with the understanding that you can increase savings and improve supply chain efficiencies by decreasing logistical operating costs. Overall, operating costs include the total money spent by a company to run the entire business. An important contributor to company operating costs is the supply chain logistics costs centers listed below. A cost center is established for each company entity or department that is authorized to incur an obligation by spending cash. The ALP examples are grouped into the following logistical cost center functions: facilities, sourcing, pricing, inventory, transportation, distribution, order fulfillment, information systems, and sustainment.

Each ALP cost center example will include a subject, status, summary, analysis, and action plan supported by a qualitative and quantitative analysis methodology detailed in section two of this chapter. This can be seen in the following:

■ **Subject:** Identifies the logistics function under assessment for an alternative logistics plan

■ **Status:** Provides the background information of the problem or issue facing a company

■ **Summary:** Details the decision-making discussion for a course of action by management

■ **Analysis:** Qualitative and quantitative method for logistics plan analysis

■ **Action plan:** Defines the recommendation and key elements of the alternative logistics plan

Note: The ALP cost center examples will focus on basic, fundamental logistics decision making and planning. Quantitative analysis for taxes, depreciation and discounts will not be included due to complexity of financial applications with tax law and state or federal regulatory requirements.

Facilities

ALP01 Subject: New facility or upgrade facility.

Status: Increased production space is required to meet customer demand.

Summary: The options are to buy a new facility, upgrade the current facility, or outsource production requirements to another.

Analysis: Comparative analysis.

Action-go: Outsource production for one year; this will cost more money in the short run but allows flexibility for a future course of action.

ALP02 Subject: Repair or replace generator.

Status: Total maintenance and repair costs for the generator exceeds the machine's lifecycle.

Summary: The options are to repair, buy, or lease a new generator.

Analysis: Cost–benefit analysis.

Action-go: Buy a new generator with performance based contract for on-time 2-day repair part delivery.

ALP03 Subject: Relocation of assembly plant to west coast.

Status: Shipping finished goods from the East coast to the West coast is expensive due to fuel costs and a limited number of qualified over the road truck drivers.

Summary: The freight costs of raw materials from the East coast to the West coast is 60% less than using multimodal rail or truck.

Analysis: Comparative analysis.

Action-go: Lease assembly plant on the West coast and lower distribution costs using rail or truck multimodal to move raw materials from the East coast.

Sourcing

ALP04 Subject: Supplier preassembly services

Status: A finish product requires the shop flow assembly of three components that must be sequenced where component A and component B are assembled first, and component C is attached last to complete the process.

Summary: The supplier of components A and B has expanded operations to provide assembly services for component A and B to remain in good standing with buyer.

Analysis: Comparative analysis.

Action-go: Contract with the supplier to provide assembly of components A and B will decrease assembly time for the finished product and will require less personnel.

Pricing

ALP05 Subject: Contracting – Long-term contracting

Status: Having a large number of suppliers without long-term sourcing contracts is not an industry best practice for maintenance, repair, and operations (MRO) parts.

Summary: Establishing two to five key MRO supplier relationships with formal contracts supports supplier-buyer partnerships and ensures supply sourcing integrity and performance.

Analysis: Benchmarking analysis.

Action-Go: Establish industry best practices for long-term sourcing contracts with a limited number of supplier partnerships for performance based sourcing and discount pricing on stock volume procurement.

Inventory

ALP06 Subject: Vendor managed inventory (VMI)

Status: Finished goods inventory for lawn mowers held at a retail store chain is sourced from one wholesale supplier (vendor). Retail store inventory labor wages and benefits represent 10% of all inventory carry costs (personnel, facility space, and retail store chain inventory on hand).

Summary: Lawn mower inventory managed by the supplier on site is a free service due to an agreement for market promotions at retail stores. VMI services to receive, stock, and handle returns will decrease retail inventory personnel requirement by 50%.

Analysis: Comparative analysis.

Action-Go: Going with the VMI plan will decrease overall inventory carry costs for wages and benefits from 10% to 5% due to less retail store inventory personnel (50% cut) that is required for lawn mower inventory.

ALP07 Subject: Just-in-time inventory (JIT)

Status: A manufacturer wants to move 10% of critical raw material inventory to just-in-time inventory; this is becoming an industry best practice. Current raw inventory is ordered on a fixed period system where inventory is only checked at fixed dates and not on a continuous basis.

Summary: JIT enables production supply and customer demand planners to align with lower inventory levels to match material requirements and production scheduling for finished goods.

Analysis: Gap analysis.

Action-go: JIT is a more efficient cost savings approach to managing inventory and requires a collaborative effort by the supplier and buyer to move 10% of critical raw material inventory from a fixed period system to JIT inventory.

Transportation

ALP08 Subject: Third party logistics (3PL) - Trucking

Status: A doll company has a private fleet of five trucks to deliver finished goods and is considering a 3PL to decrease costs related to truck maintenance, fuel, and driver wages.

Summary: A total of 40% of supply chain operating costs comes from transportation. Hiring a 3PL would cost the same and would leave more time to manage other areas of the business. There is a risk with using a 3PL regarding overall customer service with timely deliveries during peak seasonal periods.

Analysis: Cost–benefit analysis.

Action-no go: The risk associated with customer service outweighed the use of a 3PL to include limited loss of control with deliveries. Employee moral would drop due to truck driver layoffs and was also a consideration in decision making.

ALP09 Subject: Multi-modal - Truck and rail service

Status: A motor lines company has a fleet of company trucks that are used to deliver clothing apparel from the West coast to the East coast. An option to contract for multi-modal trailer on flatcar (TOFC) transportation is being reviewed for consideration.

Summary: This multi-modal operation requires four segments: origin of trailer to rail, trailer on rail, trailer off rail, and trailer to end destination. There is a need for a 3PL truck company on the East coast to make the last mile delivery once the trailer is off loaded from the rail.

Analysis: Comparative analysis.

Action-no go: There was too much dependency on multi-modal rail operations and on the need for a 3PL truck company for the last mile delivery; this will create major "dwell time" periods of waiting and delays that negatively impacts customer deliver scheduling.

Distribution

ALP10 Subject: Global networks - Air and sea delivery services

Status: A U. S.-based computer manufacturer has an air carrier service to ensure just-in-time delivery of computer parts. Sea carrier transportation is a viable option and less expensive compared to the high cost for air service delivery.

Summary: Sea carrier transportation costs when using a 20-foot shipping container are 90% less than air service costs. Just-in-time delivery requirements of computer parts are not needed due to system improvements in forecasting customer demand alignment with supply planning and production scheduling.

Analysis: Cost–benefit analysis.

Action-go: Establish a sea lane delivery network for "door to door" performance delivery and set up a contract with sea lift carrier. This contract requires the sea carrier company to pick up at origin and deliver the container to the final destination within 20 days of order.

Order Fulfillment

ALP11 Subject metric: On-time order fulfillment

Status: A shipping company wants to measure customer service by establishing a metric that will report all customer orders being shipped on time for each month.

Summary: The company creates a formula to collect and measure data. The formula is as follows: number of orders shipped on time divided by the number of orders that should have been shipped

Analysis: Comparative analysis.

Action-go: The formula was implemented for the months of January and February. The metric displayed an improvement of 30% from January to February.

January: 50 / 75 = 66%

February: 70 / 75 = 93%

Information Systems

ALP12 Subject: Information systems – Enterprise resource planning (ERP)
Status: A 3PL services company has an outdated legacy system for business operations and a separate customer service management system for reporting.

Summary: There is a need for a fully integrated ERP system to manage information of business activities or to include financial transactions and reporting.

Analysis: Gap analysis.

Action-go: Replacing the legacy system will take 1 year. The ERP system has costs two times that of the current budget for information systems. The separate customer service management system in a cost savings measure can be integrated with a bolt-on module to the open system ERP solution.

Sustainment

ALP13 Subject: Environmental – Transportation optimization
Status: Reducing the carbon footprint for supply chain companies places the focus mostly on transportation. The use of trucks, railroads, ships, and airplanes to ship goods around the global contributes to the large carbon footprint caused by burning fuel and creating harmful emissions to the environment.

Summary: For a truck company, an option to reduce emissions is the installation of wind reduction enhancements to the truck itself; these include new engines, proper tires, and tractor or trailer add-ons like trailer skirts and trailer end tails. A difficult requirement for this enhancement package is that drivers have to operate the truck at 62 miles per hour for maximum efficiency.

Analysis: Gap analysis.

Action-go: Ensuring drivers operate at 62 miles per hour is very difficult considering the tight scheduling and high demand for on-time deliveries. Payback on the enhancement package cost is attractive when considering the cost of fuel to operate an 18-wheel tractor trailer.

ALP14 Subject: Social – Product safety
   Status: Developing, marketing, and selling a consumer good of high quality and low cost is a formula for success. Companies need to ensure that cost cutting measures or lack of quality controls do not impact the safe use of the product

Summary: Product safety is paramount to a company's image and governance. Product safety for consumers must start upstream with suppliers who provide key assemblies and components for a finished product

Analysis: Cost–benefit analysis.

Action-go: Implementing a quality control program and product safety review board from one end of the supply chain to the other is required to ensure safe products are being used by consumers.

ALP15 Subject: Economic – Total supply chain performance metric
   Status: A company metric to measure supply chain performance can be to measure the supply chain as a percentage of cost. Supply chain operating costs (cost centers) can be summed up and then divided by total sales revenue.

Summary: The company creates a formula to collect and measure data. The formula is as follows: total supply chain operating cost divided by total revenue of sales, where 80k represents the total supply chain costs and 250k represents total revenue sales.

Analysis: The formula can be displayed as 80k / 250k = 32%. This percentage of 32% means that supply chain costs are 32% of total sales revenue

Action: After a company creates a 32% metric like the one above, then the next step is to establish a key performance indicator (KPI) baseline to measure the metric. An example would be if senior management wants supply chain costs to be 25% of total sales revenue. In this case, there is a need to decrease supply chain costs from 32% to 25% or to 7%.

ALP16 Subject: Economic – Individual logistics cost center performance metric.
   Status: A company metric to individually measure the performance of different logistics cost centers can be done by adding up the cost center expenditures and then dividing them by the total sales revenue.

Summary: The company creates a formula to collect and measure data. The formula is as follows: individual cost center divided by total revenue of sales, where transportation is 41k and total sales revenue is 250k.

Analysis: The formula can be displayed as 41k / 250k = 32%. This percentage of 16% means that transportation costs are 16% of total sales revenue.

Action: After a company creates a 16% metric like the one above, then the next step is to establish a key performance indicator (KPI) baseline to measure the metric. An example would be senior management wants transportation costs to be 10% of total sales revenue. In this case, there is a need to decrease transportation costs from 16% to 10% or to 6%.

DISCUSSION QUESTIONS

1. Discuss how using the five basic planning factors support a best value decision-making process for an alternative logistical plan.

2. Discuss how qualitative and quantitative analysis can enable a company to optimize sound decision making for an efficient and responsive supply chain.

3. Compare and contrast gap analysis and benchmarking analysis.

SUMMARY

Chapter 8 provided an overview of alternative logistical plans and had a focus on qualitative and quantitative assessment fundamentals that support supply chain management decision making; this decision making impacts facilities, sourcing, inventory, transportation, distribution, order fulfillment, information systems, and sustainment.

Fundamental approaches to determine a proper course of action with logistical plans were presented using qualitative and quantitative data. Four analytical methodology examples also provided a basis for effective assessment of alternative logistical plans. The four methodologies were comparative analysis, cost–benefit analysis, gap analysis, and benchmarking.

Alternative logistical plan cost center examples were presented to provide action plan requirements using timely, relevant, and actionable decision-making information. The cost centers examples focused on reducing operational costs that impact supply chain management efficiency and responsiveness.

SUPPLIER
PROCUREMENT
MANUFACTURE
SUPPLY PRODUCT
CHAIN INVENTORY
DISTRIBUTION
LOGISTIC
RETAIL

Systems in the Supply Chain

INTRODUCTION

Chapter 9 will focus on procurement, customer delivery, and the acquisition requirements of a supply chain management system. This chapter will cover supply chain concepts, processes, and applications. Section 9.1 covers procurement, 9.2 covers customer delivery, and 9.3 covers system acquisition. Section 9.3, system acquisition, will detail the acquisition guidelines, phases, and decision point milestones required for the procurement of a supply chain management system.

Partnering with vendor provided systems by collaborating with suppliers and customers to develop a world class IT infrastructure takes time, funding, and analysis. Shedding legacy or redundant systems to modernize management information systems requires true partnering of costs and services to meet the system capabilities so as to meet logistical demands for on time delivery of the perfect order.

Supply chain management, overall, is a complex operation of processes that enables the flow of materials, information, and money between suppliers and customers. In general, there are three key supply chain management information systems (MIS) required for a company to be able to optimize the supplier and customer relationship to have an efficient and responsive supply chain management system.

Enterprise Resource Planning (ERP)

This type of system integrates all aspects of the supply chain into a unified information system, providing timely analysis and reporting to support planning, procurement, order fulfillment, finance, and quality. The result is a common operating picture for key decision making. Key solution integrators in the ERP business are as follows:

- *SAP, Inc.* Based in Germany; an international ERP systems and solution integrator company
- *Oracle, Inc.* Based in the United States; an international ERP systems and solution integrator company

The next two systems listed below manage and share the supply and demand of data. This data sharing supports the inbound flow of materials or what is known as upstream requirements of sourcing (supply side). The supply side feeds the outbound flow of product (goods and services), or downstream requirements, to customers (demand side). Most people live downstream.

Supplier Relationship Management (SRM)

This supply side system manages the relationship between the company and suppliers to maximize performance and contract agreements to meet supply-sourcing requirements. The result is managing suppliers and not supplies.

Customer Relationship Management (CRM)

This demand side system manages the relationship between the company and customers to maximize communication and delivery to meet customer demand requirements; this is also known as forecasting demand. The result is a loyal customer.

Systems in Supply Chain

Information is key to developing and implementing an integrated and coordinated supply chain system. Companies must have information that is accurate, accessible, relevant, and shared. There are basically five types of systems that can be categorized to better understand the impact of MIS on supply chain logistics.

Legacy Systems

These systems are limited MIS that are adequate and meet minimum information requirements, but these systems are not modernized to fully meet current supplier and customer requirements. They lack integrated reporting capabilities and limited processing speed performance to share information efficiently with the advanced data technology systems of today.

Redundant Systems

These systems are doing the same processing requirements that other implemented systems are doing, and this creates a larger logistical MIS footprint to manage and maintain. The goal is to reduce the logistics MIS footprint by closing down these redundant systems and move to an ERP

1. Describe three key supply chain management information systems.

2. List five types of supply chain management systems that can exist in a company.

3. Identify six best value procurement guidelines for obtaining better buying power.

4. List four customer delivery processes that support order fulfillment.

5. Describe three rules for making a qualified decision for system acquisition.

system (ERP) with an enterprise data warehouse. An enterprise data warehouse system allows for logistical data to be uniform and to be configured and shared across integrated lines of business.

Unique Systems

These are specialized MIS that provides specific capabilities to meet a narrow business requirement. These systems are used for one company or group of end users. Unique systems are developed in-house by employees of the company or by contracted developers and can be called proprietary systems.

Best-of-Breed System

These systems are recognized MIS in a business sector and are sometimes called a tier one system; they provide advanced system capabilities for specific processes and reporting. These systems can have a high acquisition cost.

Enterprise Resource Planning System

These systems have a high acquisition cost MIS, requiring detailed analysis, documentation, and training to support system customization (screen displays and company jargon-industry terminology) and modification (business processes and reporting). A key understanding with ERP systems is that the business drives the ERP system and not the other way around.

Impact of Logistics and Supply Chain Systems

Logistics information systems (LIS) can be defined as a combination of computer hardware and software and data and communications that collect, process, and transmit information for planning and executing the movement of materials and services, financial transactions, and real-time reporting. There are people, policies, procedures, and practices in direct support of key LIS best practices to deliver the right product (goods and services), at the right time, at the right place, and at the right price. The optimal result is to meet and exceed customer delivery requirements by maximizing supplier-sourcing capacities to deliver the perfect order.

Logistics can be defined in this chapter as an overarching process to fulfill deliver requirements of the right product (good or service) to the right customer. Supply chain systems provide the MIS capability to activate logistical activities. To do this, a supply chain MIS must have accurate and reliable product data integrity in the database. Product data is the procurement specifications for goods and services to include life cycle management parts and costs in an MIS database.

The MIS product database impacts the process and application of procurement, customer delivery, and the acquisition processes of a collaborative supply chain system. A product database of a collaborative supply chain system includes the following:

- Single, virtual workplace for end users
- Standardized, enterprise-wide business processes supporting product data
- Technical business processes that are fully automated and modernized
- Visibility of product and technical data
- Exchange of documentation

Key supply chain management metrics that can provide logistical performance measurement are as follows:

- *On-time order fulfillment (OTOF).* The percent of orders completely filled and shipped within a specified period. This reports the perfect order measurement.
- *Order quantity fill rate (OQFR).* The percentage of orders shipped with the required quantity ordered. They are measured by the overage or underage quantity of an order delivered.
- *Time definite delivery (TDD).* The percentage of orders delivered within the contractual agreement or industry standard. It is how long it takes to satisfy a customer's order from first contact to actual delivery.
- *Logistics response time (LRT).* It is the elapsed time of a customer order to customer receipt of order. It measures the surface or air transportation capacity and efficiency to execute a customer deliver.
- *Supply chain costs as a percentage of sales (SCPS).* The percentage of total operating expenses to total of revenue generated by customer sales. This metric can be done for all customer sales or by individual customer sales.

PROCUREMENT SYSTEM ACTIVITIES
Introduction

Procurement controls a company's purchasing of goods and services. Procurement activities have a major impact when achieving optimal supply chain management; it is best used when best value policies are implemented in a company. Procurement best practices focus on a best value policy to meet supplier sourcing and customer demand to improve supply chain performance. Best value places emphasis on evaluating factors in addition to the price of an item or acquisition cost for equipment, facilities, or systems. Best value is also a process used in competitive negotiated contracting to select an offer that is advantageous to the company. The process includes evaluation and comparative factors in addition to price and cost. To make a best value decision, a company should ensure that the decision has a rational basis that is consistent with stated evaluation criteria and takes in to consideration whether or not key benefits are worth a price premium. The following best value procurement guidelines provide a focused approach to the needs of a company:

- Evaluate and compare factors against evaluation criteria
- Price and cost as an evaluation factor
- Supplier past performance as an evaluation factor
- Contract solicitation will be a best value decision
- Relevant supplier information will only be used to evaluate proposals
- Ensure consistency with procurement objectives and processes

Supply and Demand Alignment

Many supply and demand issues at the company level can escalate, causing subperformance of a supply chain operation and procurement activities. Supply can be defined as the sourcing of stock and keeping units (items, raw material, and components) that are required to manufacture or assemble a good. *Demand* can be defined as the forecasted customer need or market demand pull for that good. Supply sourcing and demand forecasting require a balance or alignment to support efficient and responsive procurement activities regarding inbound sourcing to produce the good and the outbound pricing of goods to market.

Three operational planning methods that can have a major impact on procurement and supply sourcing to meet forecasted customer demand are as follows:

- *Master production scheduling.* What is to be manufactured within a specified time horizon
- *Material requirements planning.* Phased receipt of raw materials, stock items, and assemblies to meet production schedules
- *Capacity requirements planning.* Resource analysis of manpower and machine capacity to meet customer forecasted demand requirements

When supply and demand issues escalate to a breaking point, and where resolution is not foreseeable, a demand and supply alignment meeting is required to find a solution. In a demand and supply alignment meeting, key supply and demand planners can make decisions and implement action plans to resolve inconsistencies with inbound or downstream supplier materials and services to match and or balance outbound, upstream customer demand; this is based on statistical forecasting or market surge for a product. Actions taken to resolve problematic issues include a review of current supplier performance and or improve performance while reducing or increasing inventory to meet capacity needs. Decisions in the supply demand alignment meeting can be based on the following considerations:

- *Budget allocations.* Company resource and finance managers must make decisions regarding funding requirements for supply sourcing to match demand forecasting of customer needs.
- *Demand problems.* Forecasting and projections for goods and services need to be accurate.
- *Supply problems.* Sourcing issues can cause operational constraints due to a lack of supplier discipline to deliver the right order at the right time.
- *New product procurement.* Requires product data analysis and specification documentation for quantity order point and catalog entry
- *Old product disposal.* Proper disposal includes environmental regulatory laws, secondary markets, and accounting standards to remove property from general ledger.

The demand and supply meeting can also include a review of the company procurement business plans that detail strategic goals, operational capacities and requirements, and tactical buyer level initiatives and performance objectives. Meeting with customers to better resolve issues by integrating collaborative efforts from prior meetings and by reviewing supply chain management system capabilities can also help to improve performance that can balance supply and demand.

Procurement and Demand Planning

Demand planning is designed to determine customer requirements. A demand plan will show what customers need and when they will need it. Key areas impacting procurement and demand planning are customer demand history, statistical forecasting, and application of collaborative efforts from customers and market research. Additional areas impacting procurement and demand planning include pricing policy and revenue management. Information on demand volume and customer willingness to pay for a product along with product margins allow for intelligent pricing decisions to improve overall supply chain responsiveness.

Procurement and Supply Planning

Supply planning is the process of taking a final decision demand plan and seeing what is on hand in inventory and what is needed over time. Time horizon can be 1 month to 1 year or more to include the delivery schedule to distribution sites in the future. Basically supply planning is concerned with inventory and the time-phased inventory plan to meet demand. Key areas impacting procurement and supply planning are inventory levels and sourcing of inventory. Setting inventory levels requires analysis of demand patterns, inventory carry costs, stockouts, ordering, and material and production scheduling. Overall, sourcing of supply goods and services requires information on pricing, quality, supplier lead times, and transactional data.

Procurement Processes

The following system processes enable a procurement operation to be efficient and responsive. The procurement system process capability involves automation of buyer practices, purchase agreements, issue request for quotes, purchase orders and invoicing with an end result of streamlining financial transactions and providing metric reporting:

- *Purchase requisition.* This is an internal company requirement that has cost approval levels to direct procurement to buy, for example, a stock item or request services. A requisition can start the acquisition process for large end items costing a specified amount or can be processed automatically in the case of stock requisitions when inventory levels reach a stock reorder point.
- *Purchase order.* Helps buyers streamline the ordering process and is a key audit requirement for the three way match transaction of a purchase order, receipt of goods or services, and invoicing. The buyer sends a purchase order to the supplier. The supplier sends an invoice (bill) for payment.
- *Receipt of good or service.* This key inventory process is used to accept stock items for binning or confirming service labor completed and can include inspections and invoice approval. The supplier sends goods or services to the buyer for receipt.
- *Invoicing.* The third component of a three way match identifies purchased goods, services accepted, volume or pricing discounts, and taxes to be paid and is based within an agreed time that is normally 30 days. An invoice discount term called "2 10 Net 30" means to pay in 10 days and receive a 2 % discount off of the price. The supplier sends an invoice for goods delivered or services provided to the buyer. The buyer will send the approved invoice to accounts payable, and a check is cut to pay the supplier.
- *Electronic document interface.* Automated straight through process of transmitting procurement documentation and financial transactions.
- *Accounts payable.* Expenses to be paid per an invoice document received by a company. The company is legally obligated to pay the invoice amount. This is outbound company cash flow.
- *Accounts receivable.* Revenue to be received by a company per an invoice document. This is inbound company cash flow.
- *Purchase agreements.* A contract agreement between the buyer and supplier for goods or services. Purchase agreements are also known as blanket purchase orders and allow many items to be procured at the same time, thus creating efficiencies with lead times and purchase discounts.
- *Buyer role.* Key procurement player who has the approval authority to contract with suppliers for purchases and to execute quotes, purchase agreements, and manage catalogs.

- *Catalogs.* There are several catalogs to support procurement operations. They are stock (company inventory), supplier, and manufacture catalogs. Key to maintaining catalogs is the updating of items with product specifications to include size, material, and supplier history.
- *Quotes or bidding.* A key process for a buyer when selecting suppliers to obtain best value procurement practices and long-term purchase agreements.
- *Payment terms.* A key procurement process when negotiating with a supplier for discounts, penalties, lead times, and key performance metrics for timely payments.

PROCUREMENT APPLICATIONS

Listed below are procurement applications that support supply chain operations involved with the day-to-day business side of transactions for the movement and acceptance of goods and services. The following procurement applications drive key supply chain functions:

- *Transportation.* Surface and air transportation procurement includes shipment planning and traffic management using internal transportation assets or third party logistics companies. Freight charges, insurance, and route scheduling are a part of carrier service procurements.
- *Facilities.* Acquisition of major end items like buildings for purchase or lease require procurement analysis. Analysis of facility costs can impact inventory carry costs, physical security, and maintenance and repair budgeting.
- *Inventory.* How much inventory an organization should carry is based on procurement actions in direct support of production scheduling and purchase agreement lead times with suppliers. Inventory costs can impact a company's capital funding that could be available for other company initiatives or requirements. Low inventory means more capital funding availability.
- *Sourcing.* The inbound flow of required stock items, raw materials, and assemblies per procurement actions to meet material requirements planning.
- *Procurement.* The processes of buying and selling of goods and services.
- *Order management.* An order is central to the procurement process and acts like a contract between the buyer and supplier.
- *Packaging.* Best practice packaging requirements has a major impact on costs. Smaller packaging means less cost for warehousing and distribution. Procurement of like size boxes, tape, and labels can reduce packaging costs.
- *Distribution.* Automated procurement processes for receiving, warehousing, inventory integrity, transportation, and shipping lowers distribution costs and supports environment sustainment with a smaller carbon footprint. Transportation is usually the largest carbon footprint of all operations.
- *Stock and item returns.* Ability to process reverse logistics with sound financial transaction history supports product returns and supply chain integrity. Ability to repair, refurbish, and resell for less helps the bottom line costs of accepting returns.
- *Sustainment and buying green.* Social, environmental, and economic sustainment is vital to the financial health of a company. Procurement sustainment policies start with having good stewardship of company resources for energy consumption, the buying of safety equipment for workers, and maintaining audit ready supply chain transactions. These are some examples of sustainment what works for everyone.

Conclusion

Procurement helps control the purchasing of goods and services for manufacturing requirements in a more efficient way. Procurement activities also help control the pricing of a good or service to market. Procurement activities have a major impact on achieving optimal supply chain sourcing (inbound goods and services) when best value policies are used to place emphasis on evaluating factors and the price of an item or acquisition cost for equipment, facilities, or systems.

CUSTOMER DELIVERY SYSTEM ACTIVITIES

Introduction

Customer delivery can be defined as providing goods and services to customers. The important activity with customer delivery is order fulfillment. Order fulfillment processes coordinate all efforts to move, mix, store, consolidate, assemble, label, and package items or provide services based on an agreed upon statement of work.

Order Fulfillment

Order fulfillment includes all activities throughout the supply chain system to manage the relationship between the company and the customer to include the following:

- Sales orders for goods and services
- Delivery of goods and services
- Inventory on hand
- Payments from customers

The Perfect Order

The perfect order provides a goal toward which the order fulfillment process is designed and measured against company developed metrics and key performance indicators. The perfect order includes the following:

- The right product
- At the right time
- In the right place
- In the right condition
- In the right quantity
- At the right cost
- To the right customer

Touch Points

This business concept provides the understanding that there are many points of contact with the order fulfillment process and with customer satisfaction. Customer delivery touch points of information are exchanged between the buyer and seller within the supply chain management system to successfully achieve the perfect order. Order fulfillment examples to attain customer satisfaction include order information that is executed on a scheduled basis from forecasted customer demand planning to supply planning to ensure proper levels of inventory and financial transactions are made throughout the order fulfillment process with accounts payable and accounts receivable.

Order Defined

An *order* will define goods and service purchases from a customer at a certain time and place. Legacy terms can include service order, task order, requisition, and contract call. Purchase orders help company procurement streamline the purchase order process for a customer and are as follows:

- *Order preparation.* What is the customer's need?
- *Order transmission.* How is the order received at a company?
- *Order entry.* What happens to the order after it is received?
- *Order filling.* How does the order trigger the actual selection of a good or service?
- *Order shipment.* How are the goods shipped and services delivered?
- *Order tracking.* Where is the order in the process, and when will be received by the customer?

Distribution Functions

A company distribution operation is a key activity for order fulfillment. Distribution includes receipt, storage, packing, preservation, transportation, in-transit visibility, route analysis, and final drop-off or delivery. There are customers who will not take ownership of goods delivered until the ordered items are off loaded onto the loading dock platform. Distribution functions include the following:

- *Network design.* Basic design is the hub and spoke with a main distribution center servicing forward distribution centers who then distribute to wholesale or retail stores.
- *Distribution systems.* Distribution systems support the business functions of moving and storing goods and services. Distribution performance measurement data is also collected and analyzed for freight management decision-making.
- *Administration.* Each distribution center has an administrative support staff responsible for monitoring performance and managing information systems. In addition to ensuring security requirements are in place for facilities, shipment routes and location of transportation assets are also handled.

Customer Delivery Processes

The processes supporting customer delivery start and end with customer relationship management. The most important part of a customer relationship is the execution of the order from start to finish. Responsive and efficient order fulfillment is central to customer satisfaction.

Customer Relationships

A major customer group divides customers into manageable groupings to establish customer profiles based on level of procurement activity. Important demand drivers identify customer needs for goods and services and the procurement capacity to meet these requirements. Demand data sharing shares relevant data (quantity, delivery date) for goods and services with customers.

Customer Order

Receive order is a design and methods that is used to process customers' orders into demand planning for forecasting. *Manage order* helps to provide visibility from order origin to delivery while *prioritize order* helps to determine customer priority levels. *Time standards* identify industry or company measurement to process order, and *order status* is where the order (item issued or on backorder) is.

Customer Inventory

Stock issue is a customer-specific item that is issued, and inventory levels are adjusted for stock reorder points. Avoidance of stockouts is key to limiting back ordering or orders unfilled.

Packaging and labels help prepare an item for shipment with a packing list, labels, and pack configuration; this also helps for damage control and route planning.

Customer Shipment

Supplier delivery is shipped direct from the supplier to the customer, and manufacturer delivery is shipped from the manufacturer to the customer.

Customer Delivery Applications

The applications for customer delivery involve the execution of a delivery order and the business touch points for order fulfillment. And these are as follows:

- *Delivery order*. Puts in motion the shipment with delivery instructions. Documents include a bill of lading for the consignor and consignee and any special instructions for transportation and shipment.
- *Warehousing*. Storage, issue, and release of an item that may require material handling equipment for heavy items or large size packaging.
- *Special handling*. Sensitive items prone to theft or hazardous materials requiring special permits to ship with proper labels.
- *Contracts*. Contracts are required with third party logistics companies for transportation, warehousing, and transaction technology. Purchase agreements may be required when a buyer will not take ownership of a shipment from a supplier until off loaded from truck and placed on the company's loading dock.
- *Payments*. Payment terms are complex and can involve stockouts and over and under quantity delivery penalties. The key to sound payment terms is the on-time delivery of order quantity and having a satisfied customer.

Conclusion

Customer delivery is providing goods and services to customers. The important activity with customer delivery is order fulfillment. An order fulfillment process coordinates all efforts to move, mix, store, consolidate, assemble, label, and package items or provide services based on an agreed statement of work. Key order fulfillment areas supporting customer delivery are finance, procurement, and supply and demand planning. Effective customer relationship management and order fulfillment performance measurement is based on the perfect order supported by a responsive supply chain operation.

SYSTEM ACQUISITION ACTIVITIES
Introduction

System acquisition activities will be reviewed with a focus on guiding acquisition principals, processes, and applications for the procurement of a supply chain management system. Many company acquisition programs have basic or generic acquisition phases (steps) that can be tailored to meet system procurement requirements that have complex issues regarding risk reduction with big-ticket expenditures having long-term contracts.

Acquisition activities are a focused process to plan, develop, acquire, maintain, and dispose of systems, equipment, facilities, and services. Proper fiscal stewardship is the responsibility of lead procurement managers and the chief financial officer of a company. The key to acquisition policy is ethical performance and sound decision-making with adherence to a best value policy to the company, suppliers, and customers. To make a best value decision, a company needs to ensure that the acquisition decision has a rational basis, is consistent with stated evaluation criteria, and that it takes in to consideration whether or not key benefits are worth a price premium.

Process Overview

The acquisition process for a large expenditure in direct support of procuring a supply chain management information system will have a complex set of activities across many departments of a business operation. A simplified three-phase acquisition process displayed below provides the basic steps to acquisition planning and execution with a focus on determining the need and then using a legal contract for procurement. These phases are as follows:

■ *Phase 1 – Acquisition planning*. Define the need, analyze the requirements, conduct market research, and initiate the procurement.

■ *Phase 2 – Contract planning*. Execute contract solicitation, evaluation, and sign the contract.

■ *Phase 3 – Contract administration*. Monitor contract performance, make contract payments, document contract modifications, and terminate the contract close out.

Guiding Principals

A team approach should be used to ensure the successful management and oversight of a system acquisition. The team concept of professionals having expertise in related areas supporting the procurement and delivery of a system includes, at a minimum, contracting, finance, legal and subject matter experts in operations, information systems, and supply chain management. The following are proven principals to help guide execution of a system acquisition and its related services:

■ *Team approach*. Bring together a team matrix of legal, finance, contracting, acquisition, procurement, operations, and supply chain experts.

■ *Best value*. Best value is not the lowest price but the enhanced benefit to the buyer, end users, and suppliers.

■ *Decision authority*. Have an established decision-making official or committee ready to execute the key acquisition decision points or milestones.

■ *Performance measurement*. Establish how and what the performance measurement factors are to proceed and ensure contractual agreements.

■ *System unit cost*. What is the cost of the unit (system hardware, software, and licenses) to obtain ownership and complete the acquisition?

■ *Life cycle system cost*. What are the related maintenance costs over the life of the system from implementation to final disposal?

■ *Contracting*. Legal requirements to finalize buyer (company) and seller (system vendor) agreements into a binding document

- *Affordability.* Identify all the costs associated with the acquisition to determine a viable course of action with the company's cash flow to procure and maintain a good investment.
- *Constraints.* Identify internal and external issues that may impact the acquisition. Document performance red flags during user testing or market research that would limit the scope of the implementation and fully operational capability of the system.
- *Risk management.* Identification and reduction of risks must be addressed to mitigate any concerns that are real and perceived.

Qualified Decisions

Making a qualified decision during a system acquisition process requires competitive negotiated contracting. The following three rules can ensure a final selection of the most advantageous or best value offer for a large or small system expenditure:

- Comparative analysis of all proposals
- Consistent attention with stated evaluation criteria
- Rational basis for decision documented

Acquisition Contracts

Contracts play a central role in a system acquisition. Important contractual elements for a system acquisition are defining and documenting system capabilities, vendor deliverables, lifecycle costs, and risk reduction. Buyers of a system want to ensure that they are not purchasing vaporware. A contract can be unilateral and require only that the buyers' signatures such as a purchase order for computer keyboards. A contract can also be bilateral and require the signatures of both the buyer and seller for large big-ticket systems.

Contract Basics

In general, there are basic contract terms that are required in the sections of an acquisition contract. The five basic elements that can make the contract legal and binding are below.

Offer

An offer is a specified proposal to enter into an agreement with another party. There is the offer itself, the offerer delivering said offer, and the offeree, who has the role to accept or refuse the offer and, in some cases, make a counter offer.

Acceptance

Acceptance is the verbal or written agreement to the items of a contract. Only the offeree can accept the offer. Acceptance cannot be made under duress, coercion, or fraud. All acceptances should be in writing.

Consideration

This contract term means that each party to the contract gives and receives something of value. Consideration may be unilateral or bilateral. Both parties agree to discuss the particulars of the contract. Consideration is sometimes known as striking a deal or good horse-trading. Consideration requires market research and the ability to seek leverage when trying to gain the upper hand in the contract negotiation process.

Legal

This complex term means that the contract terms and conditions meet current local, state, and federal mandated laws. In addition, the contract format and content must contain all the legal requirements under basic contract law. Judges of the court have the power to declare certain types of contract void on the grounds of improper documentation or non-compliance with regulatory guidelines.

Competent Parties

A contract may only be entered into by parties who are legally competent. An example can be the requirement to be over the age of 18.

Contract Planning

The focus of contract planning is the development of key inputs for the contract document, and it is the foundation of the entire acquisition process. Team members shape the contract requirements prior to an official offer to a competent party. The planning will depend on the size and complexity of the acquisition. The method of procurement and contract type can also be defined in contract planning. Important activities in contract panning are below.

Requirements

Qualitative and quantitative data is collected for analysis and computations in direct support of the system required for acquisition

Quality Assurance

This helps to develop specifications of the item for acquisition to measure quality during user acceptance testing.

Market Search

This is a plan to collect, organize, and review data for comparative analysis of capabilities, pricing, and competition in the marketplace. Market search can have two phases. Market surveillance is where a company conducts high-level surveys of the market for potential vendors and systems to meet current requirements. Market investigation is a more detailed approach requiring the collection of requirements data on a specific vendors and systems.

Funding

Funding is a major budget consideration that must be made for funding commitment and the release of obligated funds for payment of the acquisition total costs over an extended period of time or the life cycle of the system purchased.

Contract Development

This development of the formation of the contract activity occurs when the contract is reviewed and negotiated by both parties. There are agreed upon procedures and rules of engagement from solicitation to approval by both the buyer and seller. Key activities in contract development are the following:

- *Solicitation*. Communicating the contract terms, conditions, and most important the requirements to potential parties.
- *Quotes*. Accepting quotes or request for quotes (RFQ) allows for the review of bidding prices that then sets in motion best value analysis and a selection of a vendor and system.
- *Proposals*. The final proposal by a seller can lock in a pricing agreement for the contract to be signed.
- *Approval*. The final action is the approval and signing of the contract. Terms, conditions, and requirements are legally bidding to both parties.

Contract Administration

This administrative activity starts when the contract is signed with a start date for contract execution. There are important functions within the execution of the contract timeline to protect the buyer and the seller. A contract administrator is the designated person who has overall accountability for the term and conditions of the contract signed. There are important administrator duties and responsibilities.

Compliance

The contract meets or exceeds the terms and conditions of the contract as agreed to by two competent parties.

Payment

Ensuring payments are executed per the terms and conditions of the contract are important. Discounts periods and discount percentages may be applied based on incentive clauses in the contract.

Performance

Monitoring contract performance is a team approach with the administrator having a lead role. Performance measurement requires valid documentation and agreed to procedures to review possible contract inconsistencies.

Modification

A change (correction, deletion, or addition) to any information on the contract requires agreement by both parties.

Termination

A closeout of a contract requires all contractual issues and claims to be settled with both parties agreeing to a termination of a contract. Termination can be done for different reasons, including reaching a contract end date or termination due to poor performance.

System Acquisition Strategies

Below are five examples of system acquisition strategy models that can be tailored to the type of system required by a company. The models establish a baseline for structuring a project or program to acquire a system.

All of the models contain system requirements and system definition analysis, risk reduction, development, testing, production, implementation, deployment, and sustainment phases. In addition, each phase has major investment decisions at key project milestones and contractual decision points.

Progress through the acquisition process in the five models can be tailored depending upon obtaining sufficient knowledge about the system provided capabilities. Risks and costs also need to have an analysis to make sound business decisions to proceed to the next phase or level of commitment.

Hardware-Intensive Model

This strategy model focuses on the hardware requirements of a system acquisition that can also have software requirements. The focus can be on large hardware items like robotics, weapons systems, or heavy industry manufacturing processes. This model can include the acquisition of large mainframe computers for optimal data capacity, processing speeds, and scale ability.

Software-Intensive Model

This strategy model focuses on the software application of a system acquisition that may be unique to support a business process or the requirement to move from a client-server based application to a Web-based application.

Hardware- and Software-Intensive Model

This strategy model combines the hardware and software intensive acquisition requirements and has a focus on new technology decisions made by a company to modernize operations and bring industry standard required management information systems upgrades.

Phased Modular Software-Intensive Model

This strategy model focuses on off-the-shelf commercial software such as supply chain management ERP systems that require analysis and tailoring with a phased or modular implementation plan.

Accelerated System Acquisition Model

This strategy model uses a rapid prototype analysis and development approach. This strategy is applied when schedule considerations are more important than cost and risk considerations.

System Acquisition Procedures

System acquisition procedures can have three major activities that can be tailored to meet large and complex procurements of big expenditures like an ERP supply chain management system.

Acquisition Decision Authority

The structure of a system acquisition program and the supporting procedures should have a standard baseline document available to the members of an acquisition team. Important with all acquisition procedures is the flexibility to tailor procedures to new system acquisition requirements without the risk; this can help with sound financial approval levels and audit and accounting guidelines. Central to good acquisition procedures is the decision authority official who will make key approvals at pivotal decision points during the acquisition process.

Acquisition Categories

Important in large and small company organizations is the requirement to define acquisition categories to streamline approval levels and the scope of decision-making. Acquisition categories will define funding approval levels, reporting, documentation, and analysis to support decision-making.

Program Decision Review

The decision review activity provides assessment of the status of a decision point or milestone to proceed to the next phase of the acquisition process. Important here is the authority official who is pre-established as the final approver and is able to make a final approval. In addition, acquisition team members support the authority decision official with data to ensure the program is structured with resources for a successful acquisition.

Acquisition, Requirements, and Budgeting

Acquisition, requirements analysis, and budgeting are tied together and must be in sync operationally for acquisition program success. Validation of requirements provides priority of the acquisition and resource allocations.

Capability Requirements Process

Acquisition programs must include a validated capabilities requirement. A document detailing capabilities of the product (supply chain management system) is required during the initial phases of the acquisition. Important here is the understanding that the capabilities requirement is a dynamic process that calls for adjustment over the life cycle of the product, and changes or adjustments need to be reviewed by acquisition, budget, and requirement subject matter experts.

Budget Process

Most budgeting processes are based on an annual budget preparation cycle. The time horizon can be 12-month cycles with projected 5-year spending plans. Important to budgeting is the role of the acquisition authority decision official who makes critical decisions at key decision points during an acquisition. This authority decision official advises the budget officials so that the program is adequately funded and consistent with phased funding levels.

Phases and Decision Points Activities

This procedural step involves the core element of an acquisition and supporting key decision points. The overriding decision to commit funds to a system investment supports the development, implementation, and deployment of the system to the business users. Key decision points listed below place the primary responsibility of sound acquisition planning and management on the authority decision officials with direct support of acquisition team members.

Solution Analysis and Need Identification

The decision is made that the company needs a new system to manage an integrated supply chain operation. Courses of action, solution sets, and an action plan are analyzed to include training, testing, and user acceptance requirements.

Technology Design Review and Risk Mitigation

An investment decision to move the project forward requires a review of how advanced the technology design is and how it can meet business needs for scalability and process performance. Identification and reduction of risks associated with the system or vendor by de-conflicting any internal and external issues or concerns is reviewed and documented for acceptance.

Development and Contract

The following decision points under development and contract are the need and risk completion, request for proposal (RFP) that is developed and executed, and a contract that is finally awarded to a vendor for the system acquisition.

User and System Acceptance Testing

The hardware and software decision during user acceptance testing is based on testing all aspects of system software, performance, connectivity, and business modifications (gap analysis) as required in the contract.

Training and Documentation

Programs for quality control, training, and system documentation are developed for end users.

Production and Deployment

This decision point leads to implementation of the full capability of the system over a phased approach and has incremental modules coming online or cut during a designated time period.

Sustainment

Ongoing decisions are made during the life cycle of the system acquisition from procurement to implementation to disposal using environmental, social, and economic sustainment factors.

System Acquisition Applications

The following best of breed systems (generic) that are listed below support good acquisition program decisions to procure a supply chain management systems solution. The systems listed support the multi-dimensional dynamics of sharing real time, relevant logistical data and historical information for supply chain decision-making. Procurement procedures of these systems listed can be tailored to meet to acquisition processes involving large and complex systems.

There are two major strategic approaches to supply chain systems acquisition. One is the best of breed supply chain management system approach that focuses on a single core process of a supply chain. Another approach is the acquisition of an enterprise resource planning (ERP) system solution that integrates best of breed system processes and practices into a common operating system for supply chain management operations. Although the ERP approach provides one-stop shopping for the buyer, there can be heavy development and modifications required to match business processes. Overall, the systems listed below require sound acquisition management practices and procedures for efficient and responsive supply chain management operations. The list of these systems is as follows:

- Supplier relationship management
- Customer relationship management
- Material requirements planning
- Production schedule planning
- Capacity resource planning (operations)
- Inventory control Systems
- Purchasing and invoicing system
- Warehouse and distribution systems
- Surface and air carrier scheduling and freight claims system
- In-transit visibility with radio frequency distribution systems
- Satellite global positioning system tracking for surface transportation
- Business objects, data analysis, and measurement

Conclusion

Acquisition activities are a dynamic process to plan, develop, acquire, maintain, and dispose of systems, equipment, facilities, and services. Key to acquisition policy is ethical performance and sound decision-making with adherence to a best value policy to the company and customers. Acquisition decision-making requires a process framework of company purchasing practices that provide simplicity and uniformity in the acquisition process.

SUMMARY

Logistical information and data sharing is the key to efficient and responsive supply chain management in manual, semi-automated, and fully automated processes, and it impacts procurement, customer delivery, and system acquisition. Information must be accurate, accessible, relevant, and shared to have an efficient and responsive supply chain operation.

Overall, logistic management system supports procurement, customer delivery, and system acquisition decisions with the understanding that these systems do not make decisions for management. Management must keep the focus on supply chain decision-making by using judgment, experience, and information. The business drives the system, not the other way around.

DISCUSSION QUESTIONS

1. Three key supply chain management information systems identified are ERP, SRM, and CRM. Discuss how these systems enable a company to optimize the supplier and customer relationship to have an efficient and responsive supply chain management system.

2. There are different types of supply chain management systems. Explain how different types of systems could be operational at the same time in one company, and explain the challenges to support these systems.

3. Best value places emphasis on evaluating factors in addition to the price of an item or acquisition cost for a large, complex information system. Discuss how you would implement an acquisition policy using the six best value procurement guidelines.

4. Customer delivery processes directly support customer relationship management and customer satisfaction. Explain how customer delivery processes impact a responsive and efficient order fulfillment program.

5. Making a qualified decision during a system acquisition process requires competitive negotiated contracting. Discuss how comparative analysis of all proposals, consistent attention with stated evaluation criteria, and having a rational basis for decision documentation can ensure a final selection of the best value offer.

GLOSSARY

B

benchmarking An analytical process a company can use to evaluate its performance against the performance of another company or industry standard.

big data A huge amount of data tables that analysts examine to find trends in human behavior.

bullwhip effect A phantom demand created by inaccurate forecasts; this results in increased inventory levels throughout the supply chain as the supply chain reacts by generating more inventory requirements and adding capacity to meet increases in demand.

business strategy The plan that companies use to establish business goals and objectives; plan can include product design, process management, and collaborative business initiatives.

C

center of excellence (COE) A functional team that facilitates the gathering of standards and best practices across the enterprise.

certainty One event and one outcome.

choke point A condition where any number of shortages of material, equipment, services, or incomplete processes affect the completion of an operation.

comparative analysis A technique that looks at an item-by-item comparison of two or more comparable alternatives or processes.

competitive advantage A market position of excellence that is defined by sharp distinctions of superior processes that convert into exceptional goods and services; these goods and services are seen as superior to the competition's goods and services.

competitive strategy The plan that clearly defines a company's strategy to satisfy its customers' needs for products and services.

constraint Restricts a system from being able to achieve its goal; the term most often used is *bottleneck*.

continuous improvement Monitoring performance and processes is paramount to getting and retaining leadership within the industry; companies that continuously analyze current performance and processes for opportunities remain innovative and are prepared for changes.

cost leadership Having the lowest operating cost in the industry.

cross docking Direct distribution from a supplier or manufacturing plant to the customer or retail chain with minimal handling and storage.

D

decision theory A systematic approach to conditions of uncertainty by designing a decision

matrix chart of rows, columns, and entries and then applying moving averages, exponential smoothing, and regression statistical methods.

demand The quantity of products or services that an organization will require at a defined time period.

demand uncertainty The accuracy that a company has in projecting customer demand for products in the future.

differentiation A planned strategy of distinguishing a product and making it more attractive when compared to the competition.

digital warehouse A storage architecture designed to secure and hold massive amounts of data extracted from transaction systems, operational data stores, and external sources.

due diligence A validation process used to ensure accuracy through the evaluation of various considerations that can lead to a decision.

E

e-commerce Uses technology to conduct commercial transactions for customers and merchants and also for merchants with other merchants.

economic risks Demand shock, price volatility, currency fluctuations, and energy; these risks can be controlled or influenced with planning and management by supply chain members (for instance, fuel has had a high impact on supply chains because the cost of fuel and the supply of fuel is volatile).

economies of scale The customer attempts to reduce price by purchasing products in a sized lot to reduce cost (such as purchasing a case of cereal at your bulk store so you can get a box for half price).

efficiency The cost of delivering and producing products for the customers.

electronic data interchange Computer-to-computer communications exchanging business documents in a standardized format (purchase orders, invoices, advanced ship notices).

electronic data interchange (EDI) The submission of electronic files from one computer to another with standardized formatting to lower the need for human interaction to process documents.

end-to-end supply chain A supply chain management practice that specializes in achieving visibility of the entire end-to-end process of planning, sourcing, selecting, acquiring, receiving, paying, and the customer delivery of goods and services.

environmental risks Natural disasters, extreme weather, and disease; supply chain members have little ability to control these risks and can only plan to mitigate the risk through planning and insurance.

enterprise resource planning (ERP) A software application that help managers plan and control business functions.

enterprise resource planning (ERP) An integrated end-to-end suite of business applications that tie together finance, human resources, distribution, manufacturing, service, and supply chain functions.

ERP (enterprise resource planning) A comprehensive integrated business software system that synchronizes the entire organization's planning and resource needs.

excess inventory Materials and supplies in excess of demand; these may be inventory items such as raw materials, components, and work in process (WIP).

F

forecasting A systematic approach using statistical methods and workforce judgements (experience and knowledge) to project future service and production supply requirements to meet customer demands for services and products.

fourth party logistics (4PL) This is a non-asset independent company that brings together the resources, capabilities, and technology of its own organization to other companies, replicating and installing capabilities to design, build, and run supply chain solutions for its clients.

G

gap analysis A technique to determine what is required to move from a current state to a desired state.

geopolitical risks Political instability, trade restrictions, terrorism, theft, and piracy; these risks can be influenced but require a mitigation plan and can be controlled; the supply chain can be impacted by global situations.

greenwashing Marketing green friendly products and deceiving the consumers of green practices.

gross income Revenue minus expenses.

I

incoterms The set of rules governing international logistics defining the responsibility of sellers and buyers.

information flow The shared information in all its forms used by all stakeholders in the supply chain to manage resources; critical to the efficiency of supply chains.

internet of things (IoT) Connecting devices on humans, animals, and objects to send and receive data.

inventory management Seeks to have the right quantity on hand at the right place. The oversight of the amount of inventory to carry and how much to order.

J

just-in-time Minimizing inventory to save on costs and deliver what is needed to the next stage in the supply chain.

K

key performance indicator (KPI) A measurable value indicating a company's effectiveness in achieving its business objectives.

L

lagging indicator Indicator that follows an event.

lead time The wait time between the placement of an order and the delivery of the item to the customer.

leading indicator A signal of an event that will happen later.

learning curve States that labor hours decrease as labor operations are repeated.

linear analysis Concerned with optimal allocation of limited resources among competitive activities.

links The ways products are moved by means of the transportation system.

logistics Part of supply chain management that plans, implements, and controls the efficient flow and storage of goods, services, and related information between the point of origin and the point of consumption to meet customer requirements. Refers to the movement of materials, components, services, money, and information through a supply chain.

logistics strategy Each member of the supply chain creates one or more logistics strategies that define the service levels that the organization finds most cost-effective.

M

materials handling The processes and equipment needed to move, store, protect, and control inventory.

metric The measurement that is used to gauge a component of a company's performance.

mission statement A brief declaration about what the business exists for or what its purpose is.

N

nearshoring A form of outsourcing determined by geographical considerations in which business processes are moved to localities that are geographically nearer to the procuring group.

nodes The locations where supply chain processes happen.

O

obsolete inventory Materials and supplies that can no longer be used; this type of inventory is generated by engineering and product changes.

offshoring The process of relocating business processes (this may include, production, or manufacturing) to another country with the intent to reduce costs.

operating costs Expenses associated with conducting business on a day-to-day basis.

operations Focuses on the transformation process for products and the services needed to support these goods.

operations strategy The decisions made that cause cohesion of the team's actions, policies, programs, and systems in response to other competitors.

opportunity A shortcoming in a system or process that may allow a chance to provide or improve a product or service, gaining competitive advantage.

outsourcing A form of a make-or-buy decision where an enterprise chooses to purchase a good or service from a third party that was previously made on-site.

P

payback period The time the initial investment for the project is recouped.

picking process The process of selecting orders for the release to the warehouse for picking up the product and shipping it to customers; items are pulled from inventory and consolidated for shipment to customers.

planning Requires a broad range of skills and the understanding of resource management.

point-of-sale (POS) Technology that uses an automated system to link computers that transmit sales data to an account that can control inventory.

pricing strategy Pricing of products or services by the members within the supply chain that provides a competitive advantage.

product availability How much of a product is available at specific point in time.

product flow The movement of material from raw material to the customer end product (downstream) or in reverse (upstream); an example of upstream would be recycling or returning something to the manufacturer.

profit margin The amount of money an organization makes for each dollar of sales.

push and pull cycle The push cycle is providing product in anticipation of customer demand, and the pull cycle is providing product upon customer demand. The pull cycle is when the execution of the order is based on the customers' actual requisition.

Q

quality The ability of an organization to produce a product or service that meets or exceeds the customer's expectations consistently.

quality assurance Attempts to create confidence in the processes so that the product meets specifications and customer expectations.

quality control Checks the level of quality for creating and sustaining the products.

queuing Standing in line or waiting for services.

R

responsiveness (Sometimes known as *agility*) the speed at which a supplier reacts to a customer's request.

revenue flow The movement of funds through the supply chain to all

stakeholders; can be upstream and downstream; includes bottom-line, who is spending what where to what expectation, and how much profit is generated from the supply chain for all of the entities in collaboration.

reverse flow When a customer returns products back through the supply chain (such as returning a product or turning in a bottle for credit).

reverse logistics Moving products in the opposite flow of the intended supply chain direction that goes from natural resources to the final customer.

RFID Technology that uses tags that can transmit data to identify and track its movement.

risk Any issue that impacts the supply chain's performance; there are good risks and bad risks.

S

sourcing The organizational function that finds and coordinates the raw materials, materials, and support that is required for products moving along the supply chain.

stakeholders The entities involved in the supply chain transaction from start to finish that promote the movement of the service or product, information, or funding to the customer.

strategic fit The continuity between competitive strategy and customer supply chain strategies.

strategy The plan that guides the business to achieve its goals and mission.

supplier strategy Members of the supply chain working to improve performance by communicating effectively and integrating processes.

supply chain Consists of the suppliers all the way to the customers and everything that is in between; this includes all functions and operations. The processes for producing and supporting a product from natural resources to its final disposition.

supply chain management (SCM) A systematic management approach to the flow of goods or services from supplier to the customer and involves all of the stakeholders within the transaction.

supply chain network design The decisions suppliers make to design the configuration of the supply chain.

supply chain sustainability The actions an organization takes to minimize damaging the environment by mitigating threat risks and eliminating waste in the supply chain.

T

takt time The cycle time needed to match customer demand to the final product.

target market segment A plan by a company to specifically choose a segment of an appropriate customer market.

technological risks IT disruptions and infrastructure risks; controllable and can be influenced by the supply chain members with planning and management.

the supply chain All of the organizations that are interlinked upstream and downstream within the supply chain flow of services or products that source customer expectations.

theory of constraint Based on the premise that every system has one or more limiting factors that prevents it from attaining a specified goal.

third party logistics (3PL) These are companies that contract with shippers to manage their clients' logistics operations. The services they provide include warehousing, management of transportation software, freight bill auditing, and many more logistic elements.

time series A set of observations measured at successive points in time or over successive periods of time.

trade agreements Arrangements made by governments that give duty- and tax-free incentives to promote fair trade.

transport modes This is the methods by which a freight is transported. There are three types of transport modes: land (road, rail, and pipeline), water, and air.

transportation Moving materials and products through one or more of the following methods: water, rail, truck, air, pipeline, and digital.

transportation management systems (TMS) A subcategory of supply chain management (SCM) software that is dedicated to transportation functions.

trend analysis A measure of increasing or decreasing observations for a given time period.

U

uncertainty Risk.

V

value analysis The application of function analysis techniques to an existing product, process, or procedure to compare customer requirements at the lowest cost, specified performance, and required level of reliability.

value engineering The application of function analysis techniques during the planning or design stages of a new product before major commitments or investments are made; methodology used to execute advanced product quality planning (APQP).

vendor-managed inventory (VMI) A technique for suppliers to replenish stock for the next stage of the supply chain.

PHOTO CREDITS

Chapter 1 Opener, p. 2: © Tzido (iStock); p. 4: © Funnycreature (iStock); p. 11: © Jezperklauzen (iStock); p. 12: © didecs (iStock); p. 14: © tiero (iStock); p. 15: © sndr (iStock).

Chapter 2 Opener, p. 22: © 1971yes (iStock); p. 25, top: © sndr (iStock); p. 25, bottom: © oneblink-cj (iStock); p. 26, top: © recose (iStock); p. 26, bottom: © Bet_Noire (iStock); p. 36: © sinarp2 (iStock); p. 37: © endopack (iStock).

Chapter 3 Opener, p. 42: © vaeenma (iStock).

Chapter 4 Opener, p. 64: © Kenishirotie (iStock).

Chapter 5 Opener, p. 84: © Sashkinw (iStock).

Chapter 6 Opener, p. 102: © Jirsak (iStock).

Chapter 7 Opener, p. 122: © mikemcd (iStock); p. 138: © Riccardo_Mojana (iStock).

Chapter 8 Opener, p. 142: © Nongkran_ch (iStock).

Chapter 9 Opener, p. 160: © buchachon (iStock).

REFERENCES

Chapter 1

Alibaba. (2015). *Products*. Retrieved from http://www.alibaba.com

Alibaba Group. (2015). *About us*. Retrieved from http://www.alibabagroup.com/en/about/businesses

Ariba, Inc. (2015). *Solutions*. Retrieved from http://www.ariba.com

BMW Group. (2015). *Company portrait. Strategy*. Retrieved from http://www.bmwgroup.com

Central Intelligence Agency. (2013). *The world factbook: Pipelines*. Retrieved from https://www.cia.gov/library/publications/the-world-factbook/index.html

Container Research Institute. (2015). Retrieved from http://www.container-recycling.org/index.php/publications

EnviroMedia social marketing. (2015). Retrieved from http://www.greenwashingindex.com/about-greenwashing/

Excel. (2015). *What we do*. Retrieved from http://www.exel.com

Federal Trade Commission. (2015). *Going green*. Retrieved from http://www.consumer.ftc.gov/features/feature-0013-going-green

FedEx. (2015). *About FedEx*. Retrieved from http://about.van.fedex.com

Greenpeace. (2015). *Greenwashing*. Retrieved from http://www.stopgreenwash.org/

Home Depot. (2015). *Investor FAQ, What is Home Depot's mission statement?* Retrieved from http://ir.homedepot.com/phoenix.zhtml?c=63646&p=irol-faq#37549

Huff, B. (2014). *How to optimize supply chain operations for strong cash flow*. Retrieved from http://www.industryweek.com/cash-is-king

IKEA. (2015). *This is IKEA*. Retrieved from http://www.ikea.com/cn/en/

Lajoie, M., & Shearman, N. (2014). *What is Alibaba?* Retrieved from http://projects.wsj.com/alibaba/

NAFTA. (2012). *North American Free Trade Agreement*. Retrieved from http://www.naftanow.org/default_en.asp

Office of the United States Trade Representative. (2015). *Countries and regions*. Retrieved from https://ustr.gov

Sherman, E. (2013). *Resilient supply chain management: Turn disaster response into a competitive strength*. Retrieved from http://www.middlemarketcenter.org/expert-perspectives/resilient-supply-chain-management-turn-disaster-response-into-a-competitive-strength

SourceWatch. (2015). *Greenwashing*. Retrieved from http://www.sourcewatch.org/index.php/Greenwashing

United Parcel Service of America, Inc. (2015). *UPS supply chain solutions*. Retrieved from http://www.ups-scs.com/

Chapter 2

Apple. (2015). *Investors*. Retrieved from http://investor.apple.com

Aronow, S., Hofman, D., Burkett, M., Romano, J., & Nilles, K. (2014). The 2014 supply chain top 25: Leading the decade. *Supply Chain Management Review, 18*(5), 8–17.

British Broadcasting Corporation. (2007). *Addicted to cheap shopping? Why the real cost of goods keeps going down* [Video file]. Retrieved from http://digital.films.com/play/UJZ4L9

CNN Money. (2001, July 9). *Webvan shuts down*. Retrieved from http://money.cnn.com/2001/07/09/technology/webvan/

Commercial Section of the Canadian Embassy in the Republic of Korea. (2012, February). *Global value chain analysis on Samsung Electronics*. Retrieved from http://albertacanada.com/korea/images/GlobalValueChainAnalysisSamsungElectronics.pdf

Coyle, J., Langley, C., Novack, R., & Gibson, B. (2013). *Supply chain management: A logistics perspective* (9th ed.). Mason, OH: South-Western Cengage Learning.

D'Onfro, J. (2014, April 18). The founder of a dot-com disaster is giving his old grocery delivery idea another shot. *Business Insider*. Retrieved from http://www.businessinsider.com/louis-borders-webvan-founder-hds-2014-

FedEx. (2015). *Our story*. Retrieved from http://about.van.fedex.com/our-story/company-structure/corporate-fact-sheet/

Goldratt, E. M. (2004). *The goal: A process of ongoing improvement*. Great Barrington, MA: North River.

Inbound Logistics. (2015). *Articles*. Retrieved from http://www.inboundlogistics.com

IKEA. (2015). *About the IKEA group*. Retrieved from http://www.ikea.com/ms/en_US/this-is-ikea/company-information/index.html

Ikea Group. (2015). *Ikea Group Marketline company profile*, 1–20.

Johnson, J. R. (2015). *Supply chain, RFID 24-7*. Retrieved from http://www.rfid24-7.com/

Kovalenko, V. I., & Yarmolyuk, V. V. (1995). Endogenous rare metal ore formations and rare metal metallogeny of Mongolia, *Economic Geology, 90*(3).

Kroger Co. (2015). *Kroger Co. MarketLine company profile*, 1–36.

Kroger Company. (2015). *Investor relations*. Retrieved from http://ir.kroger.com/CorporateProfile.aspx?iid=4004136

Leger, D. L., & O'Donnell, J. (2013, December 26). UPS driver: 2013 'worst Christmas ever' for delivery. *USA Today*. Retrieved from http://archive.burlingtonfree-press.com/article/20131226/BUSINESS/312260031/More-delays-as-UPS-staggers-under-holiday-crush

Marketline. (2015, April 28). Whole Foods Market, Inc. SWOT analysis. *Business Source Complete*, 1–8.

Marketline. (2014, November 7). Wal-Mart Stores, Inc. SWOT analysis. *Business Source Complete*, 1–11

Penske. (2015). *Whirlpool Corporation: Evolution of a supply chain*. Retrieved from http://www.penskelogistics.com/casestudies/whirlpool2.html

Samsung. (2014). *Sustainability report.* Retrieved from http://www.samsung.com/us/aboutsamsung/investor_relations/corporate_governance/corporatesocialresponsibility/downloads/2014sustainabilityreport.pdf

Samsung to overhaul logistics operation. (2001). *Frontline Solutions, 2*(12), 58.

Sanders, N. R. (2012). *Supply chain management: A global perspective.* Hoboken, NJ: John Wiley & Sons.

Sengupta, S. (2013). *10 supply chain trends for the next 10 years, supply chain 24/7.* Retrieved from http://www.supplychain247.com/article/10_supply_chain_trends_for_the_next_10_years

SupplyChainOpz. (2015). *Is Apple supply chain really the no. 1? A case study.* Retrieved from http://www.supplychainopz.com/2013/01/is-apple-supply-chain-really-no-1-case.html

United Natural Foods, Inc. (2014). *Products and services.* Retrieved from https://www.unfi.com

United Natural Foods, Inc. (2014). *Sustainability reports.* Retrieved from https://www.unfi.co

United Parcel Service of America, Inc. (2015). *World wide.* Retrieved from http://www.ups.com/content/us/en/about/facts/worldwide.html

United States Postal Service. (2015). *Just one day in the life of the U.S. Postal Service... by the numbers.* Retrieved from https://about.usps.com/who-we-are/postal-facts/one-day-by-the-numbers.htm

United States Green Building Council. (2015). *Overview.* Retrieved from http://www.usgbc.org/leed#overview

Walmart. (2015). *Walmart logistics.* Retrieved from http://corporate.walmart.com/our-story/our-business/logistics

Webvan.com. (2009). *Webvan, a part of Amazon.com family.* Retrieved from http://www.webvan.com/

Westone (2014). *The in-ear experts.* Retrieved from http://www.westone.com/hhc/index.php/about/about-westone

Chapter 4

Burt, D., Petcavage, S., & Pinkerton, R. (2010). *Supply management* (8th ed.). New York, NY: McGraw-Hill Irwin.

Hitt, M. A., Ireland, R. D., & Hoskisson, R. E. (2011). *Strategic management: Competitiveness and globalization, concepts and cases: 2011 custom edition* (9th ed.). Mason, OH: South-Western Cengage Learning.

Stevenson, W. J. (2009). *Operations management* (11th ed.). New York, NY: McGraw-Hill Irwin.

Swink, M., Melnyk, S. A., Cooper, M. B., & Hartley, J. L. (2014*). Managing operations across the supply chain* (2nd ed.). New York, NY: McGraw-Hill Irwin.

Chapter 5

Burt, D., Petcavage, S., & Pinkerton, R. (2010). *Supply management* (8th ed.). New York, NY: McGraw-Hill Irwin.

Evans, J. R., & Lindsay, W. M. (2014). *Managing for quality and performance excellence* (9th ed.). Mason, OH : South-Western Cengage Learning.

Hitt, M. A., Ireland, R. D., & Hoskisson, R. E. (2011). *Strategic management: Competitiveness and globalization, concepts and cases: 2011 custom edition* (9th ed.). Mason, OH: South-Western Cengage Learning.

Stevenson, W. J. (2009). *Operations management* (11th ed.). New York, NY: McGraw-Hill Irwin.

Swink, M., Melnyk, S. A., Cooper, M. B., & Hartley, J. L. (2014*). Managing operations across the supply chain* (2nd ed.). New York, NY: McGraw-Hill Irwin.

Chapter 6

Azzimonti, M., & Sarte, P. G. (2007). Barriers to foreign direct investment under political instability. *Economic Quarterly - Federal Reserve Bank of Richmond, 93*(3), 287–315. Retrieved from http://search.proquest.com/docview/204755669?accountid=26967

Burke, H. (2007) *Mattel recall of lead-tainted Chinese toys cost $30 million.* Retrieved from http://www.bloomberg.com/apps/news?pid=newsarchive&sid=ah7cuhojMidI

Chapman, B., (2014). *Moving operations or functions to a new country? Think long term.* Retrieved from http://deloitte.wsj.com/riskandcompliance/2014/04/30/moving-operations-or- functions-to-a-new-country-think-long-term/

Drikhamer, D. (2007) *India gears up: India's logistics challenge in a nutshell.* Retrieved from http://www.jdmandassociates.com/pdfs/2007_05_SEKO_LT_India_Gears_Up.pf

Goh, M., & Ang, A. (2000). Some logistics realities in Indochina. *International Journal of Physical Distribution & Logistics Management, 30*(10), 887–911. Retrieved from http://search.proquest.com/docview/232586603?accountid=26967

GOV.UK. (2012). *Transport and distribution for international trade – Detailed guidance.* Retrieved from https://www.gov.uk/transport-and-distribution-for-international-trade

Ingersoll, R. (2009). *Global Supply Chain Essentials I* Davidson, NC: Author.

Kearney, A. T. (2014). *China's e-commerce market in 2014- Full report.* Retrieved from https://www.atkearney.com/paper/-/asset_publisher/dVxv4Hz2h8bS/content/chinas-e-commerce-market-the-logistics-challenges/10192

Knigge, R. (2013). *Freight forwarding and logistics: What the high performers know.* Retrieved from http://www.accenture.com/us-en/outlook/Pages/outlook-online-2013-freight-forwarding-and-logistics-what-high-performers-know.aspx

Kunaka, C. (2011). Logistics in lagging regions: Overcoming local barriers to global connectivity. *World Bank.* Retrieved from http://openknowledge.worldbank.org/handle/10986/2543 License: CC BY 3.0 IGO.

Maersk Line. (n.d.). *Shipping services.* Retrieved from http://www.maerskline.com/en-us/shipping-services/your-promise-delivered/your-promise-delivered/overview

Material Handling & Logistics. (2004). *Ten key challenges for the Chinese logistics industry.* Retrieved from http://mhlnews.com/global-supply-chain/ten-key-challenges-chinese-logistics-industry.

Mentzer, J. T., Stank, T. P., & Esper, T. L. (2008). Supply chain management and its relationship to logistics, marketing, production, and operations management. *Journal of Business Logistics, 29*(1), 31–38. Retrieved from http://search.proquest.com/docview/212664362?accountid=26967

O'Riordan, A. (2013). *Winning in emerging markets: Understanding the barriers.* Retrieved from http://www.accenture.com/us-en/blogs/life-sciences-blog/archive/2013/05/21/winning-in-emerging-markets-understanding-the-barriers.aspx.

Porter, M. E. (1998). *Competitive advantage: creating and sustaining superior performance* (1st ed.) New York, NY: The Free Press.

The Costco Connection. (2015, May). *30*(5). Retrieved from http://www.costcoconnection.com/connection/201505#pg1

Value analysis. (n.d.). Retrieved from http://syque.com/quality_tools/toolbook/Value/value.htm

Walters, R. (2014). Cyber attacks on U.S. companies in 2014. *Heritage Foundation.* Retrieved from http://www.heritage.org/research/reports/2014/10 cyber-attacks-on-us-companies-in-2014

Chapter 7

Ballis, A., & Golias, J. (2002). *Comparative evaluation of existing and innovate railroad freight transport terminals. Transportation research part A: Policy and practice.* Retrieved from http://www.worldtransitresearch.info/research/2100/

Banham, R. (n.d.). *Political risk and the supply chain.* Retrieved from http://www.rmmagazine.com/2014/06/01/political-risk-and-the-supply-chain/

Bubner, N., Bubner, N., Helbig, R., & Jeske, M. (2014). *Logistics trend radar.* Retrieved from http://www.dhl.com/content/dam/downloads/g0/about_us/logistics_insights/DHL_Logistics-TrendRadar_2014.pdf

Canadian Energy Pipeline Association. (2015). *Why pipelines are needed.* Retrieved from http://www.cepa.com/about-pipelines/why-pipelines

Chand, S. (2015). *Warehousing: Function, benefits and types of warehousing.* Retrieved from http://www.yourarticlelibrary.com/marketing/marketing-management/warehousing-function-benefits-and-types-of-warehousing/27952/

Chopra, S., & Sodhi, M. (2004). *Managing risk to avoid supply-chain breakdown.* Retrieved from http://sloanreview.mit.edu/article/managing-risk-to-avoid-supplychain-breakdown/

Fitzgerald, D. (2013). *Avon to halt rollout of new order management system.* Retrieved from http://www.wsj.com/articles/SB10001424052702303932504579251941619018078

Gershenhorn, A. (2004). *The making of a successful supply chain.* Retrieved from http://search.proquest.com.proxy.cecybrary.com/abicomplete/docview/228233312/33C9A3FA6B3E4A9APQ/1?accountid=26967

Ghegan, D. (2014). *Advantages of a bonded warehouse.* Retrieved from http://www.bondedservice.com/2014/07/advantages-bonded-warehouse/

Hanaoka, S., & Regmi, M. (2011). *Promoting international freight transport through the development of dry ports in Asia: An environmental perspective.* Retrieved from http://www.sciencedirect.com/science/article/pii/S0386111211000148

Holland, J. (2005). *Calculating risks in the Chinese logistics market.* Retrieved from http://search.proquest.com.proxy.cecybrary.com/docview/228322060?accountid=26967

iContainers. (2014). *5 benefits of ocean freight.* Retrieved from http://www.icontainers.com/us/2014/10/24/5-benefits-ocean-freight/

Khalid, N. (2006). *China's port development and shipping competition in East Asia.* Retrieved from http://www.japanfocus.org/-Nazery-Khalid/1649/article.pdf

Lamberti, M., Costello, M., & Getz, K. (2012). *Global supply chain management.* Retrieved from http://search.proquest.com/docview/1081340862?accountid=26967

Lee, H. (2004) *The triple-a supply chain.* Retrieved from https://hbr.org/2004/10/the-triple-a-supply-chain

Lohrey, J. (2015). *The importance of warehousing in a logistics system.* Retrieved from http://smallbusiness.chron.com/importance-warehousing-logistics-system-74825.html

Lummus, R., Melnyk, S., Vokurka, R., Burns, L., & Sandor, J. (2007). *Getting ready for tomorrow's supply chain.* Retrieved from http://search.proquest.com/docview/221200125?accountid=26967

MacDonald, A. (2006). *The difference between managing a global vs. domestic supply chain is a matter of degree.* Retrieved from http://connection.ebscohost.com/c/articles/23587854/difference-between-managing-global-vs-domestic-supply-chain-matter-degree

Manners-Bell, J., & Lyon K. (2014). *The implications of 3D Printing for the global logistics industry.* Retrieved from http://www.supplychain247.com/article/the_implications_of_3d_printing_for_the_global_logistics_industry

Mason, S., Ribera, M., Farris, J., & Kirk, R. (n.d.). Retrieved from http://citeseerx.ist.psu.edu/viewdoc/download?doi=10.1.1.19.3516&rep=rep1&type=pdf

Mizutani, M., Tsuchiya, K., Takuma, F., & Ohashi, T. (2005). *Estimation of the economic benefits of port development on international maritime market by partial equilibrium model and scge model.* Retrieved from http://www.easts.info/on-line/journal_06/892.pdf

Murray, M. (n.d.). *Less than truckload (LTL).* Retrieved from http://logistics.about.com/od/supplychainmodels/a/LTL_Carriers.htm

Nabben, H. (2014). *12 trends that are shaping the future of logistics.* Retrieved from http://blog.damco.com/2014/07/14/12-trends-that-are-shaping-the-future-of-logistics/

Pearson, M. (2012). *The dynamic supply chain.* Retrieved from http://www.industryweek.com/articles/the_dynamic_supply_chain_26771.aspx

Perez, H. D. (2013). *Supply chain strategies: Which one hits the mark?* Retrieved from http://www.supplychainquarterly.com/print/20130306-supply-chain-strategies-which-one-hits-the-mark/

RedPrairie. (2002). *The new era of digital logistics.* Retrieved from http://www.idii.com/wp/rpNewEraDigitalLogistics.pdf

Reichhart, A., & Holweg, M. (2007). *Creating the customer-responsive supply chain: A reconciliation of concepts.* Retrieved from http://search.proquest.com.proxy.cecybrary.com/abicomplete/publication/publications_36644?accountid=26967

Reuters. (2014). *China to establish $40 billion Silk Road infrastructure fund.* Retrieved from http://www.reuters.com/article/2014/11/08/us-china-diplomacy-idUSKBN0IS0BQ20141108

Runckel, C. (n.d.). *Infrastructure India: A long road ahead.* Retrieved from http://www.business-in-asia.com/asia/infrastructure_india.html#transport

Rutkowski, R. (2015). *Transportation and logistics.* Retrieved from http://www.accenture.com/Microsites/supplywatch/articles/archive/issue1/Pages/transportation-and-logistics.aspx

Storey, J., Emberson, C., Godsell, J., & Harrison, A. (2006). *Supply chain management: Theory, practice and future challenges.* Retrieved from http://search.proquest.com.proxy.cecybrary.com/abicomplete/docview/232328680/88E281B5A7214C0BPQ/1?accountid=26967

Supply Chain Digest. (2010). *Supply chain news: The five challenges of today's global supply chains.* Retrieved from http://www.scdigest.com/ASSETS/ON_TARGET/10-08-12-3.php

Takach, J. (2010). *Five priorities for supply chain success.* Retrieved from http://search.proquest.com.proxy.cecybrary.com/abicomplete/docview/903552548/7789BB25B9554DEFPQ/1?accountid=26967

The Economist. (2014). *The flow of things.* Retrieved from http://www.economist.com/news/china/21606899-export-superpower-china-suffers-surprisingly-inefficient-logistics-flow-things

Vermont Agency of Commerce and Community Development. (n.d.). *About bonded warehouses.* Retrieved from http://accd.vermont.gov/sites/accd/files/Documents/business/vgtp/AboutCustomsBondedWarehouses.pdf

World Bank. (2015). *Good practices in the inland waterways sector: Project PLATINA.* Retrieved from http://www.ppiaf.org/freighttoolkit/case-study/good-practices-inland-waterways-sector-project-platina

World Bank. (2015). *Increasing the use of inland waterways in the modal share – in China, India and Brazil.* Retrieved from http://www.ppiaf.org/freighttoolkit/case-study/increasing-use-inland-waterways-modal-share-%E2%80%93-china-india-brazil

World Bank. (2015). *Intermodal freight systems.* Retrieved from http://www.ppiaf.org/freighttoolkit/knowledge-map/road/intermodal-freight-systems

World Bank. (2015). *National plan for logistics and transport in Brazil.* Retrieved from http://www.ppiaf.org/freighttoolkit/case-study/national-plan-logistics-transport-brazil

World Shipping Council. (2015). *Benefits of liner shipping.* Retrieved from http://www.worldshipping.org/benefits-of-liner-shipping

Zigiaris, S. (2000). *Supply chain management.* Retrieved from www.adi.pt/docs/innoregio_supp_management.pdf

INDEX

R

S

T

Notes

Notes

Notes

Notes